Lecture Notes in Computer Science

Edited by G. Goos, J. Hartmanis and J. van Lee

Springer
Berlin
Heidelberg
New York
Barcelona
Hong Kong
London
Milan
Paris
Singapore
Tokyo

Brian Read (Ed.)

Advances
in Databases

18th British National Conference on Databases, BNCOD 18
Chilton, UK, July 9-11, 2001
Proceedings

 Springer

Series Editors

Gerhard Goos, Karlsruhe University, Germany
Juris Hartmanis, Cornell University, NY, USA
Jan van Leeuwen, Utrecht University, The Netherlands

Volume Editor

Brian Read
CLRC Rutherford Appleton Laboratory
Information Technology Department
Chilton, Didcot, Oxfordshire OX11 0QX
United Kingdom
E-mail: Brian.Read@rl.ac.uk

Cataloging-in-Publication Data applied for

Die Deutsche Bibliothek - CIP-Einheitsaufnahme

Advances in databases : proceedings / 18th British National Conference on
Databases, BNCOD 18, Chilton, UK, July 9 - 11, 2001. Brian Read (ed.). -
Berlin ; Heidelberg ; New York ; Barcelona ; Hong Kong ; London ; Milan ;
Paris ; Singapore ; Tokyo : Springer, 2001
    (Lecture notes in computer science ; Vol. 2097)
    ISBN 3-540-42265-X

CR Subject Classification (1998): H.2-4

ISSN 0302-9743
ISBN 3-540-42265-X Springer-Verlag Berlin Heidelberg New York

Springer-Verlag Berlin Heidelberg New York
a member of BertelsmannSpringer Science+Business Media GmbH

http://www.springer.de

© Springer-Verlag Berlin Heidelberg 2001
Printed in Germany

Typesetting: Camera-ready by author, data conversion by PTP-Berlin, Stefan Sossna
Printed on acid-free paper   SPIN: 10839443   06/3142   5 4 3 2 1 0

Foreword

The ever-expanding growth of Information Technology continues to place fresh demands on the management of data. Database researchers must respond to new challenges, particularly to the opportunities offered by the Internet for access to distributed, semi-structured and multimedia data sources.

This volume contains the proceedings of the 18th British National Conference on Databases (BNCOD 2001), held at the Rutherford Appleton Laboratory in July 2001. In recent years, interest in this conference series has extended well beyond the UK. In selecting just eleven of the submitted papers for presentation, the programme committee has included contributors from The Netherlands, Germany, Sweden, Canada and USA. In addition, two specially invited speakers address subjects of topical interest.

Our first invited speaker is Professor Dr. Rudi Studer from the University of Karlsruhe. At AIFB, the Institute for Applied Informatics and Formal Description Methods, he and his colleagues are in the forefront of work on the Semantic Web. This aims to make information accessible to human and software agents on a semantic basis. The paper discusses the role that semantic structures, based on ontologies, play in establishing communication between different agents. The AIFB web site has been developed as a semantic portal to serve as a case study.

The massive increase in data volumes from big science such as remote sensing and high energy physics means that we now contemplate the storage and processing of petabytes. Grid technology, specifically the „Data Grid" is seen as attractive. It is thus timely that our second invited speaker addresses strategy in this field. He is Professor Tony Hey, now recently appointed as Director of the UK e-Science Core Programme and well placed to expound the vision.

The contributed papers are presented in four groups. The first of these addresses performance and optimisation. This issue has always been at the core of database technology. The first paper, by Regan and Delis, reports on a practical study of space management in logs. They evaluate a technique for reclaiming log space from short transactions while retaining recoverability for long running ones. The increasing popularity of XML presents new challenges. Zhu and Lü propose an algorithm for an effective storage placement strategy for XML documents that facilitates their efficient parallel processing. The trade off between data quality and performance is an interesting topic tackled by Caine and Embury. They study algorithms for integrity checking delayed from when the system is too busy to off-peak, „lights out" hours.

The second group of papers concentrates on objects in databases and software engineering. The great variety of CASE tools prompt the adoption of standardised meta-models and transfer formats. In proposing an extension to OCL, Gustavsson and Lings further the interchange of models by defining a common, model independent notation for design transformations. Next, Zhang and Ritter investigate the state of database support for software development using object-oriented programming languages. They highlight the shortcomings in this respect of the current object-relational database paradigm and suggest how it might beneficially be enhanced. The third paper returns to the engineering design environment and tackles concurrent version control. Al-Khudair, Gray and Miles present a generalised object-oriented model that captures the evolution of design configurations and their components by supporting versioning at all levels.

In the third group of papers, we again consider optimisation. More specifically, contributors consider efficient querying in the newer domains of multimedia and distributed data sources.   The requirements and techniques of the worlds of information retrieval and transactional databases are very different. The Dutch team of Blok, de Vries, Blanken and Apers present a case study on the „top-N" queries familiar in content retrieval in the context of a database approach to the management of multimedia data. The key issues addressed, such as speed and quality of answers and the opportunities for scalability are supported by experimental results. A similar problem is of concern to Sattler, Dunemann, Geist, Saake and Conrad. They seek control over the potentially excessive data returned from a query over heterogeneous data sources. By extensions to multi-database languages, they explore ways of asking for just the „first n" results, or of asking for a *sample* of the complete result. Still with the theme of information systems relying on database technology, Waas and Kersten are concerned with a web multimedia portal based on the Monet database system. Here the optimisation challenge is query throughput. The authors report on the performance of a simple and robust scheme for the scheduling of queries in a large, parallel, shared-nothing database cluster.

The two papers in our final group are both about querying objects. However, they are very different. Trigoni and Bierman present an inference algorithm for OQL that identifies the most general type of a query in the absence of schema type information. This is relevant to where heterogeneity is encountered – for example, in any open, distributed, or even semi-structured, database environment. Distributed databases and virtual reality are combined in the ambitious work reported by Ammoura, Zaiane and Ji. They explore data mining in a virtual data warehouse.   Rendering multi-dimensional data aggregates as objects, the user flies through the data to explore and query different views.

Acknowledgements

The members of the programme committee, under the energetic leadership of Carole Goble, reviewed the submitted papers with critical thoroughness. Their enthusiastic commitment to the continued success of BNCOD is much appreciated. Susan Hilton and her team played an essential part in the practical organisation. Thanks are also due to Alex Gray and the steering committee for the invitation to host the conference and valuable guidance.

April 2001   Brian Read

Conference Committees

Programme Committee

Carole Goble (Chair)	University of Manchester
David Bell	University of Ulster
Richard Connor	University of Strathclyde
Richard Cooper	University of Glasgow
Suzanne Embury	University of Wales, Cardiff
Carole Goble	University of Manchester
Alex Gray	University of Wales, Cardiff
Mike Jackson	University of Wolverhampton
Anne James	Coventry University
Keith Jeffery	CLRC Rutherford Appleton Laboratory
John Keane	UMIST
Graham Kemp	University of Aberdeen
Jessie Kennedy	Napier University
Brian Lings	University of Exeter
Rob Lucas	Keylink Computers Ltd
Mark Levene	University College London
Nigel Martin	Birkbeck College, University of London
Werner Nutt	Heriot-Watt University
Norman Paton	University of Manchester
Alex Poulovassilis	Birkbeck College, University of London
Brian Read	CLRC Rutherford Appleton Laboratory
Nick Rossiter	University of Newcastle upon Tyne
Michael Worboys	Keele University

Additional Referees

Carsten Butz	Heriot-Watt University
Alvaro Fernandes	University of Manchester
Tony Griffiths	University of Manchester
Paulo Pinheiro da Silva	University of Manchester
Sandra Sampaio	University of Manchester

Organising Committee

Brian Read (Chair)	CLRC Rutherford Appleton Laboratory
Susan Hilton	CLRC Rutherford Appleton Laboratory
Kevin O'Neill	CLRC Rutherford Appleton Laboratory

Steering Committee

Alex Gray (Chair)   University of Wales, Cardiff
Nick Fiddian   University of Wales, Cardiff
Carole Goble   University of Manchester
Peter Gray   University of Aberdeen
Roger Johnson   Birkbeck College, University of London
Jessie Kennedy   Napier University
Brian Lings   University of Exeter
Michael Worboys   Keele University

Table of Contents

Invited Papers

Performance and Optimisation

Objects - Design & Development

Query Optimisation

Querying Objects

SEAL — A Framework for Developing SEmantic Web PortALs

Alexander Maedche[1,3], Steffen Staab[1,2], Nenad Stojanovic[1],
Rudi Studer[1,2,3], and York Sure[1,2]

[1] Institute AIFB, University of Karlsruhe, D-76128 Karlsruhe, Germany
http://www.aifb.uni-karlsruhe.de/WBS
{ama,sst,nst,rst,ysu}@aifb.uni-karlsruhe.de
[2] Ontoprise GmbH, Haid-und-Neu Straße 7, 76131 Karlsruhe, Germany
http://www.ontoprise.de
[3] FZI Research Center for Information Technologies,
Haid-und-Neu Straße 10-14, 76131 Karlsruhe, Germany
http://www.fzi.de/wim

Abstract. The core idea of the Semantic Web is to make information
accessible to human and software agents on a semantic basis. Hence,
web sites may feed directly from the Semantic Web exploiting the underlying structures for human and machine access. We have developed a
generic approach for developing semantic portals, *viz.* SEAL (SEmantic
portAL), that exploits semantics for providing and accessing information
at a portal as well as constructing and maintaining the portal.
In this paper, we discuss the role that semantic structures make for establishing communication between different agents in general. We elaborate
on a number of intelligent means that make semantic web sites accessible
from the outside, *viz.* semantics-based browsing, semantic querying and
querying with semantic similarity, and machine access to semantic information at a semantic portal. As a case study we refer to the AIFB web
site — a place that is increasingly driven by Semantic Web technologies.

1 Introduction

The widely-agreed core idea of the Semantic Web is the delivery of data on a
semantic basis. Intuitively the delivery of semantically apprehended data should
help with establishing a higher quality of communication between the information provider and the consumer. How this intuition may be put into practice is
the topic of this paper.

We discuss means to further communication on a semantic basis. For this one
needs a theory of communication that links results from semiotics, linguistics,
and philosophy into actual information technology. We here consider *ontologies*
as a sound semantic basis that is used to define the meaning of terms and hence
to support intelligent access, *e.g.* by semantic querying [5] or dynamic hypertext
views [19].

Thus, ontologies constitute the foundation of our SEAL (SEmantic portAL)
approach. The origins of SEAL lie in Ontobroker [5], which was conceived for

B. Read (Ed.): BNCOD 2001, LNCS 2097, pp. 1–22, 2001.

semantic search of knowledge on the Web and also used for sharing knowledge on the Web [2]. It then developed into an overarching framework for search and presentation offering access at a portal site [19]. This concept was then transferred to further applications [1,21,24] and is currently extended into a commercial solution[1].

We here describe the SEAL core modules and its overall architecture (Section 3). Thereafter, we go into several technical details that are important for human and machine access to a semantic portal.

In particular, we describe a general approach for semantic ranking (Section 4). The motivation for semantic ranking is that even with accurate semantic access, one will often find too much information. Underlying semantic structures, *e.g.* topic hierarchies, give an indication of what should be ranked higher on a list of results.

Finally, we present mechanisms to deliver and collect machine-understandable data (Section 5). They extend previous means for better digestion of web site data by software agents. Before we conclude, we give a short survey of related work.

2   Ontology and Knowledge Base

For our AIFB intranet, we explicitly model relevant aspects of the domain in order to allow for a more concise communication between agents, *viz.* within the group of software agents, between software and human agents, and — last not least — between different human agents. In particular, we describe a way of modeling an ontology that we consider appropriate for supporting communication between human and software agents.

2.1   Ontologies for Communication

Research in ontology has its roots in philosophy dealing with the nature and organisation of being. In computer science, the term ontology refers to an engineering artifact, constituted by a specific vocabulary used to describe a particular model of the world, plus a set of explicit assumptions regarding the intended meaning of the words in the vocabulary. Both, vocabulary and assumptions, serve human and software agents to reach common conclusions when communicating.

Reference and meaning. The general context of communication (with or without ontology) is described by the meaning triangle [15]. The meaning triangle defines the interaction between symbols or words, concepts and things of the world (*cf.* Figure 1).

The meaning triangle illustrates the fact that although words cannot completely capture the essence of a reference (= concept) or of a referent (= thing), there is a correspondence between them. The relationship between a word and

---

[1] cf. http://www.time2research.de

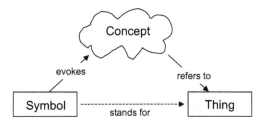

Fig. 1. The Meaning Triangle

a thing is indirect. The correct linkage can only be accomplished when an interpreter processes the word invoking a corresponding concept and establishing the proper linkage between his concept and the appropriate thing in the world.

Logics. An ontology is a general logical theory constituted by a vocabulary and a set of statements about a domain of interest in some logic language. The logical theory specifies relations between signs and it apprehends relations with a semantics that restricts the set of possible interpretations of the signs. Thus, the ontology reduces the number of mappings from signs to things in the world that an interpreter who is committed to the ontology can perform — in the ideal case each sign from the vocabulary eventually stands for exactly one thing in the world.

Figure 2 depicts the overall setting for communication between human and software agents. We mainly distinguish three layers: First of all, we deal with things that exist in the real world, including in this example human and software agents, cars, and animals. Secondly, we deal with symbols and syntactic structures that are exchanged. Thirdly, we analyze models with their specific semantic structures.

Let us first consider the left side of Figure 2 without assuming a commitment to a given ontology. Two human agents HA_1 and HA_2 exchange a specific sign, *e.g.* a word like "jaguar". Given their own internal model each of them will associate the sign to his own concept referring to possibly two completely different existing things in the world, *e.g.* the animal *vs.* the car. The same holds for software agents: They may exchange statements based on a common syntax, however, they may have different formal models with differing interpretations.

We consider the scenario that both human agents commit to a specific ontology that deals with a specific domain, *e.g.* animals. The chance that they both refer to the same thing in the world increases considerably. The same holds for the software agents SA_1 and SA_2: They have actual knowledge and they use the ontology to have a common semantic basis. When agent SA_1 uses the term "jaguar", the other agent SA_2 may use the ontology just mentioned as background knowledge and rule out incorrect references, *e.g.* ones that let "jaguar" stand for the car. Human and software agents use their concepts and their inference processes, respectively, in order to narrow down the choice of referents (*e.g.*, because animals do not have wheels, but cars have).

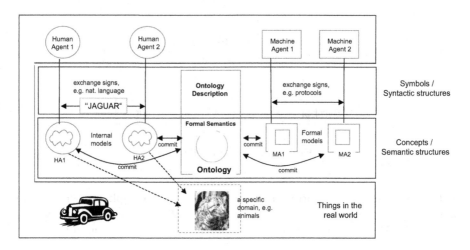

Fig. 2. Communication between human and/or software agents

A new model for ontologies. Subsequently, we define our notion of ontology. However, in contrast to most other research about ontology languages it is not our purpose to invent a new logic language or to redescribe an old one. Rather what we specify is a way of *modeling* an ontology that inherently considers the special role of signs (mostly strings in current ontology-based systems) and references.

Our motivation is based on the conflict that ontologies are for human and software agents, but logical theories are mostly for mathematicians and inference engines. Formal semantics for ontologies is a *sine qua non*. In fact, we build our applications on a well-understood logical framework, *viz.* F-Logic [10]. However, in addition to the benefits of logical rigor, user and developer of an ontology-based system profit from ontology structures that allow to elucidate possible misunderstandings.

For instance, one might specify that the sign "jaguar" refers to the union of the set of all animals that are jaguars and the set of all cars that are jaguars. Alternatively, one may describe that "jaguar" is a sign that may either refer to a concept "animal-jaguar" or to a concept "car-jaguar". We prefer the second way. In conjunction with appropriate GUI modules (*cf.* Sections 3ff) one may avoid presentations of 'funny symbols' to the user like "animal-jaguar", while avoiding 'funny inference' such as may arise from artificial concepts like the union of the sets denoted by 'animal-jaguar' and 'car-jaguar'.

2.2   Ontology *vs.* Knowledge Base

Concerning the general setting just sketched, the term ontology is defined — more or less — as some piece of formal knowledge. However, there are several properties that warrant the distinction of knowledge contained in the ontology *vs.* knowledge contained in the so-called *knowledge base*, which are summarized in Table 1.

Table 1. Distinguishing ontology and knowledge base

	Ontology	Knowledge base
Set of logic statements	yes	yes
Theory	general theory	theory of particular circumstances
Statements are mostly	intensional	extensional
Construction	set up once	continuous change
Description logics	T-Box	A-Box

The ontology constitutes a general logical theory, while the knowledge base describes particular circumstances. In the ontology one tries to capture the general conceptual structures of a domain of interest, while in the knowledge base one aims at the specification of the given state of affairs. Thus, the ontology is (mostly) constituted by *intensional* logical definitions, while the knowledge base comprises (mostly) the *extensional* parts. The theory in the ontology is one which is mostly developed during the set up (and maintenance) of an ontology-based system, while the facts in the knowledge base may be constantly changing. In description logics, the ontology part is mostly described in the T-Box and the knowledge base in the A-Box. However, our current experience is that it is not always possible to distinguish the ontology from the knowledge base by the logical statements that are made. In the conclusion we will briefly mention some of the problems referring to some examples of following sections.

The distinctions ("general" *vs.* "specific", "intensional" *vs.* "extensional", "set up once" *vs.* "continuous change") indicate that for purposes of development, maintenance, and good design of the software system it is reasonable to distinguish between ontology and knowledge base. Also, they describe a rough shape of where to put which parts of a logical theory constraining the intended semantic models that facilitate the referencing task for human and software agents. However, the reader should note that none of these distinctions draw a clear cut borderline between ontology and knowledge base in general. Rather, it is typical that in a few percent of cases it depends on the domain, the view of the modeler, and the experience of the modeler, whether she decides to put particular entitities and relations into the ontology or into the knowledge base.

Both following definitions of ontology and knowledge base specify constraints on the way an ontology (or a knowledge base) should be modeled *in a particular logical language* like F-Logic or OIL:

Definition 1 (Ontology). *An ontology is a sign system $\mathcal{O} := (\mathcal{L}, \mathcal{F}, \mathcal{G}, \mathcal{C}, \mathcal{H}, \mathcal{R}, \mathcal{A})$, which consists of*

- *A **lexicon**: The lexicon contains a set of signs (lexical entries) for concepts, $\mathcal{L}^c$, and a set of signs for relations, $\mathcal{L}^r$. Their union is the lexicon $\mathcal{L} := \mathcal{L}^c \cup \mathcal{L}^r$.*
- *Two **reference functions** $\mathcal{F}, \mathcal{G}$, with $\mathcal{F} : 2^{\mathcal{L}^c} \mapsto 2^{\mathcal{C}}$ and $\mathcal{G} : 2^{\mathcal{L}^s} \mapsto 2^{\mathcal{S}}$. $\mathcal{F}$ and $\mathcal{G}$ link sets of lexical entries $\{L_i\} \subset \mathcal{L}$ to the set of concepts and relations they refer to, respectively, in the given ontology. In general, one lexical entry*

may refer to several concepts or relations and one concept or relation may be refered to by several lexical entries. Their inverses are $\mathcal{F}^{-1}$ and $\mathcal{G}^{-1}$.

In order to map easily back and forth and because there is a n to m mapping between lexicon and concepts/relations, $\mathcal{F}$ and $\mathcal{G}$ are defined on sets rather than on single objects.

- *A set $\mathcal{C}$ of **concepts**: About each $C \in \mathcal{C}$ exists at least one statement in the ontology, viz. its embedding in the taxonomy.*
- *A **taxonomy** $\mathcal{H}$: Concepts are taxonomically related by the irreflexive, acyclic, transitive relation $\mathcal{H}$, ($\mathcal{H} \subset \mathcal{C} \times \mathcal{C}$). $\mathcal{H}(C_1, C_2)$ means that C_1 is a subconcept of C_2.*
- *A set of binary **relations** $\mathcal{R}$: $\mathcal{R}$ denotes a set of binary relations.[2] They specify pairs of domain and ranges (D, R) with $D, R \in \mathcal{C}$.*
  The functions d and r applied to a binary relation Q yield the corresponding domain and range concepts D and R, respectively.
- *A set of ontology axioms, $\mathcal{A}$.*

The reader may note that the structure we propose is very similar to the WordNet model described by Miller [14]. WordNet has been conceived as a mixed linguistic / psychological model about how people associate words with their meaning. Like WordNet, we allow that one word may have several meanings and one concept (synset) may be represented by several words. However, we allow for a seamless integration into logical languages like OIL or F-Logic by providing very simple means for definition of relations and for knowledge bases.

We define a knowledge base as a collection of object descriptions that refer to a given ontology.

Definition 2 (Knowledge Base). *We define a knowledge base as a 7-tupel $\mathcal{KB} := (\mathcal{L}, \mathcal{J}, \mathcal{I}, \mathcal{W}, \mathcal{S}, \mathcal{A}, \mathcal{O})$, that consists of*

- *a **lexicon** containing a set of signs for instances, $\mathcal{L}$.*
- *A **reference function** $\mathcal{J}$ with $\mathcal{J} : 2^{\mathcal{L}} \mapsto 2^{\mathcal{I}}$. $\mathcal{J}$ links sets of lexical entries $\{L_i\} \subset \mathcal{L}$ to the set of instances they correspond to.*
  Thereby, names may be multiply used, e.g. "Athens" may be used for "Athens, Georgia" or for "Athens, Greece".
- *a set of **instances** $\mathcal{I}$. About each $I_k \in \mathcal{I}, k = 1, \ldots, l$ exists at least one statement in the knowledge base, viz. a membership to a concept C from the ontology $\mathcal{O}$.*
- *A **membership function** $\mathcal{W}$ with $\mathcal{W} : 2^{\mathcal{I}} \mapsto 2^{\mathcal{C}}$. $\mathcal{W}$ assigns sets of instances to the sets of concepts they are members of.*
- ***Instantiated relations**, $\mathcal{S}$, are described, viz. $S \subseteq \{(x, y, z) | x \in \mathcal{I}, y \in \mathcal{R}, z \in \mathcal{I}\}$.*
- *A set of knowledge base axioms, $\mathcal{A}$.*
- *A reference to an ontology $\mathcal{O}$.*

Overall the decision to model some relevant part of the domain in the ontology *vs.* in the knowledge base is often based on gradual distinctions and driven by the needs of the application. Concerning the technical issue it is sometimes

---

[2] Here at the conceptual level, we do not distinguish between relations and attributes.

even useful to let the lexicon of knowledge base and ontology overlap, *e.g.* to use a concept name to refer to a particular instance in a particular context. In fact researchers in natural language have tackled the question how the reference function *J* can be dynamically extended given an ontology, a context, a knowledge base and a particular sentence.

3 SEAL Infrastructure and Core Modules

The aim of our intranet application is the presentation of information to human and software agents taking advantage of semantic structures. In this section, we first elaborate on the general architecture for SEAL (SEmantic PortAL), before we explain functionalities of its core modules.

3.1 Architecture

The overall architecture and environment of SEAL is depicted in Figure 3:

The *backbone* of the system consists of the *knowledge warehouse*, *i.e.* the data repository, and the *Ontobroker* system, *i.e.* the principal inferencing mechanism. The latter functions as a kind of middleware run-time system, possibly mediating between different information sources when the environment becomes more complex than it is now.

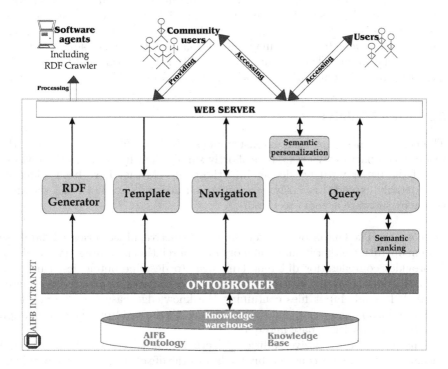

Fig. 3. AIFB Intranet - System architecture

At the front end one may distinguish between three types of *agents*: *software agents*, *community users* and *general users*. All three of them communicate with the system through the *web server*. The three different types of agents correspond to three primary modes of interaction with the system.

First, remote applications (*e.g.* software agents) may process information stored at the portal over the internet. For this purpose, the *RDF generator* presents RDF facts through the web server. Software agents with *RDF crawlers* may collect the facts and, thus, have direct access to semantic knowledge stored at the web site.

Second, community users and general users can access information contained at the web site. Two forms of accessing are supported: navigating through the portal by exploiting hyperlink structure of documents and searching for information by posting queries. The hyperlink structure is partially given by the portal builder, but it may be extended with the help of the *navigation* module. The navigation module exploits inferencing capabilities of the inference engine in order to construct conceptual hyperlink structures. Searching and querying is performed via the *query* module. In addition, the user can personalise the search interface using the *semantic personalization* preprocessing module and/or rank retrieved results according to semantic similarity (done by the postprocessing module for *semantic ranking*). Queries also take advantage of the Ontobroker inferencing.

Third, only community users can provide data. Typical information they contribute includes personal data, information about research areas, publications, activities and other research information. For each type of information they contribute there is (at least) one concept in the ontology. Retrieving parts of the ontology, the *template* module may semi-automatically produce suitable HTML forms for data input. The community users fill in these forms and the template modules stores the data in the knowledge warehouse.

3.2   Core Modules

The core modules have been extensively described in [19]. In order to give the reader a compact overview we here shortly survey their function. In the remainder of the paper we delve deeper into those aspects that have been added or considerably extended recently, *viz.* semantic ranking (Section 4), and semantic access by software agents (Section 5).

Ontobroker. The Ontobroker system [6] is a deductive, object-oriented database system operating either in main memory or on a relational database (via JDBC). It provides compilers for different languages to describe ontologies, rules and facts. Beside other usage, in this architecture it is also used as an inference engine (server). It reads input files containing the knowledge base and the ontology, evaluates incoming queries, and returns the results derived from the combination of ontology, knowledge base and query.

The possibility to derive additional factual knowledge from given facts and background knowledge considerably facilitates the life of the knowledge providers and the knowledge seekers. For instance, one may specify that if a person belongs to a research group of institute AIFB, he also belongs to AIFB. Thus, it is unnecessary to specify the membership to his research group *and* to AIFB. Conversely, the information seeker does not have to take care of inconsistent assignments, *e.g.* ones that specify membership to an AIFB research group, but that have erronously left out the membership to AIFB.

Knowledge warehouse. The knowledge warehouse [19] serves as repository for data represented in the form of F-Logic statements. It hosts the ontology, as well as the data proper. From the point of view of inferencing (Ontobroker) the difference is negligible, but from the point of view of maintaining the system the difference between ontology definition and its instantiation is useful. The knowledge warehouse is organised around a relational database, where facts and concepts are stored in a reified format. It states relations and concepts as first-order objects and it is therefore very flexible with regard to changes and amendments of the ontology.

Navigation module. Beside the hierarchical, tree-based hyperlink structure which corresponds to hierarchical decomposition of domain, the navigation module enables complex graph-based semantic hyperlinking, based on ontological relations between concepts (nodes) in the domain. The conceptual approach to hyperlinking is based on the assumption that semantic relevant hyperlinks from a web page correspond to conceptual relations, such as `memberOf` or `hasPart`, or to attributes, like `hasName`. Thus, instances in the knowledge base may be presented by automatically generating links to all related instances. For example, on personal web pages (*cf.* Figure 5) there are hyperlinks to web pages that describe the corresponding research groups, research areas and project web pages.

Query module. The query module puts an easy-to-use interface on the query capabilities of the F-Logic query interface of Ontobroker. The portal builder models web pages that serve particular query needs, such as querying for projects or querying for people. For this purpose, selection lists that restrict query possibilities are offered to the user. The selection lists are compiled using knowledge from the ontology and/or the knowledge base. For instance, the query interface for persons allows to search for people according to research groups they are members of. The list of research groups is dynamically filled by an F-Logic query and presented to the user for easy choice by a drop-down list (*cf.* snapshot in Figure 4).

Even simpler, one may apprehend a hyperlink with an F-Logic query that is dynamically evaluated when the link is hit. More complex, one may construct an `isA`, a `hasPart`, or a `hasSubtopic` tree, from which query events are triggered when particular nodes in the tree are navigated.

Personalization module. The personalization component allows to provide checkbox personalization and preference-based personalization (including profiling from semantics-based log files). For instance, one may detect that user group A is particularly interested in all pages that deal with nature-analog algorithms, e.g. ones about genetic algorithms or ant algorithms.

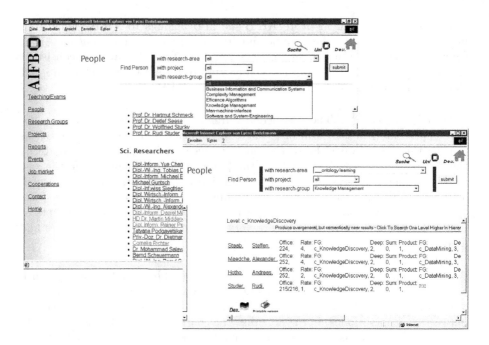

Fig. 4. Query form based on definition of concept Person

Template module. In order to facilitate the contribution of information by community users, the template module generates an HTML form for each concept that a user may instantiate. For instance, in the AIFB intranet there is an input template (*cf.* Figure 5, upper left) generated from the concept definition of person (*cf.* Figure 5, lower left). The data is later on used by the navigation module to produce the corresponding person web page (*cf.* Figure 5, right hand side).

In order to reduce the data required for input, the portal builder specifies which attributes and relations are derived from other templates. For example, in our case the portal builder has specified that project membership is defined in the project template. The co-ordinator of a project enters information about which persons are participants of the project and this information is used when generating the person web page taking advantage of a corresponding F-Logic rule for inverse relationships. Hence, it is unnecessary to input this information in the person template.

Ontology lexicon. The different modules described here make extensive use of the lexicon component of the ontology. The most prevalent use is the distinction between English and German (realized for presentation, though not for the template module, yet). In the future we envision that one may produce more

Fig. 5. Templates generated from concept definitions

adaptive web sites making use of the explicit lexicon. For instance, we will be able to produce short descriptions when the context is sufficiently narrow, *e.g.* working with ambiguous acronyms like ASP[3] or SEAL[4]

4   Semantic Ranking

This section describes the architecture component "Semantic Ranking" which has been developed in the context of our application. First, we will introduce and motivate the requirement for a ranking approach with a small example we are facing. Second, we will show how the problem of semanking ranking may be reduced to the comparison of two knowledge bases. Query results are reinterpreted as "query knowledge bases" and their similarity to the original knowledge base without axioms yields the basis for semantic ranking. Thereby, we reduce our notion of similarity between two knowledge bases to the similarity of concept pairs [23,11]. Let us assume the following ontology:

---

[3] Active server pages *vs.* active service providers.

[4] "SouthEast Asian Linguistics Conference" *vs.* "Conference on Simulated Evolution and Learning" *vs.* "Society for Evolutionary Analysis in Law" *vs.* "Society for Effective Affective Learning" *vs.* some other dozens — several of which are indeed relevant in our institute.

$$1 : \mathsf{Person} :: \mathsf{Object}[\mathrm{WORKSIN} \Rrightarrow \mathsf{Project}].$$
$$2 : \mathsf{Project} :: \mathsf{Object}[\mathrm{HASTOPIC} \Rrightarrow \mathsf{Topic}].$$
$$3 : \mathsf{Topic} :: \mathsf{Object}[\mathrm{SUBTOPICOF} \Rrightarrow \mathsf{Topic}]. \tag{1}$$
$$4 : \mathtt{FORALL}\ X, Y, Z\ \ Z[\mathrm{HASTOPIC} \twoheadrightarrow Y] \leftarrow X[\mathrm{SUBTOPICOF} \twoheadrightarrow Y]$$
$$\mathbf{and}\ Z[\mathrm{HASTOPIC} \twoheadrightarrow X].$$

To give an intuition of the semantic of the F-Logic statements, in line 1 one finds a concept definition for a Person being an Object with a relation WORKSIN. The range of the relation for this Person is restricted to Project.

Let us further assume the following knowledge base:

$$5 : \mathtt{KnowledgeManagement} : \mathsf{Topic}.$$
$$6 : \mathtt{KnowledgeDiscovery} : \mathsf{Topic}[\mathrm{SUBTOPICOF} \twoheadrightarrow \mathtt{KnowledgeManagement}].$$
$$7 : \mathtt{Gerd} : \mathsf{Person}[\mathrm{WORKSIN} \twoheadrightarrow \mathtt{OntoWise}].$$
$$8 : \mathtt{OntoWise} : \mathsf{Project}[\mathrm{HASTOPIC} \twoheadrightarrow \mathtt{KnowledgeManagement}]. \tag{2}$$
$$9 : \mathtt{Andreas} : \mathsf{Person}[\mathrm{WORKSIN} \twoheadrightarrow \mathtt{TelekomProject}].$$
$$10 : \mathtt{TelekomProject} : \mathsf{Project}[\mathrm{HASTOPIC} \twoheadrightarrow \mathtt{KnowledgeDiscovery}].$$

Definitions of instances in the knowledge base are syntactically very similar to the concept definition in F-Logic. In line 6 the instance KnowledgeDiscovery of the concept Topic is defined. Furthermore, the relation SUBTOPICOF is instantiated between KnowledgeDiscovery and KnowledgeManagement. Similarly in line 7, it is stated that Gerd is a {concPerson working in OntoWise. Ontology axioms like given in line 4 (1) use this syntax to describe regularities. Line 4 states that if some Z has topic X and X is a subtopic of Y then Z also has topic Y.

Now, an F-Logic query may ask for all people who work in a knowledge management project by:

$$\mathtt{FORALL}\ Y, Z \leftarrow Y[\mathrm{WORKSIN} \twoheadrightarrow Z]\ \mathbf{and}$$
$$Z : Project[\mathrm{HASTOPIC} \twoheadrightarrow \mathtt{KnowledgeManagement}] \tag{3}$$

which may result in the tuples $M_1^T := (\mathtt{Gerd}, \mathtt{OntoWise})$ and $M_2^T := (\mathtt{Andreas}, \mathtt{TelekomProject})$. Obviously, both answers are correct with regard to the given knowledge base and ontology, but the question is, what would be a plausible ranking for the correct answers. This ranking should be produced from a given query without assuming any modification of the query.

4.1 Reinterpreting Queries

Our principal consideration builds on the definition of semantic similarity that we have first described in [23,11]. There, we have developed a measure for the similarity of two knowledge bases. Here, our basic idea is to reinterprete possible query results as a "query knowledge base" and compute its similarity to the original knowledge base while abstracting from semantic inferences. The result of an F-Logic query may be re-interpreted as a *query knowledge base* (QKB) by the following approach.

An F-Logic query is of the form or can be rewritten into the form[5]:

---

[5] Negation requires special treatment.

$$\text{FORALL } \overline{X} \leftarrow \overline{P}(\overline{X}, \overline{k}), \tag{4}$$

with $\overline{X}$ being a vector of variables $(X_1, \ldots, X_n)$, $\overline{k}$ being a vector of constants, and $\overline{P}$ being a vector of conjoined predicates. The result of a query is a two-dimensional matrix M of size $m \times n$, with n being the number of result tuples and m being the length of $\overline{X}$ and, hence, the length of the result tuples. Hence, in our example above $\overline{X} := (Y, Z)$, $\overline{k} := (\text{``knowledge management''})$, $\overline{P} := (P_1, P_2)$, $P_1(a, b, c) := a[\text{WORKSIN} \twoheadrightarrow b]$, $P_2(a, b, c) := b[\text{HASTOPIC} \twoheadrightarrow c]$ and

$$M := (M_1, M_2) = \begin{pmatrix} \texttt{Gerd} & \texttt{Andreas} \\ \texttt{OntoWise} & \texttt{TelekomProjekt} \end{pmatrix}. \tag{5}$$

Now, we may define the query knowledge base i (QKB_i) by

$$QKB_i := \overline{P}(M_i, \overline{k}). \tag{6}$$

The similarity measure between the query knowledge base and the given knowledge base may then be computed in analogy to [23]. An adaptation and simplification of the measures described there is given in the following together with an example.

4.2   Similarity of Knowledge Bases

The similarity between two objects (concepts and or instances) may be computed by considering their relative place in a common hierarchy H. H may, but need not be a taxonomy $\mathcal{H}$. For instance, in our example from above we have a categorization of research topics, which is not a taxonomy!

Our principal measures are based on the cotopies of the corresponding objects as defined by a given hierarchy H, e.g. an ISA hierarchy $\mathcal{H}$, an part-whole hierarchy, or a categorization of topics. Here, we use the *upwards cotopy* (UC) defined as follows:

$$\text{UC}(O_i, H) := \{O_j | H(O_i, O_j) \vee O_j = O_i\} \tag{7}$$

UC is overloaded in order to allow for a set of objects M as input instead of only single objects, *viz.*

$$\text{UC}(M, H) := \bigcup_{O_i \in M} \{O_j | H(O_i, O_j) \vee O_j = O_i\} \tag{8}$$

Based on the definition of the upwards cotopy (UC) the object match (OM) is defined by:

$$\text{OM}(O_1, O_2, H) := \frac{|\text{UC}(O_1, H) \cap \text{UC}(O_2, H)|}{|\text{UC}(O_1, H) \cup \text{UC}(O_2, H)|}. \tag{9}$$

Basically, OM reaches 1 when two concepts coincide (number of intersections of the respective upwards cotopies and number of unions of the respective cotopies is equal); it degrades to the extent to which the discrepancy between intersections and unions increases (a OM between concepts that do not share common superconcepts yields value 0).

Example. We here give a small example for computing UC and OM based on a given categorization of objects H. Figure 6 depicts the example scenario. The upwards cotopy
UC(knowledge discovery, H) is given by {knowledge discovery, knowledge management}. The upwards cotopy UC(optimization, H) computes to {optimization}.

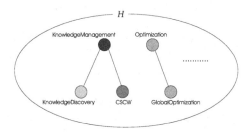

Fig. 6. Example for computing UC and OM

Computing the object match OM between KnowledgeManagement and Optimization results in 0, the object match between KnowledgeDiscovery and CSCW computes to $\frac{1}{3}$.

The match introduced above may easily be generalized to relations using a relation hierarchy H_R. Thus, the predicate match (PM) for two n-ary predicate P_1, P_2 is defined by a mean value. Thereby, we use the geometric mean in order to reflect the intuition that if the similarity of one of the components approaches 0 the overall similarity between two predicates should approach 0 — which need not be the case for the arithmetic mean:

$$PM(P_1(I_1, \ldots, I_n), P_2(J_1, \ldots, J_n)) := \sqrt[n+1]{OM(P_1, P_2, \mathcal{H}_R) \cdot OM(I_1, J_1, H) \cdot \ldots \cdot OM(I_n, J_n, H)}. \tag{10}$$

This result may be averaged over an array of predicates. We here simply give the formula for our actual needs, where a query knowledge base is compared against a given knowledge base KB:

$$Simil(QKB_i, KB) = Simil(\overline{P}(M_i, \overline{k}), KB) := \frac{1}{|\overline{P}|} \sum_{P_j \in \overline{P}} \max_{Q(M_i, \overline{k}) \in KB.S} PM(P_j(M_i, \overline{k}), Q(M_i, \overline{k})). \tag{11}$$

For instance, comparing the two result tuples from our example above with the given knowledge base: First, $M_1^T := ($Gerd, OntoWise$)$. Then, we have the query knowledge base (QKB_1):

$$\begin{array}{l} \text{Gerd}[\text{WORKSIN} \twoheadrightarrow \text{OntoWise}]. \\ \text{OntoWise}[\text{HASTOPIC} \twoheadrightarrow \text{KnowledgeManagement}]. \end{array} \tag{12}$$

and its relevant counterpart predicates in the given knowledge base (KB) are:

$$\text{Gerd}[\text{WORKSIN} \twoheadrightarrow \text{OntoWise}].$$
$$\text{OntoWise}[\text{HASTOPIC} \twoheadrightarrow \text{KnowledgeManagement}]. \tag{13}$$

This is a perfect fit. Therefore $Simil(QKB_1, KB)$ computes to 1.
Second, $M_2^T := (\text{Andreas}, \text{TelekomProject})$. Then, we have the query knowledge base (QKB_2):

$$\text{Andreas}[\text{WORKSIN} \twoheadrightarrow \text{TelekomProject}].$$
$$\text{TelekomProject}[\text{HASTOPIC} \twoheadrightarrow \text{KnowledgeManagement}]. \tag{14}$$

and its relevant counterpart predicates in the given knowledge base (KB) are:

$$\text{Andreas}[\text{WORKSIN} \twoheadrightarrow \text{TelekomProject}].$$
$$\text{TelekomProject}[\text{HASTOPIC} \twoheadrightarrow \text{KnowledgeDiscovery}]. \tag{15}$$

Hence, the similarity of the first predicates indicates a perfect fit and evaluates to 1, but the congruency of $\text{TelekomProject}[\text{HASTOPIC} \twoheadrightarrow \text{KnowledgeManagement}]$ with $\text{TelekomProject}[\text{HASTOPIC} \twoheadrightarrow \text{KnowledgeDiscovery}]$ measures less than 1. The instance match of $\text{KnowledgeDiscovery}$ and $\text{KnowledgeManagement}$ returns $\frac{1}{2}$ in the given topic hierarchy. Therefore, the predicate match returns $\sqrt[3]{1 \cdot 1 \cdot \frac{1}{2}} \approx 0.79$. Thus, overall ranking of the second result is based on $\frac{1}{2}(1 + 0.79) = 0.895$.

Remarks on semantic ranking. The reader may note some basic properties of the ranking: *(i)* similarity of knowledge bases is an asymmetric measure, *(ii)* the ontology defines a conceptual structure useful for defining similarity, *(iii)* the core concept for evaluating semantic similarity is cotopy defined by a dedicated hierarchy. The actual computation of similarity depends on which conceptual structures (*e.g.* hierarchies like taxonomy, part-whole hierarchies, or topic hierarchies) are selected for evaluating conceptual nearness. Thus, similarity of knowledge bases depends on the view selected for the similarity measure.

Ranking of semantic queries using underlying ontological structures is an important means in order to allow users a more specific view onto the underlying knowledge base. The method that we propose is based on a few basic principles:

- Reinterprete the combination of query and results as query knowledge bases that may be compared with the explicitly given information.
- Give a measure for comparing two knowledge bases, thus allowing rankings of query results.

Thus, we may improve the interface to the underlying structures without changing the basic architecture. Of course, the reader should be aware that our measure may produce some rankings for results that are hardly comparable. For instance, results may differ slightly because of imbalances in a given hierarchy or due to rather random differences of depth of branches. In this case, ranking may perhaps produce results that are not better than unranked ones — but the results will not be any worse either.

5   RDF Outside — From a Semantic Web Site to the Semantic Web

In the preceding sections we have described the development and the underlying techniques of the AIFB semantic web site. Having developed the core application we decided that RDF-capable software agents should be able to understand the content of application. Therefore, we have built an automatic RDF GENERATOR that dynamically generates RDF statements on each of the static and dynamic pages of the semantic knowledge portal. Our current AIFB intranet application is "Semantic Web-ized" using RDF facts instantiated and defined according to the underlying AIFB ontology. On top of this generated and formally represented metadata, there is the RDF CRAWLER, a tool that gathers interconnected fragments of RDF from the internet.

5.1   RDF Generator — An Example

The RDFMAKER established in the ONTOBROKER framework (*cf.* [5]) was a starting point for building the RDF GENERATOR. The idea of RDFMAKER was, that from ONTOBROKER'S internal data base, RDF statements are generated.

RDF GENERATOR follows a similar approach and extends the principal ideas. In a first step it generates an RDF(S)-based ontology that is stored on a specific XML namespace, *e.g.* in our concrete application http://ontobroker.semanticweb.org/ontologies/aifb-onto-2001-01-01.rdfs. Additionally, it queries the knowledge warehouse. Data, *e.g.* for a person, is checked for consistency, and, if possible, completed by applying the given F-Logic rules. We here give a short example of what type of data may be generated and stored on a specific homepage of a researcher:

```
<rdf:RDF
  xmlns:rdf = "http://www.w3.org/1999/02/22-rdf-syntax-ns#"
  xmlns:aifb = "http://ontobroker.semanticweb.org/aifb-2001-01-01.rdfs#">

       <aifb:PhDStudent rdf:ID="per:ama">
         <aifb:name>Alexander Maedche</aifb:name>
         <aifb:email>ama@aifb.uni-karlsruhe.de</aifb:email>
         <aifb:phone>+49-(0)721-608 6558</aifb:phone>
         <aifb:fax>+49-(0)721-608 6580</aifb:fax>
         <aifb:homepage>http://www.aifb.uni-karlsruhe.de/WBS/ama</aifb:homepage>
         <aifb:supervisor
            rdf:resource = "http://www.aifb.uni-karlsruhe.de/studer.html#per:rst"/>
       </aifb:PhDStudent>
</rdf:RDF>
```

RDF GENERATOR is a configurable tool, in some cases one may want to use inferences to generate materialized, complete RDF descriptions on a home page, in other cases one may want to generate only ground facts of RDF. Therefore, RDF GENERATOR allows to switch axioms on and off in order to adopt the generation of results to varying needs.

5.2   RDF Crawler

The RDF CRAWLER[6] is a tool which downloads interconnected fragments of RDF from the internet and builds a knowledge base from this data. Building an external knowledge base for the whole AIFB (its researcher, its projects, its publications, ...) becomes easy using the RDF CRAWLER and machine-processable RDF data currently defined on AIFB's web. We here shortly describe the underlying techniques of our RDF CRAWLER and the process of building a knowledge base. In general, RDF data may appear in Web documents in several ways. We distinguish between pure RDF (files that have an extension like "*.rdf"), RDF embedded in HTML and RDF embedded in XML. Our RDF CRAWLER uses RDF-API[7] that can deal with different embeddings of RDF described above.

One problem of crawling is the applied filtering mechanism: Baseline crawlers are typically restricted by a given depth value. Recently several new research work on so-called *focused crawling* has been published (*e.g. cf.* [3]). In their approach, they use a set of predefined documents associated with topics in a Yahoo like taxonomy to built a focused crawler. Two hypertext mining algorithms constitute the core of their approach. A classifier evaluates the relevance of a hypertext document with respect to the focus topics and a distiller identifies hypertext nodes that are good access points to many relevant pages within a few links. In contrast, our approach uses ontological background knowledge to judge the relevance of each page. If a page is highly relevant, the crawler may follow the links on the particular web site. If RDF data is available on a page, we judge relevance with respect to the quantity and quality of available data and by the existing URI's.

Example: Erdoes numbers. As mentioned above we here give a small example of a nice application that may be easily built using RDF metadata taken from AIFB using the RDF CRAWLER. The so-called *Erdoes numbers* have been a part of the folklore of mathematicians throughout the world for many years[8].

Scientific papers are frequently published with co-authors. Based on information about collaboration one may compute the Erdoes number (denoted $PE(R)$) for a researcher R. In the AIFB web site the RDF-based metadata allows for computing estimates of Paul Erdoes numbers of AIFB members. The numbers are defined recursively:

1. $PE(R) = 0$, iff R is Paul Erdoes
2. $PE(R) = \min\{PE(R_1) + 1\}$ else, where R_1 varies over the set of all researchers who have collaborated with R, *i.e.* have written a scientific paper together.

---

[6] RDF CRAWLER is freely available for download at
http://ontobroker.semanticweb.org/rdfcrawler.

[7] RDF-API is freely available at http://www-db.stanford.edu/~melnik/rdf/api.html.

[8] The interested reader may have a look at
http://www.oakland.edu/~grossman/erdoshp.html for an overall project overview.

To put this into work, we need lists of publications annotated with RDF facts. The lists may be automatically generated by the RDF GENERATOR. Based on the RDF facts one may crawl relevant information into a central knowledge base and compute these numbers from the data.

6   Related Work

This section positions our work in the context of existing web portals and also relates our work to other basic methods and tools that are or could be deployed for the construction of community web portals, especially to related work in the area of semantic ranking of query results.

Related Work on Knowledge Portals. One of the well-established web portals on the web is Yahoo[9]. In contrast to our approach Yahoo only utilizes a very light-weight ontology that solely consists of categories arranged in a hierarchical manner. Yahoo offers keyword search (local to a selected topic or global) in addition to hierarchical navigation, but is only able to retrieve complete documents, *i.e.* it is not able to answer queries concerning the contents of documents, not to mention to combine facts being found in different documents or to include facts that could be derived through ontological axioms. Personalization is limited to check-box personalization. We get rid of these shortcomings since our portal is built upon a rich ontology enabling the portal to give integrated answers to queries. Furthermore, our semantic personalization features provide more flexible means for adapting the portal to the specific needs of its users.

A portal that is specialized for a scientific community has been built by the Math-Net project [4]. At http://www.math-net.de/ the portal for the (German) mathematics community is installed that makes distributed information from several mathematical departments available. This information is accompanied by meta-data according to the Dublin Core [10] Standard [25]. The Dublin Core element "Subject" is used to classify resources as conferences, as research groups, as preprints etc. A finer classification (*e.g.* via attributes) is not possible except for instances of the publication category. Here the common MSC-Classification[11] is used that resembles a light-weight ontology of the field of mathematics. With respect to our approach Math-Net lacks a rich ontology that could enhance the quality of search results (esp. via inferencing), and the smooth connection to the Semantic Web world that is provided by our RDF generator.

The Ontobroker project [5] lays the technological foundations for the AIFB portal. On top of Ontobroker the portal has been built and organizational structures for developing and maintaining it have been established. Therefore, we compare our system against approaches that are similar to Ontobroker.

The approach closest to Ontobroker is SHOE [7]. In SHOE, HTML pages are annotated via ontologies to support information retrieval based on semantic information. Besides the use of ontologies and the annotation of web pages the

---

[9] http://www.yahoo.com
[10] http://www.purl.org/dc
[11] *cf.* Mathematical Subject Classification; http://www.ams.org/msc/

underlying philosophy of both systems differs significantly: SHOE uses description logic as its basic representation formalism, but it offers only very limited inferencing capabilities. Ontobroker relies on Frame-Logic and supports complex inferencing for query answering. Furthermore, the SHOE search tool neither provides means for a semantic ranking of query results nor for a semantic personalization feature. A more detailed comparison to other portal approaches and underlying methods may be found in [19].

Related Work on Semantic Similarity. Since our semantic ranking is based on the comparison of the query knowledge base with the given ontology and knowledge base, we relate our work to the comparison of ontological structures and knowledge bases (covering the same domain) and to measuring the similarity between concepts in a hierarchy. Although there has been a long discussion in the literature about evaluating knowledge-bases [13], we have not found any discussion about comparing two knowledge bases covering the same domain that corresponds to our semantic ranking approach. Similarity measures for ontological structures have been investigated in areas like cognitive science, databases or knowledge engineering (*cf. e.g.*, [17,16,18,9]). However, all these approaches are restricted to similarity measures between lexical entries, concepts, and template slots within one ontology.

Closest to our measure of similarity is work in the NLP community, named semantic similarity [17] which refers to similarity between two concepts in a `isA`-taxonomy such as the WordNet or CYC upper ontology. Our approach differs in two main aspect from this notion of similarity: Firstly, our similarity measure is applicable to a hierarchy which may, but not need be a taxonomy and secondly it is taking into account not only commonalties but also differences between the items being compared, expressing both in semantic-cotopy terms. This second property enables the measuring of self-similarity and subclass-relationship similarity, which are crucial for comparing results derived from the inferencing processes, that are executed in the background.

Conceptually, instead of measuring similarity between isolated terms (words), that does not take into account the relationship among word senses that matters, we measure similarity between "words in context", by measuring similarity between Object-Attribute-Value pairs, where each term corresponds to a concept in the ontology. This enables us to exploit the ontological background knowledge (axioms and relations between concepts) in measuring the similarity, which expands our approach to a methodology for comparing knowledge bases.

From our point of view, our community portal system is rather unique with respect to the collection of methods used and the functionality provided. We have extended our community portal approach that provides flexible means for providing, integrating and accessing information [19] by semantic personalization features, semantic ranking of generated answers and a smooth integration with the evolving Semantic Web. All these methods are integrated into one uniform system environment, the SEAL framework.

7   Conclusion

In this paper we have shown our comprehensive approach SEAL for building semantic portals. In particular, we have focused on three issues.

First, we have considered the ontological foundation of SEAL. There, we have made the experience that there are many big open issues that have hardly been dealt with so far. In particular, the step of formalizing the ontology raises very principal problems. The issue of where to put relevant concepts, *viz.* into the ontology *vs.* into the knowledge base, is an important one that deeply affects organization and application. However, there exist no corresponding methodological guidelines to base the decision upon so far. For instance, we have given the example ontology and knowledge base in (1) and (2). Using description logics terminology, we have equated the ontology with the "T-Box" and we have put the topic hierachy into the knowledge base ("A-Box"). An alternative could have been to formalize the topic hierarchy as an isA-hierarchy, which however it isn't and put it into the T-Box. We believe that both alternatives exhibit an internal fault, *viz.* the ontology should not be equated with the T-Box, but rather should its scope be independent from an actual formalization with particular logical statements. Its scope should to a large extent depend on soft issues, like "Who updates a concept?" and "How often does a concept change?" such as already indicated in Table 1. Second, we have described the general architecture of the SEAL approach, which is also used for our real-world case study, the AIFB web site. The architecture integrates a number of components that we have also used in other applications, like Ontobroker, navigation or query module. Third, we have extended our semantic modules to include a larger diversity of intelligent means for accessing the web site, *viz.* semantic ranking and machine access by crawling.

For the future, we see a number of new important topics appearing on the horizon. For instance, we consider approaches for ontology learning [12] in order to semi-automatically adapt to changes in the world and to facilitate the engineering of ontologies. Currently, we work on providing intelligent means for providing semantic information, *i.e.* we elaborate on a semantic annotation framework that balances between manual provisioning from legacy texts (*e.g.* web pages) and information extraction [22]. Given a particular conceptualization, we envision that one wants to be able to use a multitude of different inference engines taking advantage of different inferencing capabilities (temporal, non-monotonic, high scalability, etc.). Then, however, one needs means to change from one representation paradigm to the next [20].

Finally, we envision that once semantic web sites are widely available, their automatic exploitation may be brought to new levels. Semantic web mining considers the level of mining web site structures, web site content, and web site usage on a semantic rather than at a syntactic level yielding new possibilities, *e.g.* for intelligent navigation, personalization, or summarization, to name but a few objectives for semantic web sites [8].

Acknowledgements. The research presented in this paper would not have been possible without our colleagues and students at the Institute AIFB, University of

Karlsruhe, and Ontoprise GmbH. We thank Jürgen Angele, Kalvis Apsitis (now: RITI Riga Information Technology Institute), Nils Braeunlich, Stefan Decker (now: Stanford University), Michael Erdmann, Dieter Fensel (now: VU Amsterdam), Siegfried Handschuh, Andreas Hotho, Mika Maier-Collin, Daniel Oberle, and Hans-Peter Schnurr. Research for this paper was partially financed by Ontoprise GmbH, Karlsruhe, Germany, by US Air Force in the DARPA DAML project "OntoAgents", by EU in the IST-1999-10132 project "On-To-Knowledge" and by BMBF in the project "GETESS" (01IN901C0).

References

1. J. Angele, H.-P. Schnurr, S. Staab, and R. Studer. The times they are a-changin' — the corporate history analyzer. In D. Mahling and U. Reimer, editors, *Proceedings of the Third International Conference on Practical Aspects of Knowledge Management. Basel, Switzerland, October 30-31, 2000*, 2000. http://www.research.swisslife.ch/pakm2000/.
2. V. Richard Benjamins and Dieter Fensel. Community is knowledge! (KA)^2. In *Proceedings of the 11th Workshop on Knowledge Acquisition, Modeling, and Management (KAW '98), Banff, Canada, April 1998*, 1998.
3. S. Chakrabarti, M. van den Berg, and B. Dom. Focused crawling: a new approach to topic-specific web resource discovery. In *Proceedings of WWW-8*, 1999.
4. W. Dalitz, M. Grötschel, and J. Lügger. Information Services for Mathematics in the Internet (Math-Net). In A. Sydow, editor, *Proceedings of the 15th IMACS World Congress on Scientific Computation: Modelling and Applied Mathematics*, volume 4 of *Artificial Intelligence and Computer Science*, pages 773–778. Wissenschaft und Technik Verlag, 1997.
5. S. Decker, M. Erdmann, D. Fensel, and R. Studer. Ontobroker: Ontology Based Access to Distributed and Semi-Structured Information. In R. Meersman et al., editors, *Database Semantics: Semantic Issues in Multimedia Systems*, pages 351–369. Kluwer Academic Publisher, 1999.
6. D. Fensel, S. Decker, M. Erdmann, and R. Studer. Ontobroker: The Very High Idea. In *Proceedings of the 11th International Flairs Conference (FLAIRS-98), Sanibel Island, Florida, May*, 1998.
7. J. Heflin and J. Hendler. Searching the web with shoe. In *Artificial Intelligence for Web Search. Papers from the AAAI Workshop. WS-00-01*, pages 35–40. AAAI Press, 2000.
8. A. Hotho and G. Stumme, editors. *Semantic Web Mining — Workshop at ECML-2001 / PKDD-2001, Freiburg, Germany*, 2001.
9. E. Hovy. Combining and standardizing large-scale, practical ontologies for machine translation and other uses. In *Proc. of the First Int. Conf. on Language Resources and Evaluation (LREC)*, 1998.
10. M. Kifer, G. Lausen, and J. Wu. Logical Foundations of Object-Oriented and Frame-Based Languages. *Journal of the ACM*, 42:741–843, 1995.
11. A. Maedche and S. Staab. Discovering conceptual relations from text. In *Proceedings of ECAI-2000*. IOS Press, Amsterdam, 2000.
12. A. Maedche and S. Staab. Ontology learning for the semantic web. *IEEE Intelligent Systems*, 16(2), 2001.
13. T.J. Menzis. Knowledge maintenance: The state of the art. *The Knowledge Engineering Review*, 10(2), 1998.

14. G. Miller. Wordnet: A lexical database for English. *CACM*, 38(11):39–41, 1995.
15. C.K. Odgen and I.A. Richards. *The Meaning of Meaning: A Study of the Influence of Language upon Thought and of the Science of Symbolism.* Routledge & Kegan Paul Ltd., London, 10 edition, 1923.
16. R. Rada, H. Mili, E. Bicknell, and M. Blettner. Development and application of a metric on semantic nets. *IEEE Transactions on Systems, Man, and Cybernetics*, 19(1), 1989.
17. P. Resnik. Knowledge maintenance: The state of the art. In *Proceedings of IJCAI-95*, pages 448–453, Montreal, Canada, 1995.
18. R. Richardson, A. F. Smeaton, and J. Murphy. Using wordnet as knowledge base for measuring semantic similarity between words. Technical Report CA-1294, Dublin City University, School of Computer Applications, 1994.
19. S. Staab, J. Angele, S. Decker, M. Erdmann, A. Hotho, A. Maedche, H.-P. Schnurr, R. Studer, and Y. Sure. Semantic community web portals. *Proc. of WWW9 / Computer Networks*, 33(1-6):473–491, 2000.
20. S. Staab, M. Erdmann, and A. Maedche. Engineering ontologies using semantic patterns. In A. Preece, editor, *Proc. of the IJCAI-01 Workshop on E-Business & the Intelligent Web*, 2001.
21. S. Staab and A. Maedche. Knowledge portals — ontologies at work. *AI Magazine*, 21(2), Summer 2001.
22. S. Staab, A. Maedche, and S. Handschuh. An annotation framework for the semantic web. In *Proceedings of the First Workshop on Multimedia Annotation, Tokyo, Japan, January 30-31, 2001*, 2001.
23. S. Staab, A. Maedche, and S. Handschuh. Creating metadata for the semantic web: An annotation framework and the human factor. Technical Report 412, Institute AIFB, University of Karlsruhe, 2001.
24. Y. Sure, A. Maedche, and S. Staab. Leveraging corporate skill knowledge - From ProPer to OntoProper. In D. Mahling and U. Reimer, editors, *Proceedings of the Third International Conference on Practical Aspects of Knowledge Management. Basel, Switzerland, October 30-31, 2000*, 2000. http://www.research.swisslife.ch/pakm2000/.
25. S. Weibel, J. Kunze, C. Lagoze, and M. Wolf. *Dublin Core Metadata for Resource Discovery.* Number 2413 in IETF. The Internet Society, September 1998.

E-Science and the Grid

Tony Hey

EPSRC, Polaris House, North Star Avenue, Swindon SN2 1ET, UK
`tony.hey@epsrc.ac.uk`

Abstract. The relentless advance of Moore's Law for both processor and memory chips will continue to transform both the academic and commercial world for some years to come. Multi-Teraflop parallel computers and Petabyte databases will increasingly become the norm for frontier research problems. Even more startling has been the growth in bandwidth so that a 'Trans-Atlantic Terabit Testbed' is now under discussion based on WDM optical fibre technology and Erbium Doped Fibre Amplifiers. The scale of these enterprises will also mean that such large science problems are likely to become increasingly international and multidisciplinary. This is the vision of 'e-Science' proposed by John Taylor, Director General of the UK Office of Science and Technology. To support such global e-Science collaborations a more general infrastructure is required. Not only do researchers need to access html web pages for information but also they need transparent remote access to computing resources, data repositories and specialist experimental facilities. The Grid of Foster and Kesselman aims to provide such an environment. The Grid is an ambitious project that has immense momentum and support world-wide. In the UK, the OST and the DTI are investing over £120M in helping make this Grid vision become a reality. It is vital that sensible and secure lower level infrastructure standards are agreed upon and high-quality Open Source/Open Standard middleware delivered as soon as possible. Once these are in place there will be great scope for innovative research into new tools to support data curation, information management and knowledge discovery. Making dependable and secure Grid software to manage and exploit the intrinsically dynamic and heterogeneous Grid environment is an exciting challenge for many sections of the UK academic Computer Science community.

B. Read (Ed.): BNCOD 2001, LNCS 2097, p. 23, 2001.
© Springer-Verlag Berlin Heidelberg 2001

An Analysis of Main-Memory and Log Space Usage in Extended Ephemeral Logging

Richard D. Regan[1] and Alex Delis[2]

[1] IBM T. J. Watson Research Center
P.O. Box 704, Yorktown Heights, NY 10598, USA
reganr@us.ibm.com
[2] Computer and Information Science, Polytechnic University
Brooklyn, NY 11201, USA
ad@naxos.poly.edu

Abstract. Extended Ephemeral Logging (XEL) is a database logging and recovery technique which manages a log of recovery data by partitioning it into a series of logically circular generations. XEL copies longer-lived log data from one generation to another in order to reclaim more quickly the space occupied by shorter-lived log data. As a result of copying, records in the log lose their original ordering; this leads to main-memory and log space overhead for obsolete recovery data. In this paper, we quantify the effects of reordering log records by introducing the notion of *Garbage Removal Dependencies (GRDs)*. We develop a classification of log records based on GRDs and use it to characterize main-memory and log space allocation during normal system operation. Through simulation, we demonstrate how main-memory and log space allocation vary with changes in database and workload parameters.

1   Introduction

Database systems use data written to a nonvolatile log to recover from transaction, system, and media failures [2]. Logged data that is used to recover from transaction and system failures is ephemeral; that is, it only needs to be retained until the updates of committed transactions are propagated to the database and the updates of aborted transactions are removed from the database. When the database becomes current with respect to a given log record, that log record is obsolete and is no longer required for recovery. In order to reduce recovery time — and in particular, system recovery time — it is necessary to manage the log during normal system operation so that obsolete log records are removed from the log or are recorded as being obsolete. The goal is to do this with as little impact as possible to transaction processing performance.

Ideally, from the point of view of recovery, log records should be removed from the log as soon as they become obsolete. However, this is not possible, since in-place updates to the log are prohibited. This means that at any given time, the log will contain some number of obsolete log records. Obsolete log records increase the size of the log and may result in additional overhead during

B. Read (Ed.): BNCOD 2001, LNCS 2097, pp. 24–42, 2001.

normal system operation and system recovery. For example, system recovery processing may spend time trying to determine that a given log record is obsolete (by inspecting some portion of the log, database, or both) or it may re-apply a change that is already present in the database.

To reduce overhead, steps must be taken to limit the number of obsolete records residing in the log. Since log records can't be removed individually from arbitrary places within the log, they are removed periodically in contiguous groups from the beginning of the log — through a process known as **truncation**. The log can be truncated only up to its oldest "live" log record; thus, the rate of truncation depends on the lifetimes of log records.

Although log records are ephemeral, some may be longer-lived than others. The lifetime of a log record depends on such factors as transaction duration, the rate at which individual objects are updated, and the rate at which updates are flushed to the database. For example, the "after image" of a frequently updated object is short-lived, whereas the "before image" of an object updated by a long running transaction is longer-lived.

Through the course of normal transaction processing activity, both short-lived and long-lived log records will become intermingled throughout the log; thus, contiguous segments of obsolete data will not form "naturally." A longer-lived log record will prevent the truncation of obsolete log records that follow it, thus increasing the number of obsolete records that are retained in the log. Therefore, explicit actions are required to deal with long-lived log records so that they do not cause the amount of log to be recovered to grow without bound.

One way to handle the effects of long-lived log records is to record additional information during normal system operation which allows recovery processing to ignore or bypass obsolete log records. For example, in the ARIES logging and recovery method [10], information useful in determining which log records are obsolete is periodically written to the log in an operation called a **checkpoint**. The location of the most recent checkpoint information in the log is recorded durably outside of the log itself so that the checkpoint can be located quickly upon system recovery. In addition, log records for a given transaction are chained together (each new log record is written with a "pointer" to the prior record) so that live log records for a transaction can be located directly without scanning the log. Although the log space may be longer than it need be due to lingering obsolete log records, checkpointing and log record chaining can reduce the amount of recovery time spent processing obsolete log records.

Another way to deal with long-lived log records is to force them to become obsolete so that larger contiguous segments of the log can be truncated. The most intrusive options include flushing a change to the database just to make REDO information obsolete or aborting a long running transaction and undoing its updates just to make UNDO information obsolete. A less intrusive option is to copy log records from the beginning of the log (the **head**) to the end of the log (the **tail**) to make their original copies obsolete.

An approach based on copying log records is described in [3]. In this method, the physical log space is managed as logically circular. Logical head and tail pointers are maintained which track the oldest and newest log records, respectively. New log records are written to the tail, and whenever the tail gets within a certain threshold of the head, live log records at the head are copied to the tail [1] (whenever the head and tail pointers reach the physical end of the log, they are advanced to the physical beginning of the log). Copying live log records from the head allows the log to be truncated — that is, *overwritten* with new log data. By truncating the log on a regular basis, overall log size is reduced by reducing the amount of time shorter-lived log records reside in the log. A potential drawback to this approach is that long-lived log records may need to be copied repeatedly.

Another logging method based on copying log records is Extended Ephemeral Logging (XEL) [8]. To reclaim obsolete log space more aggressively and make the log even smaller, XEL manages the log as a *series* of logically circular **generations**. XEL reclaims log space at a rate commensurate with log record lifetimes; space occupied by shorter-lived log records is reclaimed more quickly than space occupied by longer-lived log records. By successively copying longer-lived log records from one generation to the next and truncating each generation separately, XEL attempts to reduce log size while reducing the number of times longer-lived log records must be copied. By keeping the log small, the entire log space can be recovered in its entirety; thus, there is no need for techniques such as checkpointing and log record chaining to help bypass obsolete log records.

In this paper, we study the effects that reordering log records has on an XEL-managed log. We introduce the notion of *Garbage Removal Dependencies (GRDs)* to explain why XEL incurs main-memory and log space overhead for obsolete recovery data. We develop a classification of log records based on GRDs and use it to characterize main-memory and log space allocation during normal system operation. Through simulation on an XEL implementation we have developed, we demonstrate how main-memory and log space allocation vary with changes in database and workload parameters. Our main result is showing that main-memory overhead for obsolete recovery data is proportional to the amount of log space not occupied by live recovery data.

1.1   Database System Architecture

We are evaluating XEL in the context of disk-resident database systems consisting of **pages** of objects. Recently accessed pages are cached in (volatile) main-memory and managed by the **cache manager**. Transactions update objects **in-place**; that is, directly in the cache. Objects are accessed by obtaining **object locks** in accordance with the strict two-phase locking (**strict 2PL**) protocol. For each individual access to a locked object, the **page latch** [10] for the object's page is held. We say that an updated cache object (and its containing

---

[1] Only the log records of *active* transactions ever need be copied in this method; log records of completed transactions are guaranteed to have had their corresponding changes flushed to the database by the time the head is reached.

page) is **dirty** [2] if the transaction that updated it is still active (we say the object is **clean** when the transaction completes). Updated cache pages are eventually made persistent when they are **flushed** to the disk-resident database (as a result of demand paging). Pages can be flushed regardless of whether they are dirty or clean (i.e., the **STEAL/NO-FORCE** policy is used [2]).

A disk-resident log managed by the **log manager** captures log records which describe recent updates to the database. Log records are written to a main-memory buffer (one buffer per generation) before eventually being forced to disk. Each generation of the log (and its associated main-memory data structures) is serialized by its own log lock [1]. Logged information is used by the **recovery manager** in the event of failure to restore the database to a state that reflects only (and all) committed updates.

2   XEL

XEL is a logging and recovery method that protects a database against transaction and system failures (an integrated media recovery scheme is not supported). It manages the log for databases consisting of objects which need not contain sequence numbers (i.e., timestamps). It is designed to be most effective for database workloads generating some long-lived but mostly short-lived log records.

XEL partitions a log space statically into n fixed-size generations, with generations allocated across one or more disks (assuming a disk-based log is used). A log record is initially written to the first generation (G_0) and is copied to subsequent generations as required. If the log record is short-lived, it should become obsolete during its stay in G_0; if so, the space it occupies is reclaimed automatically when G_0 is truncated. If the log record remains live when its portion of G_0 is due for truncation, it is copied to G_1 (**forwarded**) to make its original copy obsolete. Subsequently, if the log record remains live when its portion of G_1 is due for truncation, it is copied to G_2. This is repeated as necessary until the log record becomes obsolete or reaches the last generation (G_{n-1}); if the log record reaches G_{n-1}, it is copied within G_{n-1} (**recirculated**) as often as necessary until it becomes obsolete. If the entire log space is allocated to only a single generation (which XEL allows), live log records are copied within G_0.

XEL logs three types of log records: REDO Data Log Records (**REDO DLRs**), UNDO Data Log Records (**UNDO DLRs**), and Commit Transaction Log Records (**COMMIT TLRs**). Logging is done *physically*; in particular, *entire* object images are logged. A REDO DLR contains the **after image (AFIM)** of an object, and is written to the log whenever an object is updated. All REDO DLRs for a transaction are logged before the transaction's COMMIT TLR is logged (the force-log-at-commit rule [1]). An UNDO DLR contains the **before**

---

[2] Unfortunately, the term *dirty* has two different meanings in the recovery literature. One definition (e.g., [10]) defines cached data as dirty if it has been changed but not flushed to disk. Another definition (e.g., [1]) defines cached or disk-resident data as dirty if it contains the updates of an uncommitted transaction. We adopt the latter definition in this paper.

image (BFIM) of an object, and is written to the log whenever an uncommitted change to an object is about to be written to the database (the latter being the write-ahead logging (WAL) protocol [1]). A single transaction may log multiple REDO DLRs for a given object; however, only a single UNDO DLR (maximum) may be logged for a given object for a given transaction. Since XEL copies log records around in the log, each DLR contains an object-level timestamp so that DLRs can be put in their correct order during system recovery.

XEL maintains a main-memory resident (i.e., volatile) "directory" to track the contents of the log. This directory consists of two main components — the **Logged Object Table (LOT)**, which tracks DLRs by object, and the **Logged Transaction Table (LTT)**, which tracks TLRs by transaction. An entry exists in the directory for each live log record and any log record otherwise relevant to proper recovery of the database. Each entry points to the location of a log record on disk. The directory is updated continuously as log records are written, made obsolete, or removed from the log. The directory itself is not recorded durably since a "semantically equivalent" version of it can be reconstructed from the log in the event of a system crash.

3   Lifetime of Log Data

When we refer to the **lifetime** of logged recovery data we must consider both the **logical lifetime** and **physical lifetime** of log records. The logical lifetime of a log record is the span of time during which the log record is required for recovery of the database. A log record becomes **logically live** when it is written to the log and becomes **logically dead** when it is no longer needed for recovery. The logical lifetime of a log record is determined by transaction activity, cache management, and as we'll see, log management. The physical lifetime of a log record is the span of time during which the log record resides in the log. A log record becomes **physically live** when it is written to the log and becomes **physically dead** when it is removed from the log. The physical lifetime of a log record is determined by its logical lifetime and the rate at which logically dead log records are removed from the log.

Taking both the logical and physical lifetimes of log records into account, we classify a log record's lifetime into three phases: **live**, **garbage** (heretofore referred to as obsolete), and **dead**. A log record is *live* when it is both logically and physically live, *garbage* when it is logically dead but physically live, and *dead* when it is both logically and physically dead. Garbage log records exist because log records can be removed only through truncation. A log record is garbage when it is no longer needed for recovery but is present in the log nonetheless.

3.1   Ideal Logical Lifetimes

We first consider the **ideal logical lifetimes** of log records; that is, logical lifetimes when only transaction and cache management activity is considered (the
effects of log management — for example, copying live log records and removing
garbage log records — are ignored for now). Under these conditions, live log
records become garbage when transactions commit or abort, when objects are
flushed to the database, and when a new log records supersede them. For example: a REDO DLR written by a transaction becomes garbage when the update
it describes is flushed to the database, an UNDO DLR written by a transaction
becomes garbage when the transaction commits, and a COMMIT TLR written
by a transaction becomes garbage when the last REDO DLR for the transaction
becomes garbage.

Before we can summarize the types of live log records, we need to introduce
some definitions. We say that a REDO DLR is **dirty** if the transaction that
wrote it is still active, and we say that a REDO DLR is **clean** if the transaction
that wrote it has committed. When an object is written to the disk-resident copy
of the database, we say that it is **flushed**; we say that the object is **unflushed**
otherwise (similarly, we say that a DLR is flushed when its corresponding object
has been written to the database and we say that it is unflushed otherwise).
A DLR (flushed or unflushed) containing the most recent image of an object is
said to be **current**; a DLR (flushed or unflushed) containing a prior image of
an object is said to be **stale**.

Given these definitions, we can describe concisely the four types of live log
records that may exist:

- **Live clean REDO**. This is the current, unflushed REDO DLR for a given
  object, written by a transaction that has committed.
- **Live dirty REDO**. This is the current, unflushed REDO DLR for a given
  object, written by a transaction that is still active.
- **Live UNDO**. This is the current, unflushed UNDO DLR for a given object,
  written by a transaction that is either still active or has aborted.
- **Live COMMIT**. This is the COMMIT TLR of a transaction for which at
  least one *live clean REDO* exists.

Stale and *flushed* DLRs are considered garbage, as are UNDO DLRs written
by committed transactions and REDO DLRs written by aborted transactions.

3.2   Effects of Garbage Log Records

Garbage log records become an issue when system recovery is considered. While
the system is operating normally, live log records can be identified by consulting
the main-memory log directory. However, since the directory is lost after a system
crash, the recovery manager may not be able to distinguish between live and
garbage log records based on logged information alone. Therefore, during system
recovery, the recovery manager may have no choice but to assume that certain
garbage log records are live. In this case, we say that these log records are

recycled. Recycled log records — although they may waste recovery resources — will not hinder the ability to recover the database as long as means exist to deal with them.

The ability to recover the database in the presence of recycled log records is due in part to the idempotence of physical REDO and UNDO. For example, suppose transaction t_1 updates object o_1 and commits. Suppose then that o_1 is flushed to the database. At this point, there are no live log records, although there is a garbage REDO and garbage COMMIT in the log. If the system crashes and then recovers, these two log records will be recycled. Because objects do not contain timestamps, what was a *current flushed clean REDO* with respect to normal system operation is now considered a *current unflushed clean REDO* — a live log record. Accordingly, the garbage COMMIT is now considered a *live COMMIT*. As a result, the database is restored with the image found in the REDO log record. This causes no problem, however, since restoring the database with an object image is an idempotent operation.

The ability to recover the database in the presence of recycled log records is also dependent on the removal (truncation) of garbage log records in their correct order. For correct recovery, the following **Garbage Removal Rules (GRRs)** must be obeyed:

GRR1: **Remove stale DLRs before current DLRs**. If the log contains a current flushed DLR and one or more stale versions of it, the stale DLR(s) must be removed from the log before the current flushed DLR.

GRR2: **Remove UNDO DLRs before COMMIT TLRs**. If the log contains a garbage COMMIT TLR and one or more garbage UNDO DLRs written by the committed transaction, the UNDO DLR(s) must be removed before the COMMIT TLR.

GRR1 is a consequence of database objects not containing timestamps. Without timestamps in objects, the recovery manager has no way of knowing whether a logged image is the current image or not; the best it can do is apply the most recent clean DLR (determined based on DLR timestamps) to the database. GRR2 is a consequence of the presumed abort protocol [1]. Without a COMMIT TLR in the log, the recovery manager would assume incorrectly that the transaction aborted; as such, it would apply the committed transaction's UNDO DLRs to the database.

To enforce the GRRs, dependencies between individual garbage log records must be taken into account. We say that garbage log record L_2 *depends on* garbage log record L_1 if L_2 can be removed only *after* L_1 is removed. In this case, we write $L_1 \rightarrow L_2$, which reads "remove L_1 before L_2." Based on the GRRs, we define the following **Garbage Removal Dependencies (GRDs)**:

GRD1: **Stale DLR→Current DLR**. A stale DLR must be removed before its corresponding current flushed DLR. (This follows directly from GRR1.)

GRD2: **Current REDO DLR→COMMIT TLR**. A current flushed REDO DLR participating in a GRD1 must be removed before its associated garbage COMMIT TLR. To illustrate, suppose L_1 is a stale DLR, L_2 is a current flushed REDO DLR, $L_1{\rightarrow}L_2$ is a GRD1, and L_3 is the garbage COMMIT TLR associated with L_2. This means that a GRD2 $L_2{\rightarrow}L_3$ exists. (This is a "cascaded" dependency following from GRR1.)

GRD3: **UNDO DLR→COMMIT TLR**. A garbage UNDO DLR must be removed before its associated garbage COMMIT TLR. (This follows directly from GRR2.)

Given GRDs, garbage removal becomes another "event" upon which the logical lifetimes of log records depend.

3.3   Lifetimes in an Ordered Log

An **ordered log** [3] is a log in which log records retain their original ordering; that is, a log in which log records are never copied. In an ordered log, GRDs are satisfied implicitly. An object's stale DLRs will always precede [3] its current DLRs, a committed transaction's current REDO DLRs will always precede its COMMIT TLR, and a committed transaction's UNDO DLRs will always precede its COMMIT TLR (assuming the flushing of UNDO information is synchronized with the commit of its corresponding transaction). Since dependent log records always follow the log records on which they depend, garbage log records will be removed in their correct order. This is because truncation always proceeds from head to tail. As such, the presence of garbage log records does not affect the logical lifetimes of log records in an ordered log. Therefore, the logical lifetimes are the same as the ideal logical lifetimes described in Sect. 3.1.

3.4   Lifetimes in an Unordered Log

An **unordered log** [3] is a log in which log records are copied. In an unordered log, GRDs are *not* satisfied implicitly; GRRs need to be enforced with **explicit GRDs**. An explicit GRD is needed when a garbage log record *precedes* a garbage log record on which it depends.

The presence of explicit GRDs has negative implications regarding log management. One problem is that log records that would otherwise be garbage are kept live, thus extending their logical lifetimes. For example, if a committed transaction's COMMIT TLR appears before one of its UNDO DLRs, the COMMIT TLR must be treated as live — even if there are no *live clean REDO* DLRs for the transaction. The COMMIT TLR must remain live until the UNDO DLR is removed, and the only way the UNDO DLR can be removed is if the COMMIT TLR is copied "ahead" of the UNDO DLR in the log.

---

[3] To say that log record L_1 *precedes* log record L_2 in a circularly managed log means that L_1 appears before L_2 logically with respect to time.

Log records that are kept live due to explicit GRDs are referred to as **live-garbage**. This is a hybrid classification. On the one hand, the log record is garbage, at least with respect to the database. On the other hand, the log record is live, at least with respect to the log. To ensure that the log record stays in the log and is recycled after a system crash, it must be treated as live — and thus tracked in main-memory — during normal system operation. A live-garbage log record is thus viewed as a garbage log record needed for correct recovery. Live-garbage log records increase the amount of log space consumed, increase the amount of main-memory used to track log records, and increase the number of log records that need to be copied.

Another problem with explicit GRDs is that garbage log records that are depended upon must be tracked in main-memory until they are removed from the log (i.e., overwritten with new log records or copies of old ones). We refer to such log records as **tracked-garbage**. Tracked-garbage log records are garbage in that they can be removed from the log at the next opportunity; however, unlike garbage log records, their entries remain in the main-memory log directory until they are removed from the log. This increases the amount of main-memory consumed.

Whether a garbage log record is classified as live-garbage or tracked-garbage depends on whether there are any existing tracked-garbage log records on which it depends. If there is no existing tracked-garbage, the garbage log record is classified as tracked-garbage; otherwise, the garbage log record is classified as live-garbage. Live-garbage log records become tracked-garbage when the tracked-garbage on which they depend is removed.

To summarize, garbage UNDO DLRs and garbage REDO DLRs (written by active and committed transactions) must be tracked. A DLR with the most recent image of an object must be removed from the log last. To keep a clean REDO DLR containing the most recent image of an object recyclable, its associated COMMIT TLR must be kept in the log as well. Finally, to enforce the presumed abort protocol, a COMMIT TLR must be kept in the log until all associated UNDO DLRs are removed. This results in extra log and main-memory overhead for transactions that have already completed and changes that have already been propagated to the database.

Figure 1 compares the lifetimes of log records in an ordered vs. unordered log. Note that in an unordered log, not all log records pass through all lifetime phases. For example, a live log record could go directly to garbage, or a tracked-garbage log record could go directly to dead (for the latter, this is the most common case). In any case, lifetime phases must proceed from left to right in the diagram.

3.5   Lifetimes in a Partitioned Log

XEL introduces the notion of a **partitioned log**, a log divided into $n \geq 2$ generations. Live log records are copied from one generation to the next (forwarded) and within the last generation (recirculated). A partitioned log is like

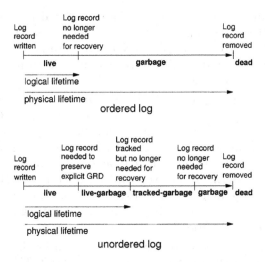

Fig. 1. Log record lifetimes in an ordered vs. unordered log.

an unordered log in that it has the same explicit GRDs and lifetimes. An explicit GRD $L_1 \to L_2$ can exist between generations G_i and G_j, $i \neq j$, or *within* generation G_{n-1}. Explicit GRDs within G_{n-1} are due to G_{n-1} being unordered. Explicit GRDs between generations are due to garbage removal being done separately by generation; without explicit GRDs, garbage log records could be removed out-of-order. An explicit GRD ensures that a dependent log record is forwarded or recirculated, as necessary, until the log record upon which it depends is removed.

3.6   Lifetimes in an XEL Log

Log record lifetimes in XEL are as described in the previous section. In addition, XEL introduces — unnecessarily — extra live-garbage by tracking *all* GRDs as explicit. XEL's behavior with respect to GRDs is the same regardless of whether the log is partitioned or non-partitioned (i.e., single-generation).

To track and enforce GRDs, XEL assigns a **status** to each log record, which is stored in each log record's main-memory directory entry. The status reflects whether the log record is live, live-garbage, or tracked-garbage (according to our classification). For example, a REDO DLR is live if its status is **unflushed**, live-garbage if its status is **required**, or tracked-garbage if its status is **recoverable** (a garbage REDO DLR has status **non-recoverable**, but that is not recorded since a garbage log record has no main-memory representation). The presence of a *required* REDO DLR implies the presence of a GRD1; for example, *recoverable* REDO DLR→*required* REDO DLR. UNDO DLRs and COMMIT TLRs also have statuses assigned to them, although they do not map one-to-one with our classification in all cases. For example, an **annulled** UNDO DLR is unambiguously tracked-garbage; however, a *required* COMMIT TLR may be live or live-garbage, depending on the status(es) of its associated DLR(s). A live-garbage *required* COMMIT TLR implies that a GRD2 (*required* REDO DLR→*required* COMMIT TLR) or GRD3 (*annulled* UNDO DLR→*required* COMMIT TLR) or both are present. Log records with statuses that make them live or live-garbage can be forwarded or recirculated.

XEL treats *all* GRDs as explicit, even GRDs that are otherwise implicit. This can lead to extra overhead due to the way the log is managed. Recall that n pages of free space are maintained between the tail and head of each generation [8]. If the log records involved in an implicit GRD both appear in the current n page range, the dependent log record will be treated as live-garbage and forwarded or recirculated unnecessarily. If the log records involved in the GRD do not appear in the current n page range, then no extra overhead is incurred; the log record depended upon will be removed before the dependent log record is considered for forwarding or recirculation.

As an example, suppose we have a two-generation log and that a given transaction's UNDO DLR is followed by its COMMIT TLR in G_0. This gives an *implicit* GRD3. Suppose further that both log records appear within the currently advanced n page window. XEL will forward the COMMIT TLR to G_1, not recognizing that the UNDO DLR is guaranteed to be removed first. The result is that a *real* explicit GRD3 is actually created (fortunately, the UNDO DLR will in all likelihood be removed before the forwarded COMMIT TLR becomes a candidate for recirculation).

To summarize, GRDs ensure that the log — and ultimately the database — remains recoverable when log records get reordered. GRDs extend the log and main-memory lifetimes of log records. Using GRDs, we can classify log records into four types: live (L), live-garbage (LG), tracked-garbage (TG), and garbage (G).

Figure 2 gives an example of all six GRD combinations and their effect on log record lifetimes in XEL. Suppose we have a two-generation XEL log. Transaction t_1 updates object o_1 and REDO DLR $R_{o_1 t_1}$ and UNDO DLR $U_{o_1 t_1}$ are logged. Then, before t_1 commits and logs COMMIT TLR C_{t_1}, $R_{o_1 t_1}$ and $U_{o_1 t_1}$ are forwarded to generation G_1. Suppose that transactions t_2 and t_4, running in succession, each update object o_4 and commit. Finally, suppose transaction t_7 updates object o_1 and then commits. If objects o_1 and o_4 are flushed to the database, three implicit GRDs and three explicit GRDs exist as depicted in the figure. Since XEL treats implicit GRDs as explicit, unnecessary LG is maintained (unnecessary LG is marked with '*'s).

We'll end our discussion of log record lifetimes with a few additional comments on GRDs. One thing to note is that a GRD1 can be broken prematurely if a stale REDO DLR's associated COMMIT TLR is removed first. This is because a REDO DLR without a corresponding COMMIT TLR is G and cannot be recycled. Also note that there is no LG UNDO in XEL. This is because XEL retains a stale REDO DLR as LG even if it is superseded by a current flushed UNDO DLR. Although this means XEL handles UNDO and REDO dependen-

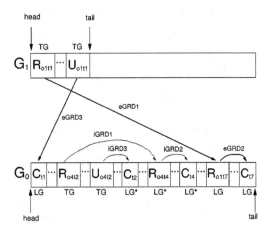

Fig. 2. An example showing all six GRD combinations (explicit GRDs are prefixed with an 'e', and implicit GRDs are prefixed with an 'i').

cies asymmetrically, it has no effect on its correctness (a current UNDO contains the same image as the previously current REDO). Finally, note that XEL relies on GRDs to set DLR timestamps correctly. A given object's timestamp can be reset to zero only when there are no more L, LG, or TG DLRs for the object.

4 Simulation Environment and Methodology

To quantify the effects of GRDs, we implemented a version of XEL based on details found in [8,5]. We built it on top of a detailed database simulation environment which includes object locking, page latching, LRU cache page replacement, and log disk simulation (including read and write buffering and group commit [1] for batching writes to disk). We use CSIM18 [9] as our discrete-event simulation engine. In our model, simulation time advances as a result of disk I/O.

Our goal is to demonstrate how main-memory and log space allocation vary with changes in workload and database parameters. We run sets of experiments that vary transaction duration, object size, object skew, and log size. For easy comparison across all experiments, we vary only one parameter value at a time in each experiment; all remaining parameters take their default values (as specified in Table 1). Although the database we model is small, our results demonstrate the basic effects that GRDs have in XEL.

For each experiment, we measure the average main-memory and log space allocation. We classify main-memory allocation into three categories: L, LG, and TG. We classify log space allocation into these same three categories plus an additional one — G. L, LG, and TG are measured by periodic sampling throughout each experiment; G is derived as the size of the log less the sum of the other three components. Main-memory is measured by assigning sizes to

Table 1. Default parameter values.

Parameter	Value
txRate	100 tx/sec
txDuration	1 sec
txNumUpdates	4
txObjectSkew	0.1
txCommitProbability	0.95
diskPageSize	4096 bytes
databaseObjectSize	100 bytes
databaseSize	10000 pages
cacheSize	500 pages
cachePolicy	LRU
logSize	250 pages

each data structure element that varies in number with transaction load: LOT entries, LTT entries, cells, and "transaction object id set elements" (we used the same values as in [8]). We update the classification of each data structure element as the classifications of its related log records change. Due to specifics of our implementation — for example, because we use Log Sequence Numbers (LSNs) [10] instead of object-level timestamps — our DLR header size and TLR size (43 bytes and 28 bytes, respectively) are bigger than in [8]. While this may affect the absolute values of our results, it should have little or no effect on the relative trends.

For each experiment, we wait until a steady state is reached before recording data (most of the experiments reported here stabilize after two passes of the log; some, like those with longer transaction durations, take longer). We record data for a minimum of ten passes over the log. For experiments running in a partitioned log, the minimum pass requirement is met by all generations.

5   Experimental Results

We perform four sets of experiments using a non-partitioned log (referred to as *XEL-1*) where we vary transaction duration, object size, object skew, and log size. We perform two sets of experiments using a two-generation partitioned log (referred to as *XEL-2*) where we vary transaction duration and object size. For the *XEL-2* experiments, the log is partitioned such that G_0 has 20% of the total log space.

5.1   *XEL-1* Results

Figures 3(a) and 3(b) show the results for *XEL-1* when transaction duration d is varied at 1, 3, 5, 7, and 9 seconds. As transaction duration increases, the L components of both main-memory and log space increase. This is due primarily to the increased number and lifetime of UNDO DLRs. The "spike" in main-memory at $d = 1$ in Fig. 3(a) is due indirectly to the disproportionately low number of UNDO DLRs in the log for this case relative to the others. At $d = 1$, there is a relatively low probability that a dirty page will be flushed to the database; hence, a relatively small number of UNDO DLRs are logged. At $d = 3$, it turns out that the rate at which dirty pages are flushed increases substantially when compared to $d = 1$. Beyond $d = 3$, the dirty page flush rate increases, but not as rapidly (in fact, there is a bit of a jump at $d = 5$, but beyond that it starts to level out).

To understand how the amount of UNDO information in the log affects main-memory requirements, consider as an example two extremes: either no UNDO DLRs are written or an UNDO DLR is written for each REDO DLR. In the first case, the number of objects represented in the log is effectively double that of the second (ignoring duplicate updates). Consequently, the number of transactions represented in the log is also double. This effectively doubles the amount of main-memory overhead for the object and transaction related data structures. This phenomenon explains the higher amount of TG main-memory at $d = 1$.

An additional phenomenon takes effect starting at the $d = 3$ second case. Because of the jump in UNDO information in the log, there is a corresponding jump in LG main-memory for the transaction related data structures. This is due to the increase in the number of COMMIT TLRs that must be retained as LG.

Figures 4(a) and 4(b) show the results for XEL-1 when object size o is varied at 50, 100, 150, 200, and 250 bytes. L main-memory usage is flat since the main-memory representation of an object is independent of its size (there are the same number of L DLRs in the log for each experiment). The most interesting result is that $total$ main-memory usage decreases as object size increases. The shape of the LG and TG curves in Fig. 4(a) is explained by observing that the total number of objects represented in main-memory is $inversely\ proportional$ to object size. As objects get bigger, less DLRs fit in the log. If we ignore the overhead of TLRs, we can approximate the number of DLRs in the log as

$$numDLRs = \frac{logSize}{objectSize + dlrHeaderSize} . \tag{1}$$

Total main-memory overhead is proportional to $numDLRs$.

Figures 5(a) and 5(b) show the results for XEL-1 when object access skew s is varied at 0.5, 0.4, 0.3, 0.2, 0.1 (skew is defined as in [8]; $s = 0.5$ means uniform access to database objects, whereas $s = 0.1$ is a highly skewed access meaning 90% of the updates go to 10% of the database). With increased skew, there is increased locality of access. This means that pages will be flushed less frequently from the cache and thus REDO DLRs will remain L a little longer. In addition, since more objects get repeat updates, there is increased LG due to increased GRDs. These effects start to magnify at the higher skews of 0.2 and 0.1.

Figures 6(a) and 6(b) show the results for XEL-1 when log size l is varied at 250, 300, 350, 400, and 450 pages. L main-memory and log space usage is flat since the same workload is run for all experiments. However, since more objects fit into more log space, there is more LG and TG main-memory and log space overhead.

5.2 *XEL-2* Results

Figures 3(c) and 3(d) show the results for *XEL-2* when transaction duration d is varied at 1, 3, 5, 7, and 9 seconds. The L components are the same as in the *XEL-1* experiments since the same parameters are used. However, partitioning the log changes the way in which the LG and TG components react.

The first thing to notice is that TG main-memory *increases* as we go from $d = 1$ to $d = 3$. This is the opposite of what happens for *XEL-1*, although it happens for the same underlying reason — a low number of UNDO DLRs at $d = 1$. With little UNDO, there are many more transactions with just REDO in the log. However, since a pass over G_0 is much faster in *XEL-2* than in *XEL-1*, COMMIT TLRs are removed faster and hence more REDO DLRs become G sooner. The larger G component at $d = 1$ displaces what would otherwise be TG.

Another interesting result is the jump in LG main-memory at $d = 5$. This is due to many more UNDO DLRs being forwarded to G_1 than for $d = 3$. This is because at $d = 5$ (and beyond), transaction duration exceeds the average time it takes to complete a pass over G_0. As a result, the number of COMMIT TLRs that must be retained as LG (and subsequently forwarded) increases. Moreover, since it takes about ten times as long to complete a pass over G_1 as it does to complete a pass over G_0, the lifetimes of TG UNDO DLRs — and hence their corresponding LG COMMIT TLRs — are greatly extended.

Interestingly enough, overall main-memory for the $d = 5$ case *decreases*. This is because the increase in LG is more than offset by a decrease in TG. First of all, the increase in LG for the transaction related main-memory data structures is accompanied by a corresponding decrease in TG for those same structures. In addition, TG is reduced further because the dirty page flush rate increases enough at $d = 5$ so that an increased amount of UNDO in the log displaces a corresponding amount of REDO (as explained earlier for *XEL-1*). Beyond $d = 5$, main-memory continues to decrease slightly. This is because pass time over G_1 decreases, resulting in quicker removal of TG UNDO DLRs and hence their corresponding LG COMMIT TLRs.

Figures 4(c) and 4(d) show the results for *XEL-2* when object size o is varied at 50, 100, 150, 200, and 250 bytes. Since the same parameters are used as for *XEL-1*, the L components are the same as in *XEL-1*. As in *XEL-1*, the shape of the main-memory curve in Fig. 4(c) is due to the inverse relationship between main-memory and object size. One notable difference is the increased LG for *XEL-2*. LG is relatively large at $o = 50$, drops off abruptly at $o = 100$, and then drops off more smoothly beyond that. This is because logging bigger DLRs consumes the log faster (since the same *number* of DLRs are logged for each experiment). The result is that pass time, and in particular G_1 pass time, varies inversely with the size of objects. Cycling through G_1 when $o = 50$ takes about five times as long as it does when $o = 100$ (cycling through G_1 when $o = 100$ takes only about twice as long as it does when $o = 150$). For $o = 50$, the considerably longer lifetime of TG in G_1 results in the extra LG reported.

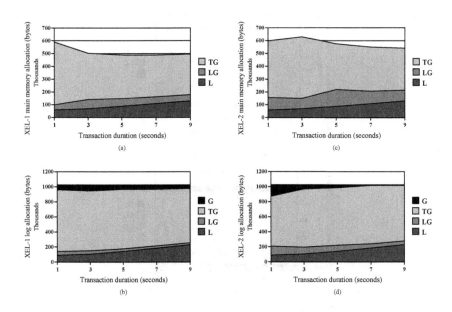

Fig. 3. Main-memory and log space allocation for increasing transaction duration.

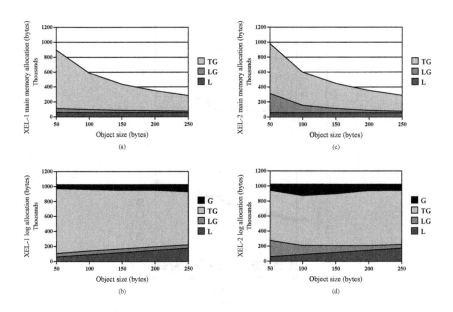

Fig. 4. Main-memory and log space allocation for increasing object size.

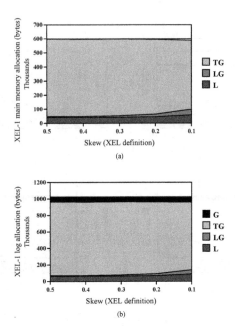

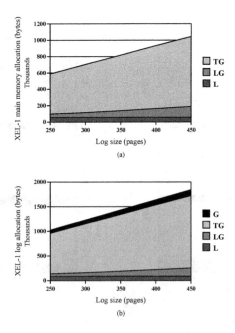

Fig. 5. Main-memory and log space allocation for increasing object skew.

Fig. 6. Main-memory and log space allocation for increasing log size.

5.3 Discussion

One consequence of a common set of parameters is that log size cannot be "tuned" ad hoc to the minimum required to support the workload of each experiment (as is done in [8,4]). This means that the amounts of TG (and to a lesser extent LG) reported are higher than they would be if the size of the log were minimized. On the other hand, it is unlikely that a log used within the context of a real database system would (or could) be tuned in this manner. More likely, log size would be fixed and would incorporate extra space to accommodate peaks in workload. In addition, there will be times when the amount of L in the log is low and thus the amount of TG and LG in the log is high (such as when the workload quiesces temporarily). Also, in the interest of choosing generation sizes such that 'only a small fraction of log records need to be forwarded or recirculated' [8], log space utilization [11] would need to be kept low. This can be accomplished by increasing the size of the log beyond the workload's capacity needs. Therefore, we expect that in a real system a nontrivial amount of main-memory will always be dedicated to tracking obsolete recovery data.

6 Summary and Future Work

We analyzed XEL qualitatively and quantitatively to show how main-memory and log space allocation are affected by copying log records within the log. When the log becomes unordered, dependencies among log records must be tracked explicitly to constrain the order in which log records are overwritten. This results in log records that remain live past their ideal logical lifetimes, thus increasing main-memory and log space usage. In addition, we've shown that overall main-memory usage increases as the log gets bigger or objects get smaller.

It would be interesting to repeat our experiments for Ephemeral Logging (EL) [6]. In EL, database objects contain timestamps. In [7], it is stated that this would result in less main-memory and log space usage. Using our analysis — for example, noting that only GRD3s would exist in EL — this difference in main-memory and log space usage could be quantified. Also, it would be worthwhile to investigate how changes in workload parameters, database parameters, and log partition affect transaction throughput (in both XEL and EL).

Acknowledgements. The work of the second author was partially supported by the National Science Foundation under grant NSF IIS-9733642.

References

[1] J. Gray and A. Reuter. *Transaction Processing: Concepts and Techniques*. Morgan Kaufmann, 1993.

[2] T. Haerder and A. Reuter. Principles of Transaction-Oriented Database Recovery. *ACM Computing Surveys*, 15(4):287–317, December 1983.

[3] R. B. Hagmann and H. Garcia-Molina. Implementing Long Lived Transactions Using Log Record Forwarding. Technical Report CSL-91-2, Xerox Palo Alto Research Center, Palo Alto, CA, February 1991.

[4] P. Hennessey, M. T. Ibrahim, and A. M. Fedorec. Formal Specification, Object Oriented Design, and Implementation of an Ephemeral Logger for Database Systems. In *Proceedings of the 7th International Conference on Database and Expert Systems Applications*, pages 333–355, September 1996.

[5] J. S. Keen. Logging and Recovery in a Highly Concurrent Database. Technical Report AITR-1492, Massachusetts Institute of Technology, Artificial Intelligence Laboratory, June 1994.

[6] J. S. Keen and W. J. Dally. Performance Evaluation of Ephemeral Logging. In *Proceedings of the 1993 ACM SIGMOD International Conference on Management of Data*, pages 187–196, May 1993.

[7] J. S. Keen and W. J. Dally. XEL: Extended Ephemeral Logging for Log Storage Management. In *Proceedings of the Third International Conference on Information and Knowledge management*, pages 312–321, November 1994.

[8] J. S. Keen and W. J. Dally. Extended Ephemeral Logging: Log Storage Management for Applications with Long Lived Transactions. *ACM Transactions on Database Systems*, 22(1):1–42, March 1997.

[9] Mesquite Software, Inc. *User's Guide: CSIM18 Simulation Engine (C++ Version)*.

[10] C. Mohan, D. Haderle, B. Lindsay, H. Pirahesh, and P. Schwarz. ARIES: A Transaction Recovery Method Supporting Fine-Granularity Locking and Partial Rollbacks Using Write-Ahead Logging. *ACM Transactions on Database Systems*, 17, number 1:94–162, March 1992.

[11] M. Rosenblum and J. K. Ousterhout. The design and implementation of a log-structured file system. *ACM Transactions on Computer Systems*, 10(1):26–52, February 1992.

An Effective Data Placement Strategy for XML Documents

Yuanling Zhu and Kevin Lü

SCISM, South Bank University
103 Borough Road
London SE1 OAA
zhuy@sbu.ac.uk

Abstract. As XML is increasingly being used in Web applications, new technologies need to be investigated for processing XML documents with high performance. Parallelism is a promising solution for structured document processing and data placement is a major factor for system performance improvement in parallel processing. This paper describes an effective XML document data placement strategy. The new strategy is based on a multilevel graph partitioning algorithm with the consideration of the unique features of XML documents and query distributions. A new algorithm, which is based on XML query schemas to derive the weighted graph from the labelled directed graph presentation of XML documents, is also proposed. Performance analysis on the algorithm presented in the paper shows that the new data placement strategy exhibits low workload skew and a high degree of parallelism.

Keywords: Data Placement, XML Documents, Graph Partitioning, and Parallel Data Processing.

1   Introduction

As a new markup language for structured documentation, XML (eXtensible Markup Language) is increasingly being used in Web applications because of its unique features in data representation and exchange. The main advantage of XML is that each XML file can have a semantic schema and makes it possible to define much more meaningful queries than simple, keyword-based retrievals. A recent survey shows that the number of XML business vocabularies has increased from 124 to over 250 in six months [1]. It can be expected that data in XML format would be largely available throughout the Web in the near future. As Web applications are time vulnerable, the increasing size of XML documents and the complexity of evaluating XML queries pose new performance challenges to existing information retrieval technologies. The use of parallelism has shown good scalability in traditional database applications and provides an attractive solution to process structured documents [2]. A large number of XML documents can be distributed onto several processing nodes so that a reasonable query response time can be achieved by processing the related data in parallel.

B. Read (Ed.): BNCOD 2001, LNCS 2097, pp. 43–56, 2001.

In parallel data processing, effective data placement has drawn a lot of attention because it has a significant impact on the overall system performance. The data placement strategy for parallel systems is concerned with the distribution of data between different nodes in the system. A poor strategy can result in a non-uniform distribution of the load and the formation of bottlenecks [3]. In general, determining the optimal placement of data across nodes for performance is a difficult problem even for the relational data model [4]. XML documents introduce additional complexity because they do not have a rigid, regular, and complete structure. Although some XML documents may have a DTD (Document Type Definition) file to specify their structures and the W3C (World Wide Web Consortium) is working on the XML Schema standard, either DTD or XML Schema is an optional companion to the XML documents. We cannot expect that every XML document on the Web is a *valid* XML file, which means that it conforms to a particular DTD or XML Schema.

In this paper, we use the labelled directed graph model to represent XML data. A graph partition algorithm is explored to maximise the parallelism among the different processing nodes in a shared-nothing architecture where each node has its own memory and disks. The distribution of the data is dependent on the queries applied to the data. XML queries are based on path expressions because of its lack of schema information. As path expressions access data in a navigational manner, elements along the objective path should be placed together to minimise communication cost. At the same time, data relative to the same query should be distributed evenly to different nodes to achieve the load balance. These two objectives are both considered in the new proposed data placement strategy. Moreover, the new strategy is based on the unique features of XML documents and the distribution of XML query sets. This paper also presents the performance analysis on the new data placement strategy.

The remainder of the paper is organised as follows: Section 2 presents the related work and motivations of the study. Section 3 describes the XML data model and the algorithm for deriving the weighted graph of XML documents. Section 4 proposes a new graph-partitioning algorithm based on the features of XML documents. Section 5 analyses the performance of the new algorithm. Section 6 concludes the paper and discuss pending research issues.

2   Related Work and Motivations

Effective parallelisation of data queries requires a declustering of data across many disks so that parallel disk I/O can be obtained to reduce response time. A poor data distribution can lead to a higher workload, load imbalance and hence higher cost.

Various data placement strategies have been developed by researchers to exploit the performance potential of shared-nothing relational database systems. Since the complexity of the problem is NP-complete [5], heuristics are normally used to find a nearly optimal solution in a reasonable amount of time. According to the criteria used in reducing costs incurred on resources such as network bandwidth, CPUs, and disks, data placement strategies can be classified into three categories, which are network traffic based [6], size based [7], and access frequency based [8]. The main idea of these approaches is to achieve the minimal load (e.g. network traffic) or a balance of load (e.g. size, I/O access) across the system using a greedy algorithm. Our algorithm is a combination of the network traffic based and access frequency based strategy, because it aims to minimise the communication cost and to maximise the intra-operation parallelism.

In parallel object-oriented database systems, data placement strategy is also critical to the system performance and is far more complex. [9] pointed out that in designing a data placement method for a parallel object-oriented databases, two major factors that most of the time contradict each other must be taken into account: minimising communication cost and maintaining load balance. [4] used a greedy similarity graph partitioning algorithm to assign object into different processing nodes aiming to minimise inter-node traversals and maximise parallelism. This algorithm attempts to place objects that have a higher degree of similarity on different disks, where two objects are more similar if they are accessed together in a navigational manner but less similar if the two objects can be accessed together in a parallel manner. Although the paper gives an equation to compute the similarity between two nodes, there's no definite method for getting the weights between two nodes.

Data placement strategies in both relational and object-oriented parallel database systems could be helpful to the study of the data placement strategy for XML documents. The idea of our data placement strategy for XML data is similar to those in parallel object-oriented databases. But we focus on how to construct the weighted graph from the original XML document, which forms the basis of the graph partitioning algorithm. The objective of the research is trying to find a nearly optimal data distribution so that the system throughput and resource utilisation can be maximised. Our graph partition algorithm is based on the multilevel graph partition algorithm for its efficiency and accuracy. The unique features of XML documents and XML queries have been studied to provide the foundation for the graph partition.

3   Graph Model of XML Data

3.1   Labelled Directed Graph

The latest W3C working draft on XML Information Set (InfoSet) [10] provides a data model for describing the logical structure of a well-formed XML 1.0 document. In this model, an XML document's information set consists of a number of Information Items, which are abstract representations of some components of an XML document. For example, in the XML document of figure 2, there are three different types of information item: document information items, element information items, and attribute information items. The specification presents the information set as a tree and accordingly the information items as the node of the tree. Any information item in the XML document can be reached by recursively following the properties of the root information item. Similar to the data model used in Lore [11], we extended the InfoSet data model to a directed labelled graph, where the vertices in the graph represent the information items and arcs represent the semantic links between the information items.

```
<Publications>
   <Proceeding>
        <Conference>VLDB</Conference>
        <Year>1999</Year>
        <Location>Edinburgh</Location>
        <Article id='A1' reference='A2 A3' >
            <Title>Query Optimization for XML </Title>
            <Author>Jason McHugh </Author>
            <Author>Jennifer Widom</Author>
        </Article>
   </ Proceeding >
   <Proceeding>
        <Conference>ICDT</Conference>
        <Year>1997</Year>
        <Article id="A2">
            <Title>Querying Semi-Structured Data</Title>
            <Author>Serge Abiteboul</Author>
        </Article>
</ Proceeding >
   <Proceeding>
        <Conference>ICDE</Conference>
        <Year>1998</Year>
        <Article id='A3' Reference='A2' >
            <Title>Optimizing Regular Path Expressions Using Graph
                    Schemes</Title>
            <Author>Mary F. Fernandez</Author>
            <Author>Dan Suciu</Author>
        </Article>
   </ Proceeding >
</Publications>
```

Fig. 1. An example for XML documents

Figure 2 describes the graph presentation of the XML document in Figure 1. We use the definition in [12] as our definition for the labelled directed graph:

Definition 3.1 Let L be an arbitrary set of labels. A tuple $G = (V, A, s, t, l)$ is a L-labelled directed graph, if V is a set of vertices, A is a set of arcs, s and t are total functions from A to V assigning each arc its source and target vertex, and l is a total label function from A to L assigning each arc a label.

We can see that the labelled directed graph of single XML document is actually a graph with a unique root. Any vertex in the graph can be reached from the root by following a certain *path*.

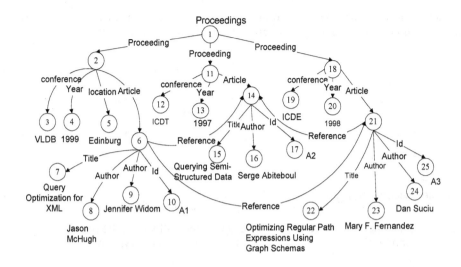

Fig. 2. The labelled directed graph representation for the XML document in Figure 1.

Definition 3.2 A nonempty sequence $(v_{i0}, a_{i1}, v_{i1,...}, a_{im}, v_{im})$ is called a *path* in the graph $G = (V, A, s, t, l,)$ if $s(a_{ij}) = v_{ij}$ 1 and $t(a_{ij}) = v_{ij}$ for all positive j m, and all arcs and all vertices in that sequence are pair wise distinct.

3.2   Weighted Graph

Query languages for XML documents generally utilise *path expressions* to exploit the information stored in XML documents. Path expressions are algebraic representations of sets of paths in a graph and are specified by a sequence of nested tags.   For example, the path expression „proceeding.article.title" for the XML document in Figure 1 refers to the titles of all articles published in all proceedings. As shown in [12], an XML query can also be presented by a labelled directed graph. Two XML queries and their graph presentations were shown in Figure 3. The elements in the graph are labelled with predicates, where the predicate *true()* serves as a wildcard.

Definition 3.3 Given a set of unary predicates P , a tuple $G_q = (V_q, A_q, s_q, t_q, l_q)$ is a query schema if the elements are labelled with predicates $(l : V_q$ A_q $P)$.

The graphs in Figure 3 can act as schemas, which partly describe the structure of the XML document. If the predicate in a schema is true for the corresponding vertices and arcs in an instance, we say that the instance conforms to the schema. The answer to a query of XML documents is the union of all instances conforming to the query schema. If those instances could be evenly distributed among several different disks and therefore could be accessed in parallel during the query processing, the response time for a query would be largely shortened. Meanwhile, one instance should avoid spanning multiple partitions to reduce the communication cost. These two objectives conflict because the first one tries to distribute vertices across as many partitions as possible, while the second one tries to group the relevant vertices together.

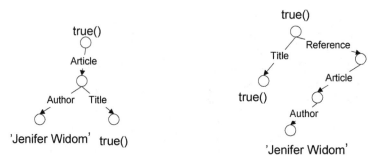

Q1: select all papers authored by   Q2: select all papers that cite the papers
        'Jenifer Widom'   authored by 'Jenifer Widom'

Fig. 3. Two typical XML queries and their corresponding graph based presentation

The data placement of XML documents over different sites can be viewed as a graph partitioning problem. Each edge between two vertices in the graph is associated with a *weight* to describe the frequency of traversals on it. The higher the weight is, the more possible it is to assign the two vertices to the same partition. In our algorithm, the weight between two vertices reflects two factors. One is the possibility of the two vertices to be accessed together in sequential manner, and another one is the likelihood of two vertices to be access together in parallel manner.

With the knowledge on the distribution of the XML query set, a weighted graph could be derived based on the labelled directed graph defined in section 3.1.

Definition 3.4 $G_w = (V, E, r, w)$ is the weighted graph for a labelled directed graph $G = (V, A, s, t, l)$, if E is a set of edges, r is a total functions from A to V assigning each edge its vertices, and w is a total weight function assigning each edges in E a number to describe the traversal frequency of that edge. For each e E, there exists at least one arc a A with the same vertices as e.

Algorithm 3.1 describes the method to derive the weighted graph from the original labelled directed diagram based on the query distributions. In this algorithm, if the arcs in the labelled directed graph are traversed in a query, the weights between the corresponding vertices are computed based on the query frequency. If there is more than one instance that conforms to a query schema, the arcs between any two instances are studied to compute the weight of the edges that connect these two instances. The value of parameter   is an adjustable number between zero and one, which indicates the relative benefit by increasing the degree of parallelism compared with lowering communication cost. If the communication overhead is high, a higher value for   can be chosen.

Algorithm 3.1 Assigning Weight Algorithm

```
Input:
```

The labelled directed graph $G = (V, A, s, t, l)$

The graph presentation $G^q = \{G_1^q, G_2^q, ..., G_n^q\}$

Where, $G_i^q = (V_i^q, A_i^q, s_i^q, t_i^q, l_i^q), i = 1, 2, ..., n$

Query distribution: $= \{1, 2, ..., n\}$, where $\sum_{i=1}^{n} = 1$

Adjustable parameter $, 0 < < 1$

```
Output:
```
the weighted graph $G^w = (V, E, r, w)$

```
Begin
```
Initialise the weight for each edge with zero

For each query G_i^q in the query set

For each $G_{ij} = (V_{ij}, A_{ij}, s, t, l), j = 1, 2 ..., m$ conforms to G_i^q

```
        For each  a   Aij
            If  s(a) > t(a)  Then  u = t(a), v = s(a)
                Else  u = s(a), v = t(a)
            End If
```
$w(u, v) = w(u, v) + {}_i 100$
```
        End For
        For each  Gik = (Vik, Aik, s, t, l), j < k   m
            If exists a   A ,{s(a)  Vij, t(a)  Vik | t(a)  Vij, s(a)  Vik}
                If  s(a) > t(a)  Then  u = t(a), v = s(a)
                    Else  u = s(a), v = t(a)
                End If
```
$w(u, v) = w(u, v) \quad (1 \quad) \quad {}_i 100$
```
            End If
        End For
    End For
End For
End
```

4 Graph Partitioning Algorithm

The graph partitioning problem is NP-complete [13], and heuristics are required to obtain reasonably good partitions. The problem is to decluster the graph into n partitions, such that each partition has roughly equal number of vertices and the number of traversals between different partitions is minimised. In the case of XML parallel processing, we aim at achieving lowest communication cost and gaining load balance among different processing nodes.

[13] introduced a multilevel graph partitioning algorithm, which generally consists of three phases: coarsening phase, partitioning phase, and uncoarsening phase. The graph is first coarsened down to a few hundred vertices, a bisection of this much smaller graph is computed, and then this partition is projected back towards the original graph. This algorithm is suitable for XML graph partitioning because vertices to be accessed in navigational manner could coalesce firstly to make sure that they are assigned to the same processing nodes. Experiments presented in [13] also showed that the multilevel algorithm outperforms other approaches both in computation cost and partition quality. Our new data placement strategy is based on a multilevel graph partitioning approach with the consideration of features of XML documents and XML query distributions.

The goal of the coarsening phase is to reduce the size of a graph by collapsing the matching vertices together. The edges in this set are removed, and the two vertices connected by an edge in the matching are collapsed into a single vertex whose weight is the sum of the weights of the component vertices. The method used to compute the matching is crucial, because it will affect both the quality of the partition, and the time required during the uncoarsening phase. [13] described a heuristic known as heavy-edge matching (HEM) which tries to find a maximal matching that contains edges with large weight. The idea is to randomly pick an unmatched node, select the edge with the highest weight over all valid incident edges, and mark both vertices connected by this edge as matched. Because it collapsed the heaviest edges, the resulting coarse graph is loosely connected. Therefore, the algorithm can produce a good partition of the original graph.

[14] argued that the HEM algorithm may miss some heavy edges in the graph because the nodes are visited randomly. To overcome this problem, they proposed a heaviest-edge matching by sorting the edges by their weights and visiting them in decreasing order of weight. HEM and its variants reduce the number of nodes in a graph by roughly a factor of 2 at each stage of coarsening. If r (instead of 2) nodes of the graph are coalesced into one at each coarsening step, the total number of steps can be reduced form $\log_2(n/k)$ to $\log_r(n/k)$. [14] used an algorithm called heavy-triangle matching (HTM), which coalesces three nodes at a time so that they can get 20% time saving.

We call our coarsening algorithm HSM (Heaviest Schema Matching). Algorithm 4.1 describes the details of the algorithm. In HSM, the vertices are no longer visited in random order. The edges are sorted by their weight and the vertices with the maximum weighted edge are selected to do the matching first. According to algorithm 3.1, there is an edge between two vertices in the weighted graph only if there is an arc between them in the labelled directed graph. In the other word, the neighbour of a vertex v in the weighted graph can be accessed together with v by following a certain path. It is reasonable to collapse the matching vertex with its neighbour together as many as possible if the weight between them is high enough. This strategy can improve the efficiency of the coarsen phase.

The coarsen phase stops when the number of nodes in the coarser graph is small enough. The coarsened graph G_i is made of *multivertices* and edges that have not been merged. A vertex in graph G_i is called multivertices if it contains more than one vertex of G. In a weighted graph, the weight of each edge indicates the possibility for the corresponding vertices to be accessed together both in sequential mode and in parallel mode. On the other hand, the weight also reflects the workload under the query distribution. When two vertices are collapsed together, we need to keep the weight information of the edge being merged. Therefore, we introduced a new notation $\overline{w}$ to denote the weight of the multivertices in the coarsened graph. The workload of each partition will be determined by the sum of the weight of edges and multivertices in that partition.

Definition 3.5 $G_k^w = (V_k, E_k, r_k, w_k, \overline{w})$ is the coarsened graph of a weighted graph $G^w = (V, E, r, w)$, if $V_k \quad V \quad \overline{V}$, where $\overline{V}$ is mad up of multivertices that are created by collapsing vertices from V, and $\overline{w}$ is a total weight function assigning each multivertices in $\overline{V}$ a number to describe the workload of that vertex.

Algorithm 4.1 Coarsening Graph

```
Input:  The labelled directed graph  G = (V0, A, s, t, l)
           The weighted graph  G0 = (V0, E0, r, w)  for  G
Output: Coarser graph  Gn = (Vn, En, w) with  N vertices
Begin
```
$\quad i = 0$

$\quad$ Do while the number of vertices in $G_i = (V_i, E_i, r, w)$ is greater than N

$\qquad$ Sort the edges of E_i in descending order by their weights

$\qquad$ Assume $(u, v) \quad E_i$ is one of edges with maximum weight

$\qquad$ Call *collapse_vertices(u,v)* to get the new vertices v' V_{i+1}

$\qquad i = i + 1$

$\quad$ End Do

End

collapse_vertices(u, v) {

$\quad V_{i+1} = V_i \quad \{u, v\}$

$\quad E_{i+1} = E_i \quad (u, v)$

$\quad$ Build a new vertex v'

$\quad$ Compute the workload for the new vertex:

$\quad \overline{w}(v') = \overline{w}(v') + w(u, v)$

$\quad$ For each neighbour $x \quad V_i$ of u and v

$\qquad$ If $(u, x) \quad E_i$ and $(v, x) \quad E_i$ Then

$$E_{i+1} = E_i \quad \{(u,x),(v,x)\} + (x,v')$$
$$w(x,v') = w(u,x) + w(v,x)$$
```
Else
```
$$E_{i+1} = E_i \quad (\{u \mid v\}, x) + (x,v')$$
$$w(x,v') = w(\{u \mid v\}, x)$$
```
End If
If  w(u',x)   w(u,v) then
```
      `Call` $collapse\_vertices(u,v)$ to get the new vertices v' V_{i+1}
```
    End If
  End For
}
```

The second phase of a multilevel graph partitioning algorithm is to compute a balanced bisection of the coarsened graph. [13] evaluated four different algorithms for partitioning the coarser graph. The basic idea of those algorithms is to form a cluster of highly connected nodes. We choose the *graph growing* heuristic for the partitioning phase. The heuristic computes a partition by recursively bisecting the graph into two sub-graphs of appropriate weight. To bisect a graph, we pick up a multivertices with the highest weight first, find its neighbours and neighbours' neighbours in a heaviest-edge-first manner until the workload of the new partition reach the average workload of the graph.

Algorithm 4.2 Partitioning Graph
```
Input:   Coarser graph  Gn = (Vn, En, w) with  N vertices
         The number of processors: m
Output:  The partition function  P assigning each vertex  v   Vn  to
         one of  m partitions
Begin
```
   $i = 2$

   $workload\,(G_n) = \quad w(e) + \quad \overline{w}(v)$
                        $e\ E_n$ $v\ V_n$

```
   Do while  i < m
```
     $Average\_workload = \dfrac{worklaod\,(Gn)}{i}$

     `For` $j = 1\ \text{to}\ \tfrac{1}{2}\ \text{do}$

        Sort the multivertices in $V_n^{\,j}$ in descending order by their weights

        Assume v $V_n^{\,j}$ is one of multivertices with maximum weight

        $workload\,(G_n^{\,j}) = \overline{w}(v)$

        $V_n^{\,j*2} = \{v\}$

```
Do while        w(e) +      w(v)) < Average _ workload
          e E_n^{j 2}        v V_n^{j 2}
```

Assume u is the neighbour of $V_n^{j\,2}$ with the maximum edge weight

$$V_n^{j\,2} = V_n^{j\,2}\quad \{u\}$$

```
      End Do
    End For
      i = i  2
  End Do
End
```

During the third phase of multilevel graph partitioning, the partition of the coarsest graph G_k is projected back to the original graph by going through the graphs $G_{k\;1}, G_{k\;2},..., G_1$. The purpose of a partition refinement algorithm is to select two subsets of vertices, one from each part such that when swapped the resulting partition has smaller edge-cut. Many algorithms associate with each vertex v a quantity called *gain*, which is the decrease in the edge-cut if v is moved to the other part. These algorithms proceed by repeatedly selecting vertices with the highest gains from each part and updating the gains of the remaining vertices. Assuming P is the initial partition of the graph, the gain of a vertex is defined as the following:

$$g_v =\quad w(v,u)\qquad w(v,u), \text{where } (v,u)\quad E$$
$$\quad P(v)\;P(u)\qquad P(v)=P(u)$$

$$(1)$$

If v is moved to the other partition, the gain of its neighbours should be modified. The algorithm stops when there's no vertex with positive gain value left.

5   Performance Analysis

We used the DBLP [15] data set as our experiment data. The DBLP data set collects about 140,000 entries for published literature on database research area. The original DBLP database stored each entry in a separate XML file and organised them by multiple directories according to its origination. We parsed the files into entities, which represent the vertices in the graph, and tags, which are the labels in the graph. The hierarchy of the directories is also reflected in the graph representation. We specially checked the *cite* entity in each document and linked it to the corresponding vertices in the graph. The final graph for partitioning test contains 1,693,444 vertices and 1,802,158 arcs. We used the query set in [16] to test our algorithms, and the query frequency was also specified.

Table 1. Description of query sets and relative query fequencies for the experiment

	Query Description	Result Number	Frequency			
			Case1	Case2	Case3	Case4
SQ_1	Select the authors for a given title	8	30%	20%	20%	10%
SQ_2	Select all papers authored by Michael Stonebraker	169	20%	10%	5%	10%
SQ_3	Select all papers authored by Michael Stonebraker or Jim Gray	242	20%	10%	10%	15%
SQ_4	Select all papers published between 1990 and 1994	47,527	5%	5%	10%	10%
JQ_1	Select all papers by Jim Gray that are quoted by Michael Stonebraker	2	10%	30%	20%	10%
JQ_2	Select all papers that quoted Michael Stonebraker's papers and were published between 1990 and 1994	513	10%	20%	25%	30%
JQ_3	Select all pairs of papers that cite one another	108,717	5%	5%	10%	15%

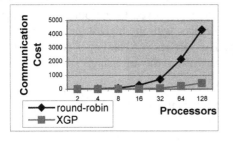

Fig. 4. Communication costs of different numbers of processors

Fig. 5. Workload skews of different numbers of processors.

For convenience, we briefly called our XML graph partitioning algorithm XGP. As the objectives of the XGP algorithm are to reduce the communication cost and lower workload skew, these two measures have been tested to check the quality of the algorithm. Figure 4 compares the communication costs when the round-robin algorithm and the XGP algorithm are used for data partitioning. The communication cost is indicated by the numbers of remote requested pages. We can see that the XGP algorithm produces less communication cost than the round-robin algorithm does. Figure 5 shows workload skews among the processing nodes. The workload skew is indicated by the difference between the workload of each partition to the average workload. It is defined in formula (2) and (3).

$$Avg\_workload = \frac{\underset{e \ E}{w(e)}}{m} \qquad (2)$$

$$workload\_skew = \frac{\sum_{i=1}^{m} |workload(Pi) \quad avg\_wokload|}{m} \quad (3)$$

It can be seen that the workload skew for the XGP algorithm doesnot change much with the increase of the number of processing nodes. XGP also produces a low workload skew, which is much less than the round-robin algorithm does.

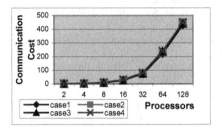

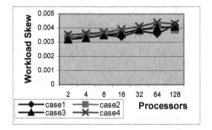

Fig. 6. Communication costs of different numbers of processors.

Fig. 7. Workload skews of different numbers of processors

The last experiment was to test the impact of query distributions to the workload balance. We tested the communication costs and workload skews caused by partitioning with different query frequency distributions. Figure 6 and Figure 7 show that XGP algorithm performs well under all the four cases showed in table 1. We can see that the communication costs and workload skews of four cases are quite close. Because the weight used in the XGP algorithm is dependent on the query frequency, the partitions for different query distributions will change accordingly.

6   Conclusion

In this study, we have developed a data placement strategy for the XML documents on parallel processing systems. This approach is based on the multilevel graph partitioning algorithm with consideration of the unique features of XML data and XML queries. A new algorithm is proposed for deriving the weighted graph from the labelled directed graph by using the implied schema information from XML queries. According to our approach, entities to be accessed by navigation in a query would be assigned to the same processing node, and instances accessed by the same query are distributed evenly along all the processing nodes. In the coarsening phase of the multilevel graph partitioning algorithm, all vertices in the neighourhood of the selected matching vertex are coalesced based on their edge weight. This criterion speeds up the procedure of the coarsening and reduces the possibility of assigning vertices to be accessed by navigation to different processing nodes. In the partitioning phase, the weights of multivertices are used to evenly distribute the workload of a query. The performance analysis shows that the partition produced by our algorithm could greatly reduce the communication cost and lower workload skew. In our future work, we will focus on the parallel processing of XML queries and the XML query optimisation with the consideration of different data placement strategies.

References

[1] Alan Kotok, An updated Survey of XML Business Vocabularies, http://www.xml.com/lpt/a/2000/8/02/ebiz/extensible.html, August 2000.

[2] D.B. Skillicorn, Structured Parallel Computation in Structured Documents, external technical Report, 1995.

[3] Manish Mehta, David J. DeWitt, Data placement in shared-nothing parallel database systems, VLDB Journal (1997) 6: pages 53–72.

[4] Zhen He and Jefferey Xu Yu, Object Placement in Parallel OODBMS, Proceedings of the Tenth Australasian Database Conference, pages 101-114, Auckland, New Zealand, January 1999.

[5] D. Sacca and G. Widerhold, Database partitioning in a cluster of processors. In proceedings of the 9th VLDB Conference, pages 242-247, Florence, Italy, Oct 31-Nov2, 1983.

[6] P. Apers. Data allocation in distributed database systems. ACM Transactions on Database Systems, 13(3): 263-304, September 1988.

[7] K.A. Hua, C. Lee, and H.C. Young, An efficient load balancing strategy for shared-nothing database systems. In proceedings of DEXA'92 conference, pages 469-474, Valencia, Spain, 1992.

[8] G. Copeland, W. Alexander, E. Boughter, and T. Keller, Data placement in Bubba, in Proceedings of ACM SIGMOD Conference, pages 99-108, Chicago, Illinois, June 1988.

[9] David Taniar, Toward an Ideal Data Placement Scheme for High Performance Object-Orented Database Systems, Proceedings of high-performance Computing and Networking, International Conference and Exhibition, HPCN Europe, pages 508-517, Amsterdam, 1998.

[10] Roy Goldman, Jason McHugh, Jennifer Widom, From Semistructured Data to XML: Migrating the Lore Data Model and Query Language, Proceedings of the 2nd International Workshop on the Web and Databases (WebDB '99), pages: 25-30, Philadelphia, Pennsylvania, June 1999.

[11] XML Schema Part1: Structures, W3C Candidate Recommendation, http://www.w3.org/TR/xmlschema-1, 24 October 2000.

[12] A. Bergholz. "Querying Semistructured Data Based On Schema Matching", Doctoral dissertation, Department of Computer Science, Humboldt University Berlin, Berlin, Germany, January 2000.

[13] George Karypis and vipin Kumar, A Fast and High Quality Multilevel Scheme for Partitioning Irregular graphs, SIAM Journal on Scientific Computing, Vol. 20 Number 1, pages: 359-392. 1998.

[14] A. Gupta, Fast and Effective Algorithms for Graph Partitioning and Sparse-matrix Ordering, Vol. 41, NO. 1-2, IBM Journal of Research & Development, pages: 171-184, 1997.

[15] DBLP maintained by M. Ley. http://www.informatik.uni-trier.de/~ley/db/index.html, December 2000.

[16] Feng Tian, David J. Dewitt, Jianjun Chen, and Chun Zhang, The Design and Performance Evaluation of Alternative XML Storage Strategies, http://www.cs.wisc.edu/niagara/vldb00XML.pdf, December 2000.

LOIS: The "Lights Out" Integrity Subsystem

Nicholas J. Caine and Suzanne M. Embury

Department of Computer Science, Cardiff University, The Parade,
Cardiff CF24 3XF, Wales, U.K., N.J.Caine@cs.cf.ac.uk

Abstract. Despite many years of research into mechanisms for checking integrity in databases, current commercial systems provide support for checking only the simplest forms of integrity constraints. However, both the users and developers of database applications are increasingly aware of the problems that can arise when poor quality data is allowed to enter, and remain within, large scale databases. Clearly, some form of integrity checking is required for such applications, but it must be packaged in a way that respects the business context in which the application is to operate. In particular, this means acknowledging that mission critical transaction processing cannot be delayed while integrity checks are made. In this paper, we propose an approach which makes use of periods of low database activity for integrity checking. We present a range of algorithms for scheduling integrity checks during these periods, and describe the results of our initial experiments with the system.

1 Introduction

Over recent years, both users and developers of information systems (IS) have become increasingly aware of the problems that can arise when poor quality data is allowed to enter, and remain within, large scale databases [19]. Studies place the proportion of bad data maintained by organisations at anything between 10% and 70% (e.g. [14]). The situation can be worse for some individual systems. For example, a recent BBC Radio 4 programme reported that when the contents of one U.K. metropolitan police database was compared with paper-based records 100% of the records were found to contain some form of discrepancy [2]. There is also an accumulating body of anecdotal evidence highlighting the increasing effect of data quality problems on the lives of individuals [11].

These errors, many of which have hitherto lain "dormant", are now coming to light as companies attempt to use their data in new and unanticipated ways. Perhaps, the most prominent example of this phenomenon is the data warehouse. The integration of data from different database systems, produced by different applications and managed by different parts of the organisation, into a single coherent framework typically reveals a surprising number of inconsistencies and errors within the original data sources [3]. Cleaning up the data prior to loading it into the warehouse requires a great deal of data processing effort (running queries to detect potential errors in the data) and human effort (correcting the errors found, in consultation with domain experts). While one-off improvement

B. Read (Ed.): BNCOD 2001, LNCS 2097, pp. 57–74, 2001.

efforts of this kind can result in dramatic reductions in error rates in databases, they are expensive and time-consuming. Moreover, since few organisations can afford to repeat the exercise regularly, they do nothing to maintain data quality in the long term. Once data cleansing is complete, the existing IS processes will continue to allow bad data to enter the system.

An alternative approach is to monitor data quality continuously, and to insist that all errors are corrected before data can be entered into the system. This is exactly what an integrity constraint mechanism promises to do. The database owner describes the conditions that should be held by all reasonable and consistent data sets. The DBMS and application programs then check all updates executed against the database, and refuse to allow any that would violate those conditions. However, despite nearly thirty years of research into mechanisms for checking data integrity, application developers are still reluctant to implement any but the simplest and cheapest integrity constraints. The problem is that a generalised integrity checking mechanism is very expensive, and most developers have taken the view that they cannot afford to include even hand-coded integrity checks in their applications. They would prefer to live with the possibility of bad data entering the system rather than hold up the processing of mission critical transactions — something that might lead to a direct loss in revenue for the organisation in question [1].

In fact, the problem with integrity checking is not so much that it is slow, but that it is slow at the most inconvenient of times. Because of the insistence that bad data must be prevented from entering the system at any cost, all integrity checking activities occur at update-time or on transaction commit. However, most updates are made during periods of high business activity, when the organisation's revenue is critically dependent upon the rate at which transactions can be processed. During periods of normal business activity, the application cannot afford to spend time processing complicated integrity checking queries, or for business transactions to be blocked until the integrity checker releases its shared read locks. In contrast, during the night, when the transaction processing rate is much lower, the database system will often sit idle for several hours at a time.

In this paper, we propose a "middle way" for data quality assessment, between the two extremes of one-off data cleansing activities and continuous integrity checking. Under this approach, constraint checking is delayed until periods when the load on the system is expected to be low, thus achieving a regular pattern of checking but without incurring an unacceptable cut in the rate at which the system can process important business transactions. We present the basic architecture of our system (called LOIS - the "Lights Out Integrity Subsystem"), a selection of the algorithms used to coordinate periodic constraint checking and the results of our initial experiments with the system. We begin, in Section 2, by surveying the range of methods for checking integrity. In Section 3, we describe the overall architecture of the LOIS system, while Section 4 presents the algorithms for scheduling constraint checking. Our experimental framework and results are given in Section 5, and Section 6 concludes.

2   A Comparison of Approaches to Integrity Checking

Traditional integrity checking (which we call *immediate integrity checking*) and data cleansing can be seen as two ends of a spectrum of possible approaches to data integrity. At one end, we check relevant constraints on every state change, no matter how small and insignificant; at the other end, constraints are not checked until some major new use for the data is identified that is hampered by the poor state of the data. Further, at one end of the spectrum, violations are never allowed to enter the database whereas, at the other, violations may exist in the database both before and after constraint checking. Unsurprisingly, each approach has advantages and disadvantages when applied in practice.

2.1   Immediate Constraint Checking

In immediate integrity checking, constraints are typically defined using a high-level declarative language. Each constraint is compiled into fragments of procedural code which check the constraint, and directives to the DBMS to execute these fragments when events occur which might violate it. One very common way of achieving this is to use the declarative constraint to generate a collection of active rules that will fire when potentially violating updates takes place [7,10]. Researchers working on techniques for immediate integrity checking have recognised the difficulty of producing efficient translations of integrity constraints, and have directed much effort at the problem of avoiding unnecessary integrity checking whenever possible (e.g. [7,9,16]).

We have already mentioned the major problems with immediate checking; namely, that it can be very time-consuming, and occurs at times when processing capacity is at a premium. Clearly, however, some constraints are so important that it is worth the processing time required to enforce them continuously. The basic structural constraints typically associated with relational databases, such as key integrity and referential integrity are good examples of this kind of constraint, as are "hard" constraints that ensure that an organisation's activities comply with the law, or that patients in a hospital are not prescribed lethal doses of drugs, for example. For many constraints, however, immediate checking is overkill, requiring that considerable processing effort be expended to check validity of data that may not be used again for some weeks or months.

A further factor that reduces the applicability of immediate integrity checking in practice is that it is too unforgiving for use in real applications. Inconsistent data is never allowed to enter the system, no matter what the context or consequences. All too often, however, such inconsistencies can reflect a failure in the design of the system rather than in the data itself. If they are to be usable in the real world, database systems must be capable of storing exceptional data that violates one or more of the system constraints [4,5].

2.2   Data Cleansing

Data cleansing is the process of identifying and removing errors and inconsistencies in data sets, in order to prepare them for some new task; for example, feeding the data into a data warehouse or using it for some form of analysis that is sensitive to errors in data (e.g. data mining). Detection of errors in the input data set(s) typically involves either:

- guessing at the types of error that might occur, and writing customised queries to detect any instances of these types,
- using a data profiling tool, such as EvokeSoft's Axio [15], or
- using sampling to produce a subset of values for a human expert to examine manually [17].

Once errors are identified, they must be corrected. Unlike in immediate checking, where we expect to correct each error as it occurs, in data cleansing it is common to find the same error in many hundreds or thousands of records. Because of the large numbers of errors, it is necessary to apply some sort of transformation to the data to correct them "in bulk" [12,18].

The principal advantage of data cleansing is that it typically has only a minor impact on standard business processing. Rather than work with the original data source, it is much more common for data cleansing staff to extract relevant sets of data (e.g. as flat files), which are then examined and corrected entirely off-line. Extracts from mission critical systems can be performed overnight, so that day-to-day processing is completely unaffected.

The principal disadvantage of data cleansing as a means of maintaining data quality over the long term is that it is not performed frequently enough, (i.e. it consumes too few data processing resources). Effectively, we allow all errors to enter the system unhindered, and then apply panic measures to remove the most expensive when their presence threatens to cost more than their detection and removal. In addition, data cleansing attacks the symptoms rather than the cause of the data quality problems. Once the cleansing effort is complete, errors can continue to enter the database system as frequently as they could before it. Moreover, due to pressure on resources, it is rare for corrections to be propagated back to the original source data sets. A further disadvantage of this approach is that the errors that are found may have been introduced many years before they are detected. This makes it very difficult to determine the correct repair strategy for the errors, as their original context may be lost completely. In contrast, the context of entry of errors is often (though not always) available to immediate checking techniques.

2.3   Less "Extreme" Forms of Integrity Checking

Despite the problems described above for the two ends of the integrity checking spectrum, very little attention has been paid to approaches which attempt to find a compromise between them. If immediate checking requires too frequent checking, and data cleansing too infrequent checking, what is the "optimum" frequency for checking constraints? The simplest answer to this question is to say that the user must decide. For example, both Cremers and Domann [8] and Cammarata et al. [6] have proposed integrity checking functions that can be invoked by the user on demand. As this would seem to be placing both too much responsibility on the user, these authors have independently proposed that constraints could be checked periodically, at times set in advance by the user (e.g. at lunchtime or overnight). However, this is no guarantee that integrity checking will not have a detrimental effect on normal business processing, as both authors assume that the entire database will be checked for all constraints whenever the integrity function is invoked. This may be realistic for small databases, which can be checked in a short time, but could interfere with mission critical transactions in large-scale databases.

Rather than relying on the user to request regular integrity checks, it would be better if the DBMS could decide whether an immediate check is necessary or whether a check could safely be made at some later time. Lafue has proposed a method for achieving this in a limited form, based on *semantic integrity dependencies* [13]. This proposal is founded on the observation that while there are theoretically many repairs for a given constraint, in practice the number of repairs is often much more limited and, in some cases, focusses on only one or two of the variables appearing in the constraint. For example, violations of a constraint which relates the modules chosen by an undergraduate student to the number of credits available from those modules would always be repaired by changing the module choices of the student, and not by changing the number of credits available from the module.

In Lafue's system, the user identifies the variables which can be changed in order to repair a constraint violation (called *dependent* variables) and those which cannot (*independent* variables). If a change occurs to some object which appears as a dependent variable in a constraint, then that constraint must be checked immediately. However, if an independent variable object changes, there is no need to check the constraint, as it cannot be that object which is at fault. Instead, the check can be deferred until the next time someone accesses the dependent variable objects associated with that constraint. Essentially, by specifying the dependent and independent variables for each constraint, the user is telling the DBMS when it is "safe" to delay an integrity check. However, this method only provides a way of cutting down the amount of integrity checking that is required. Business processing will still be interrupted and delayed by the remaining integrity checks. An alternative approach is to adapt the idea of asking the user to specify the times when constraint checking will be allowed, but to leave the DBMS with the task of deciding which constraints should be checked at each of these times. This is the approach that we have explored, and which we describe in the remainder of this paper.

3   The "Lights Out" Integrity Subsystem

As we have said, traditional approaches to integrity checking place unacceptable demands on the system resources during the peak business hours. The "Lights Out" Integrity Subsystem (LOIS) attempts to overcome this problem by making use of "off-peak" time to process the integrity constraints in a dynamic manner.

Table 1. Example timetable for controlling LOIS

Time	00	01	02	03	04	05	06	07	08	09	10	11	12	13	14	15	16	17	18	19	20	21	22	23
Sun	H	H	H	H	H	H	H	L	L	L	L	L	L	L	L	L	L	L	L	L	L	L	L	L
Mon	H	H	H	H	L	L	L	L	L	L	H	H	H	H	L	H	H	H	H	L	L	H	H	L
Tue	H	H	H	H	L	L	L	L	L	L	H	H	H	H	L	H	H	H	H	L	L	H	H	L
Wed	H	H	H	H	L	L	L	L	L	L	H	H	H	H	L	H	H	H	H	L	L	H	H	L
Thu	H	H	H	H	L	L	L	L	L	L	H	H	H	H	L	H	H	H	H	L	L	H	H	L
Fri	H	H	H	H	L	L	L	L	L	L	H	H	H	H	L	H	H	H	H	L	L	H	H	L
Sat	H	H	H	H	H	H	H	L	L	L	L	L	L	L	L	L	L	L	L	L	L	L	L	L

The periods which constitute this "off peak business time" are specified in advance (by the database administrator) in the form of a timetable showing the start and end points of periods of expected low activity. An example of such a timetable is shown in Table 1, where hours when the load on the system is expected to be high are marked with an 'H', and hours when the system is expected to be sitting idle are marked with an 'L'. Effectively, the timetable states when the system administrator is prepared to release processing resources for integrity checking and when she/he is not. Within each low-activity time slot, the DBMS decides dynamically which constraints to check. In general, there can be no guarantee that all of the integrity constraints can be checked completely within each time slot. Therefore, constraint checking must be scheduled across several time slots (i.e. periods of low system activity), hopefully in a way that ensures that all serious constraint violations are detected before the bad data is used by some major business process.

The architecture of LOIS (Figure 1) comprises two main components:

- the System Utilisation Monitor (SUM): this component waits for periods of low activity, as defined by the current system activity timetable, and initiates constraint checking when such a period begins or ends.
- the Constraint Selector: when awakened by the SUM, this component selects a constraint to check (according to some predefined criteria), extracts the query which implements the constraint from the constraint metadata, executes it and records details of any violations found. This process then repeats until the Constraint Selector is closed down by the SUM.

One of the aims of our work is to determine the most effective set of criteria that can be used for selecting the constraints to be checked in any given time slot. We have therefore constructed the Constraint Selector component in such a way that different selection algorithms can easily be plugged in to the system. This has allowed us to experiment with a variety of different selection criteria, as described later in Section 4 of this paper.

The LOIS components are supported by three sets of metadata:

- the Constraint Metadata: stores details of the constraints that are to be checked against the database. For each constraint, a unique identifier, an

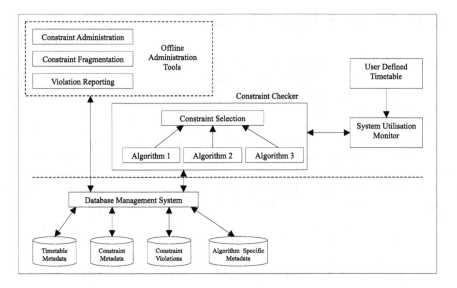

Fig. 1. Overview of the LOIS Architecture

SQL query that can be used to detect violations of the constraint, and an estimate of the time required to execute the query are stored:

constraint(ConstraintID, SQLQueryString, Estimate)

– the Constraint Violation Log: violations found during the constraint checking process are stored in a constraint violation log table, for subsequent browsing or analysis by the database administrator. The violation log table has the following structure:

violation(ViolationId, ConstraintId, TableName, TableNameRowId, TimeDetected)

– the Timetable Metadata: the start and end times of the expected periods of low activity are stored within the following table:

timetable(PeriodId, StartTime, EndTime, TimetableLength)

A timetable may be of arbitrary length (a week or a month are typical lengths) and may contain an arbitrary number of low and high periods of activity. The timetable metadata records the start and end times of each period of low activity, as a relative time (in minutes) from the start of the timetable cycle. The timetable length (in minutes) is also stored with each period for convenience.

Additional metadata is required by some of the selection algorithms that we have experimented with. This is described in the following section.

4   Constraint Selection Criteria

The heart of LOIS is the constraint selector component, which determines which constraints will be checked in any given period of low system activity. Since, in general, it will not be possible to check all constraints in each time slot, LOIS must use some selection criteria in order to identify the subset of constraints that can most usefully be checked in any one period. Clearly, one obvious element of these criteria is the amount of time required to check a constraint: there is no point in wasting time trying to check a constraint that requires 3 hours of processing in a time slot that lasts for 1 hour. Another element might be the degree of importance attached to each constraint by the user, so that more important constraints are checked more quickly (or more frequently) than less important ones.

The basic algorithm used by the LOIS constraint checker is as follows:

> *load selected constraint metadata into in-memory structures*
> *loop*
> > *determine amount of time left in low activity period*
> > *select a constraint according to the current selection criteria*
> > *if no such constraint can be found then*
> > > *exit*
> > *else*
> > > *evaluate the constraint query*
> > > *log any violations found*
> > > *update constraint metadata if appropriate*
> > *end if*
> *end loop*

This simple algorithm is invoked every time the constraint checker receives a signal indicating that a period of low activity has begun, and continues to execute until interrupted by a signal that the period has ended or until no more constraints can be found to check.

In order to determine the most useful selection criteria in practice, we have experimented with three different selection algorithms, based on different characteristics of the integrity constraints to be checked:

- an estimate of how long each constraint will take to check,
- a user-defined partial ordering on constraints, describing their relative importance, and
- user-supplied information about the maximum amount of time that may elapse between checks of each constraint.

We now describe how these characteristics are exploited by each of our three constraint selection algorithms.

4.1   Trivial Constraint Selection

The principle underlying the simplest of the three selection algorithms is that we should choose the largest constraint[1] that can be evaluated in the time remaining within the current time slot. In order to support this, we store an estimate of how long each constraint query takes to evaluate in the constraint metadata. The estimate is automatically maintained by LOIS, which keeps track of how long each constraint query takes to run in practice, and computes a sliding average of the time required over each execution.

However, an algorithm which simply chose the largest available constraint at each point would repeatedly select the same set of constraints to check over and over again, when we would prefer LOIS to systematically work through the whole set of constraints. We therefore keep track of which constraints have been checked by LOIS, and modify the selection criterion to be:

> *Choose the largest constraint that can be checked in the time remaining that has not been checked in the current round.*

Once all constraints have been checked, we mark all constraints as "unchecked" and the cycle of checking can begin again.

This selection criterion will eventually check all constraints, but it has a disadvantage that some time available for constraint checking may be wasted unnecessarily. For example, suppose that 15 minutes of checking time remain, but that no unchecked constraint can be found that can be executed in this amount of time. In this case, it would be more productive to recheck one of the constraints that can be checked in this time. This is far from pointless, as the constraint in question may have been checked in some previous period of low activity, and violations may have been created in the database in the meantime. We therefore extend our earlier selection criteria to take this possibility for rechecking into account:

> *Choose the largest constraint that can be checked in the time remaining that has not been checked in the current round. If no such constraint exists, then choose the largest constraint that can be checked in the time remaining.*

The algorithm which schedules constraints according to these criteria is given in Appendix A.

4.2   Prioritised Constraint Selection

The philosophy underpinning the previous algorithm is that "all constraints are equal", and that therefore equal weight should be given to the checking of each. In reality, however, some violations are potentially more serious than others, and therefore some constraints should be given priority over others. Our

---

[1] By 'largest' here, we mean the constraint which will take the longest to check.

second algorithm recognises this fact, by making use of a user-defined partial ordering over constraints (stored in the constraint metadata) to ensure that the more important constraints are checked more frequently. With this additional information, our selection criteria become:

> *Choose the highest priority constraint that can be checked in the time remaining that has not been checked in the current round. If more than one such constraint exists, then choose the "largest" such constraint. If no such constraint exists, then choose the largest, highest priority constraint that can be checked in the time available.*

We use the same algorithm for prioritised selection as for trivial selection, except that the constraints are orded first by their priority, and then (when several constraints have the same priority) by their size (i.e. query estimate).

4.3   Cyclic Constraint Selection

While a priority mechanism such as that described above is helpful, it can only affect the *order* in which constraints are checked. In reality, it may be more useful to try to control the *frequency* at which they are checked. For example, a constraint which guards against important violations in frequently updated data should be checked on a more regular basis than a constraint that prevents a minor error in a more static set of data. For our final algorithm, therefore, we allow the user to associate a "cycle time" with each constraint, which indicates the maximum amount of time that can be allowed to go by without checking the constraint. This is stored in the constraint metadata, along with details of when each constraint was last checked by LOIS.

LOIS then uses this information to select constraints whose cycles are almost over in preference to those that have longer to wait before they must be checked. As with the other algorithms, only constraints which are small enough to be checked within the period are selected, and when there is a choice of constraints with the same cycle deadline, the largest possible constraint is selected. Of course, we cannot always guarantee that every such deadline will be met, particularly if constraint cycle times are too small or the timetable is too tight. The constraint checker must therefore behave appropriately when some deadlines are missed. We have chosen to give highest priority to constraints which are most overdue, so that the algorithm attempts to "catch-up" on missed deadlines as soon as possible. The risk with this approach is that more and more constraints may not be checked by their deadline, as the algorithm tries to catch up on its backlog of overdue work.

The algorithm used for Cyclic Selection is given in Appendix B. For this form of scheduling, the constraints are ordered by ascending amount of time remaining before each constraint must be checked. For constraints which are overdue, this value will be a negative number, and therefore the most overdue constraint will appear at the very beginning of the list of constraints to be checked. However, unlike the other two algorithms, this form of selection has the added overhead

Table 2. Example constraints derived from the CAS schema

If PersonTitle = Mr then PersonGender = M
TotalStudentsEnrolled = Sum(TotalFemale + TotalMale)
If RegDisabled = N then DisabilityCode = 00
If RegDisabled = Y then DisabilityCode != 00 and in Range (01 - 99)

of having to update this ordering dynamically throughout each time period, whereas the other algorithms assume that the ordering will remain fixed within each low activity period.

5   Experimental Framework

In order to evaluate the performance of the three selection algorithms we have constructed an experimental framework, based on a real legacy database system, that allows us to compare the patterns of constraint checking achieved by each one. The legacy system that our framework simulates is the Course Administration System (CAS) used by the Department of Lifelong Learning at Cardiff University [20]. CAS holds detailed information on courses, tutors, students and mailing lists for marketing purposes, and currently contains something in the region of 70,000 records. Typical transaction volumes are low, at about 200 per day. The system is implemented in COBOL on top of the TurboIMAGE/3000 Database Management System from Hewlett Packard. Unfortunately the source code to CAS is not available, and as a result it was not possible to determine the integrity constraints enforced by the original application. Instead, we analysed the schema and samples of the data, and identified some eighty useful integrity constraints of varying degrees of complexity. From these, we excluded all structural constraints of the kind better implemented using the declarative constraint facilities provided by most commercial DBMSs, and simple constraints on individual tuples as these are better checked using immediate checking. This left some sixty-two more complex constraints (e.g. those involving multiple tables or aggregate functions), which are more appropriate for checking under the LOIS approach. Table 2 shows some examples of the types of constraints identified for checking with LOIS.

To further develop the simulation of the legacy system, we analysed a number of key business processes within the Department of Lifelong Learning in order to determine typical data set sizes and transaction patterns. Using this information, we constructed a program to generate a sequence of random transactions representative of six months' worth of data updates within CAS, scaled down in volume so that they can be executed in just six hours within the LOIS system. We also constructed a scaled-down timetable to simulate the periods of low and high activity in the CAS working week (see Figure 1).

We then executed the simulated transaction sequence three times (starting from the same starting state each time), with LOIS configured to use a different selection algorithm for each run. The graphs in Figure 2 show the number of times each constraint was checked using trivial selection (top graph), prioritised selection (middle graph) and cyclic selection (bottom graph). Each bar on each graph represents a constraint, and in each case constraints are ordered by size, with the most time-consuming constraint appearing at the left and the least at the right.

Using trivial selection, LOIS managed to check almost all the constraints at least once, with just four constraints never being checked. These are all quite large constraints which do not fit easily into any of the available time slots. In addition, the algorithm seemed to "get stuck" on three constraints, which it checked a very large number of times. The performance of the prioritised selection algorithm is much better. Again, four constraints are never checked, but the vast majority of constraints are checked at least five times. The algorithm only got "stuck" on one particular constraint. Interestingly, cyclic checking was least successful of the three. It clearly checks some of the constraints more frequently than the other two algorithms, but also ignored twenty-nine of the constraints completely. This is partly due to the additional overhead involved in this third selection algorithm, which means that less time is available for constraint checking, but it may also reflect the difficulties of specifying a set of cycle time deadlines which can be achieved within a given timetable.

These results raise the question as to why prioritised selection seems to spend more time in checking constraints than trivial selection, when the two algorithms are so similar. In order to understand this, it is necessary to consider the amount of time "wasted" by each algorithm when it is interrupted in the middle of checking a constraint, at the end of the period of low activity. This is shown by the set of graphs in Figure 3, which gives the number of times each constraint was aborted during checking by each of the three algorithms. We can see from these graphs that trivial selection results in far more time being wasted by aborted constraint checks, when compared to prioritised selection. Cyclic selection wastes still less time, but this again would seem to be due to the increased overhead of this algorithm[2]. These initial results would seem to indicate that the use of priorities is the most effective means to select constraints for "lights out" integrity checking.

6   Conclusions

We have described the design and evaluation of a new approach to integrity checking. Unlike traditional integrity checking mechanisms, which do all checking at the time the update is made, our approach makes use of the times when normal database activity is low to undertake constraint checking and therefore does not

---

[2] This diagnosis can be further supported by our results. Since we know how long each constraint takes to check, we can use these results to estimate how long each algorithm spent doing "useful" constraint checking activity. Prioritised selection spends 3288s, trivial selection spends 2740s while cyclic selection spends just 2660s in successful constraint checking.

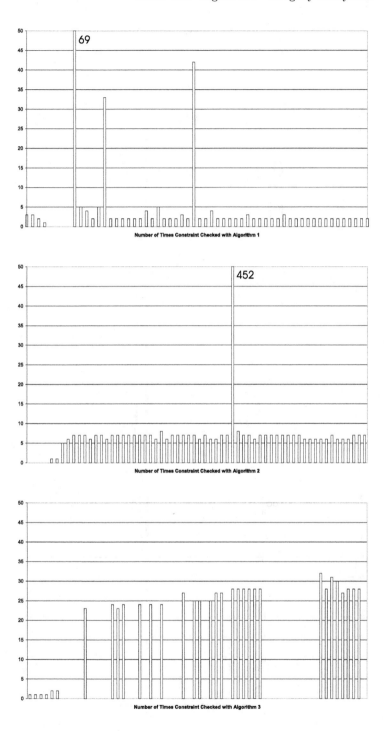

Fig. 2. Results showing the number of checks on constraints

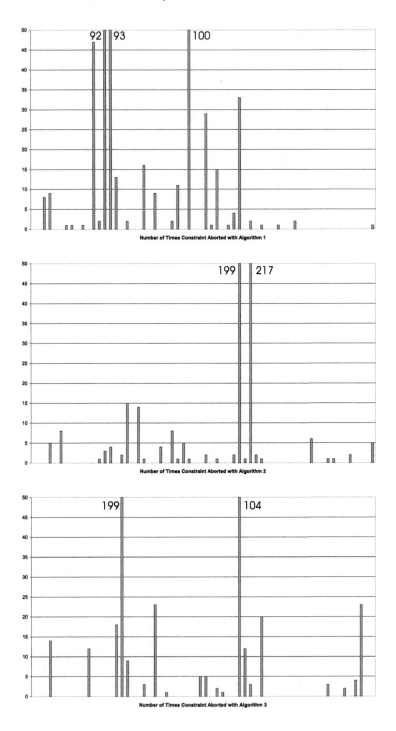

Fig. 3. Results showing the number of aborts on constraints

interfere with the processing of critical business transactions. This has a number of additional advantages:

- The system allows inconsistent data to be entered into the database. While this might appear to be a disadvantage, experience from real database applications indicates that the stringent requirements of full data integrity imposed by traditional approaches is unworkable in practice [5].
- The responsibility for repairing integrity violations is moved from the end-user/data entry point (where the information required to make appropriate corrections is often not available) to the data quality or database administration team.
- LOIS allows "low priority" constraints to be entered into the system to check for rare errors, or to report occurrence of data patterns that might be indicative of an anomalous situation, without impacting on business-critical processing rates.

A major disadvantage of the LOIS approach is that certain important kinds of error may not be discovered until after the time at which they can be corrected. For example, a telephone sales operator may have been able to correct an error through dialogue with the customer, if warned at the time of data entry. This is exactly the sort of situation that traditional approaches to integrity checking handle well. However, it is important to recognise that the LOIS approach is complementary to, and not a replacement for, traditional methods of integrity control. The developer of the database system can choose to implement some constraints using immediate checking (e.g. checks on allowed value ranges, checks that some data values are unique or non-null) and others using LOIS (e.g. complex constraints involving aggregates, or navigation across several tables) — thus gaining the advantages of both approaches.

Having established the basic feasibility of a system based on "lights out" integrity checking, we are now investigating ways in which constraint selection can be made more appropriate for use in practice. For example, more efficient constraint selection could be performed if LOIS made use of the timetable information to pre-plan optimal (or near optimal) schedules for constraint checking off-line. Or, one could make use of the transaction log to focus constraint checking on areas of the database which have been updated recently. In addition, we are investigating the alternative approach of using a real-time monitor to switch on integrity checking when the load on the DBMS falls below some pre-determined threshold value. This will enable constraint checking to occur in *actual* periods of low activity, rather than in *predicted* periods of low activity. A further potential application of LOIS is in fraud detection, where the LOIS engine could be used to search for data patterns that may indicate fraudulent usage of the system, without impacting on day-to-day business processing.

Acknowledgements. This research is supported by a grant from the EPSRC and TenFold Solutions Ltd. The original idea for checking integrity constraints during periods of low activity was suggested by Jeff Walker of TenFold, Inc., and further input was provided by Steve Clark and Mike Bermeister, of TenFold Solutions Ltd. We are also grateful to Professor Alex Gray, Dr Iain Sutherland and the Department of Lifelong Learning at Cardiff University for access to their legacy database.

A   Trivial Constraint Selection Algorithm

NC ← total number of constraints
N ← NC
load constraint IDs into array constraints[] in descending order of size
load estimates into array estimates[]
load checked table into array checked[]

loop
    if N = 0 then
        % All constraints have been checked. Begin the cycle again
        N ← total number of constraints
        delete all tuples in checked table
        reinitialise checked[] with false values
    end if

    % Calculate time left in period
    TL ← end of period - now
    % Find the first constraint that has not been checked and
    % that can be checked within the remaining time
    I ← 1
    while (checked[I] or estimate[I] > TL) and I ≤ NC do
        I ← I + 1
    end while

    % If no such constraint exists
    if I > NC then
        % Find the next constraint that can be checked in the time left
        I ← 1
        while estimate[I] > TL and I ≤ NC do
            I ← I + 1
        end while

        if I > NC then
            % No constraint will fit in the remaining time
            exit
        else
            % Check the selected constraint
            retrieve and evaluate query for constraint[I]
            log details of any violations found

```
            end if
      else
            retrieve and evaluate query for constraint[I]
            log details of any violations found
            add checked(constraint[I]) to constraint metadata
            checked[I] ← true
            N ← N - 1
      end if
end loop
```

B   Cyclic Constraint Selection Algorithm

```
NC ← total number of constraints
calculate time to next deadline for each constraint (now - timeLastChecked
+ frequency)
load constraint IDs into array constraints[] ordered by time to next deadline
load estimates into array estimates[] ordered by time to next deadline

loop
      % Calculate time left in period
      TL ← end of period - now
      % Find the first constraint that can be checked within the time left
      I ← 1
      while estimate[I] > TL) and I ≤ NC do
            I ← I + 1
      end while

      if I > NC then
            % No such constraint can be found
            exit
      else
            % Check the selected constraint
            retrieve and evaluate query for constraint[I]
            log details of any violations found
            update timeLastChecked of constraint[I] (= now)

            % Recreate arrays based on new time to deadline for each constraint
            calculate time to next deadline for each constraint
            load constraint IDs into array constraints[] ordered by time to next
            deadline
            load estimates into array estimates[] ordered by time to next deadline
      end if
end loop
```

References

1. R. Barquin and H. Edelstein. *Building, Using and Managing the Data Warehouse.*
   Prentice Hall, 1997.

2. BBC Radio 4. File on Four. Broadcast on 10th December 2000.

3. A. Bischoff. *Data Warehouse: Practical Advice from the Experts*. Prentice Hall, 1997.

4. A. Borgida. Language Features for Flexible Handling of Exceptions in Information Systems. *ACM Transactions on Database Systems*, 10(4):565–603, December 1985.

5. I. Boydens, A. Pirotte, and E. Zimanyi. Managing Constraint Violations in Administrative Information Systems. In S. Spaccapietra and F. Maryanski, editors, *Data Mining and Reengineering*, pages 353–377. Chapman & Hall, 1998.

6. S.J. Cammarata, P. Ramachandra, and D. Shane. Extending a Relational Database with Deferred Referential Integrity Checking and Intelligent Joins. In J. Clifford, B. Lindsay, and D. Maier, editors, *Proceedings of the 1989 ACM SIGMOD International Conference on Management of Data*, pages 88–97, Portland, Oregon, June 1989. ACM Press.

7. S. Ceri and J. Widom. Deriving Production Rules for Constraint Maintenance. In D. McLeod, R. Sacks-Davis, and H. Schek, editors, *Proceedings of 16th International Conference on Very Large Databases*, pages 566–577, Brisbane, 1990. Morgan Kaufmann Publishers, Inc.

8. A.B. Cremers and G. Doman. AIM - An Integrity Monitor for the Database System INGRES. In M. Schkolnick and C. Thanos, editors, *Proceedings of 9th International Conference on Very Large Databases*, pages 167–170, Florence, Italy, 1983. Morgan Kaufmann Inc.

9. S.M. Embury and P.M.D. Gray. Compiling a Declarative, High-Level Language for Semantic Integrity Constraints. In R. Meersman and L. Mark, editors, *Proceedings of 6th IFIP TC-2 Working Conference on Data Semantics*, pages 188–226, Atlanta, USA, May 1997. Chapman and Hall.

10. S.M. Embury and P.M.D. Gray. Database Internal Applications. In N.W. Paton, editor, *Active Rules in Database Systems*, chapter 19, pages 339–366. Springer, New York, 1999.

11. L.P. English. *Improving Data Warehouse and Business Information Quality*. John Wiley & Sons, Inc., 1999.

12. H. Galhardas, D. Florescu, D. Shasha, and E. Simon. AJAX: An Extensible Data Cleaning Tool. Internal report, 2000. http://caravel.inria.fr/~galharda/ajax.html.

13. G.M.E. Lafue. Semantic Integrity Dependencies and Delayed Integrity Checking. In *Proceedings of 8th International Conference on Very Large Databases*, pages 292–299, Mexico City, 1982.

14. K.C. Laudon. Data Quality and Due Process in Large Interorganisational Record Systems. *Communications of the ACM*, 29(1):4–11, January 1986.

15. Migration Architect. http://www.evokesoft.com/products/ProdDSMA.html.

16. J.-M. Nicolas. Logic for Improving Integrity Checking in Relational Databases. *Acta Informatica*, 18:227–253, 1982.

17. V. Raman, A. Chou, and J.M. Hellerstein. Scalable Spreadsheets for Interactive Data Analysis. In K. Shim and Srikant R, editors, *Proceedings of ACM SIGMOD Workshop on Research Issues in Data Mining and Knowledge Discovery*, Philadelphia, USA, May 1999.

18. V. Raman and J.M. Hellerstein. Potters Wheel: An Interactive Framework for Data Cleaning and Transformation. Working Draft. Available from: http://www.cs.berkeley.edu/ rshankar/pwheel/pwheel5.pdf, 2000.

19. T.C. Redman. *Data Quality for the Information Age*. Artech House, Inc., 1996.

20. I. Sutherland. The course administration system: A legacy problem. Master's thesis, Cardiff University, 1997.

CASE-Tool Interchange of Design Transformations

Henrik Gustavsson [1] and Brian Lings [2]

[1] University of Skövde, Sweden
henke@ida.his.se
[2] University of Exeter, UK
B.J.Lings@exeter.ac.uk

Abstract. The great variety of CASE tools available on the market implies a need for data interchange. One approach to satisfying this need is the export and import of models. For this to be vendor independent requires standardized common interchange formats, either in the form of meta-models or a common transfer format. CASE tools use some type of explicit or implicit design transformations to transform different types of models, for example conceptual to logical. The transformations are important for interchange since a set of models which are consistent in one tool may be inconsistent in another tool that does not support the same set of transformations. Subsequent modification in the latter tool may lead to irresolvable inconsistencies. In this paper we define a common, model independent notation for design transformations to facilitate interchange between tools so that the meaning of different transformations can remain consistent between different CASE tools. The proposal is made in the form of a conservative extension to OCL. A run-time interpreter for the extension has been built.

1 Introduction

Currently there is great variety in the different CASE tools marketed by a large number of vendors. It is common in practice for design teams to use more than one CASE tool to support the different phases of design in their proprietary design life-cycles. There is thus a need for data interchange between the tools offered by different CASE tool vendors [4]. In order to interchange models between different CASE tools, standardized common meta-models and common transfer formats have been defined. Transfer formats such as CDIF [8] and XMI [11] case tool interchange formats allow interchange of CASE tool models using a standardized, vendor independent format.

However, many CASE tools use some type of explicit or implicit design transformations to transform different types of models. For example, a conceptual ER design may have been transformed by one tool into a specific logical RM. Such transformations are important for interchange since a set of models which is consistent in one tool may be inconsistent in another tool that does not support the same set of transformations. If the models produced using one tool are modified by a tool that does not support the design transformations from that tool, irresolvable inconsistencies could potentially be introduced between the tools.

B. Read (Ed.): BNCOD 2001, LNCS 2097, pp. 75–88, 2001.
© Springer-Verlag Berlin Heidelberg 2001

We maintain that there is a need for a representation of design transformations which allows such transformations to be shared and interchanged between different tools. Such transformations are, however, rarely made explicit. While the metadata in a tool can be interchanged using standardized interchange formats, to our knowledge, no standard notation for language and platform independent definition and subsequent interchange of transformations exists.

The goal of the work reported here is to define a common, model independent notation for design transformation interchange between tools, so that the meaning of different transformations will remain consistent between different CASE tools.

The result of this is a proposed extension of the MOF UML-based meta-model [13] which will allow the interchange of transformations as part of a model, together with an extension of the OCL language that can be used with the meta-model to describe transformations. A prototype system has been implemented, which supports the representation and execution of transformations. Extensions to the OCL interpreter to support transformations amount to less than 10% of the complete interpreter code.

2 Previous Work

In recent years, work in the development of tools for database applications has shown that various types of transformations can be used to perform many of the common modelling tasks in database design. A survey of various approaches to database design that utilise transformation can be found in [5]. Support for such design transformations is now expected of tools in the area. However, little progress has been made in the area of general interchange of design transformations between CASE tools.

One important characteristic of the database design processes that utilise design transformations as presented in textbooks [2,3] is that they are often defined in the form of a set of steps which together form a transformation procedure. Some of these steps specify alternative transformations which can be selected by the user of the procedure.

Very few approaches have tried to represent transformations and transformation procedures directly. The DB-main meta-CASE environment [6] offers support for alternative design transformations and transformation procedures. The main flaw in the approach from the perspective of this paper is the use of a proprietary procedural programming language called Voyager [6] for the implementation of the various transformations. Interchange of the transformations and the transformation procedures would thus be a very difficult task, since the constructs expressed in the Voyager Language would have to be translated to the specific language of the target CASE tool.

An alternative approach to design transformations [10] utilises logics and graph-oriented constructs to define transformations, making the transformations declarative and thus less dependent on specific programming languages. The approach utilises a graph-oriented meta-model with a logic programming implementation. However, their graphical model is proprietary and, as presented in the literature, does not directly support transformation procedures and the use of alternative transformations.

Our own concern has been to develop a declarative transformation language for supporting Object-Oriented information systems design. In this context, one language which is an obvious contender for defining transformation constraints is the OCL language, developed for defining constraints in UML models. OCL is declarative, platform and language independent, and has the advantage of being a part of the UML standard [12]. Different implementations of OCL interpreters exist, one implementation of the OCL language is provided by IBM [7], which contributed the OCL language for UML 1.1. The largest problem with using the OCL language to define design transformations is that it is, in its original guise, side effect free. It thus requires extension to support design transformations for inter-tool development of designs incorporating transformations. Another extension of the OCL language which supports side effects does exist [9]. However, that extension does not allow the modification of models; rather it provides the language with a shorthand for posting events. Since it is not guaranteed that the source and destination CASE tools support the same set of events or methods, such an extension does not actually convey the semantics of the modification and is thus not sufficient for transformation interchange.

3 A Conservative Extension of the OCL Language

In line with OCL's status as a standard language requiring implementation in any compliant CASE tool, any suggested changes to OCL must be kept to a minimum. In recognition of this, the proposed extensions of the language have been designed to be localised to a small set of concepts. Migration of an existing OCL interpreter should be straightforward, and require modest effort.

The proposed extensions form two distinct categories: extensions that are needed to update models, and extensions that will allow the specification of rules.

Extensions to Provide Support for Object Modification

The extensions in this category together form the set of extensions that are required to perform updates to models.

The first and most important extension is the addition of an assignment operator. The assignment operator, denoted by the symbol ':=', is used to assign values to properties or roles. Since the same operator is used both to assign properties and roles, the extension is localised to a very small part of an OCL interpreter.

The semantics of the assignment of *properties* is very straightforward. When an assignment statement is executed, the relevant repository object is modified to reflect the change of state.

The semantics of the assignment of roles, i.e. the various types of collections, is not as simple. When an assignment of a *collection* is performed, the old content of the collection is removed, and the new content is inserted in its place. This means that if a new entry is to be added to a collection, that new object is added to the existing collection by assigning the collection the value of the old collection but including the new value.

In order to perform any transformation of a schema, it is necessary to be able to create new schema objects. An operation has thus been added to the language which creates a new object. The *create* operator can be applied only to aliases which originate from rule declaration statements. It is thus illegal to change the object which is referred to by the *self* alias by calling the create method.

Analogous to object creation, it is also desirable to be able to delete a modelling object from a model. In order to maintain schema consistency, the object deletion operation should also preserve referential integrity by cascading the delete. When an object is deleted, it is thus simultaneously removed from all collections which refer to it. The application restrictions of the creation operator do not apply to the deletion operator. It is thus possible to delete the object that the *self* alias refers to, given that no modifications of the object occur after it has been deleted.

In order to be able to group several modifications together within a single extended OCL expression a symbol was introduced to delineate the components of an expression that are to be interpreted separately. This *separator symbol* is denoted by ';'. In order to comply with the basic design of the OCL language, all successful components evaluate to „true„. The ';' symbol is thus only a shorthand for the logical AND operator.

Extensions to Support Rules

The OCL language supports aliases, which allow the creation of conditions which span several levels of operations. The most well known alias is the *self* alias, which refers to the context object. Declarations of such aliases can be made in the rule declaration part of a transformation rule.

If the OCL language is to be used to specify rules that create objects and modify the newly created objects, the language must include some means of declaring the objects that are to be created. The ordinary alias mechanism can thus be extended in scope to allow *declaration aliases*, maintaining the standard aliases without any modification to the OCL interpreter. When a declaration alias is passed to an OCL interpreter the only difference from a standard alias is that it can be used to create new objects in a model.

4 Extending the Meta-model to Support Transformations

A language for expressing transformations is not sufficient on its own for the representation and subsequent interchange of models and the transformations which make the constraints between the models explicit. To express a transformation in a transferable way requires a common meta-model for expressing OCL rules as well as other model components.

The chosen representation must support a representation of the transformation procedure, the individual transformation rules which together make up the procedure, and the patterns which supply a user with a choice of alternative transformations for a specific object.

Any object in a meta-model, such as the ER entity class, is associated with a single model which groups all of the associated classes together. A transformation procedure groups a set of transformation rules together and associates the procedure with a set of models between which it performs some type of transformation. The instantiated classes contained in the model, for instance an EREntity with the name *person*, may also refer to a transformation pattern which will allow the user to select a specific transformation for that particular modelling object. This will allow interchange of the choices of transformation that a user has made together with the meta-model and the transformation procedures.

The extended meta-model features needed for handling the proposed extension appear in figure 1. The transformations are thus represented at the model level. This allows a model element to directly refer to the transformation patterns. The transformation information would then be interchanged as part of the model; it is thus model specific rather than general. The interpretation of the OCL statements, however, must take place at the meta-model level, i.e. at a level that is higher than that at which they are represented. The only limitation with this is that the transformations cannot transform the procedures or the rules, because such self modification would potentially introduce anomalies.

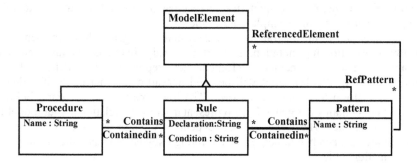

Fig. 1. Transformation meta-model framework.

5 Example Schemas

In order to demonstrate the proposed approach we present a concrete example.

An Example Meta-model

One type of transformation which is common and well described in textbooks on database design (Insert reference!) concerns the transformation of an enhanced entity-relationship diagram into a corresponding set of tables for the relational model. In the textbooks this type of transformation requires the designer to follow a specific procedure, described as a number of steps. For each of these steps there is often a set of alternative transformations which can be used to produce different sets of tables for the same entity-relationship diagram. One of the most complicated steps in such an algorithm is the transformation of inheritance hierarchies. For each inheritance connection there are at least three main categories of transformation possible. One option is to represent inheritance by using a foreign key. A second option is to move the attributes of the supertype into the subtype. A third option involves moving the attributes from the subtypes into the supertype. In the two last options either the supertype or the subtype will not have a directly corresponding table, and the attributes and relationship associated with that entity need to be redirected to the correct corresponding table. The behaviour of this transformation can become even more complex, since the supertype relationship is potentially recursive, allowing supertypes of other supertypes. In order to show the function of the transformation language in a somewhat realistic setting, the example was devised to illustrate this complex behaviour.

The meta-model devised is an exemplar, designed explicitly as a representative test-bed of the transformation procedures developed. Its representation of entity relationship models and relational tables is necessarily simplified to reduce the complexity of the examples; additional interconnections could have been added to give an even higher degree of modelling transparency. The provision for alternative transformation patterns has been restricted in the example to the case of the subtype relationship. Furthermore, the pattern reference has been simplified in the example by using a property (see, for example, rule 1 below).

The upper part of the diagram (Figure 2) contains the generalised representation of an Entity Relationship notation, supporting binary relationships and inheritance hierarchies. The class named ERDependency represents dependencies between entities, defining which entities will be used instead of another entity if it does not directly transform to a table on its own. The lower part of the diagram, below the dashed line, contains the generalised representation of the relational data model used for this example. The Primary key dependency class is used to represent a dependency between two tables where the foreign key is also made the primary key in the destination table.

Example Rules

The transformations are specified using the OCL language to create the condition for the transformation and the extended OCL language to specify the action of the transformation rule. The main outline of the rules is similar to the transformation procedures that are provided in common textbooks in the database area. There are, however, some differences. Due to the nature of the procedures as they are presented in a textbook (namely, as algorithms) they do not directly correspond to transformation rules.

The most obvious difference is that the subtype/supertype relationships are transformed in the beginning of the transformation process as opposed to at the very end of a transformation algorithm. This is because the associated transformations will effect the creation of tables for the entities, and will thus need to be performed before transformations which modify them. One other notable difference is the transformation of the attributes as separate objects and not as part of an entity. It was decided to have separate transformations for the attributes in order to gain flexibility of transformations. Finally, support for inherited relationships would require separate transformations.

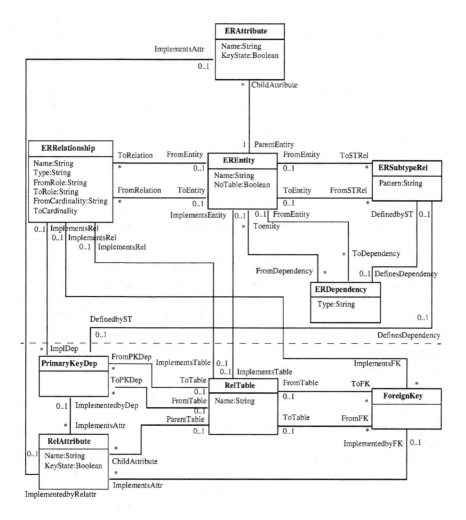

Fig. 2. The example meta-model[1]

A few simplifications of the rules and the meta-models have been made in order to make the example easier to read and understand. In this example, the separate class for transformation patterns has been reduced to a property. This property is furthermore only present in the supertype relationship class. All references to the transformation patterns are thus reduced to conditions that work with this property. In a more realistic schema, patterns would be represented as classes and references, and patterns for all of the classes would be provided. In order to reduce the size of the rules and the size and complexity of the example meta-model, the *model* class, which represents the models containing the other modelling concepts, has been removed. In a more realistic schema, all other modelling objects would be contained in a *model*.

---

[1] ModelElelement has been omitted for simplicity; it is a superclass of all classes.

A few relationships between classes, such as for example the fact that a primary key dependency defines a foreign key, have also been removed to reduce the size of the model. The absence of these relationships reduces the modeling transparency [1] of the models, but the information can still be derived from data that is present in the models.

A transformation algorithm for models of the complexity of the example meta-model in this paper requires a large set of rules. The set of transformation rules presented in this paper is thus only a subset of those required. The set of rules selected for the example contains the rules that are required by the example schema; all rules not necessary for the example schema have been left out of the example set. The ordering among the rules is, however, the same as it would be in the complete set for the schema.

Rule 1: Performs the transformation of downward inheritance into downward dependencies. A rule that is similar to this rule performs the upward inheritance transformations. The condition of this rule will assure that the inheritance relationship is only transformed if the supertype has no supertypes that have not yet been transformed, and that the object that is to be transformed is of the correct type. The action performs the creation of a dependency going from the supertype to the subtype entity, and ensures that all dependencies of the supertype are inherited by the subtype. The action statement also ensures that no table will be generated for the supertype.

```
Class: ERSubtypeRel
Condition:FromEntity.FromSTRel->forall(Pattern="D"
implies DefinesDependency->notempty AND
FromEntity.ToSTrel->Forall(Pattern="U" implies
DefinesDependency-> notempty) AND pattern = "D" AND
DefinesDependency->isempty
Declaration: ERDependency E1
Action: FromEntity.NoTable:=true; E1.create;
DefinesDependency:=E1; E1.Type:="D";
E1.FromEntity:=FromEntity; ToEntity.FromDependency:=
Toentity->FromDependency->union
(FromEntity.FromDependency)->including(E1)
```

Rule 2: Transforms an entity definition into a table definition. The condition for this rule ensures that only the entities that should have a corresponding table will be transformed. The action statement generates the table and connects the table with the corresponding entity.

```
Class: EREntity
Condition: NoTable=false and ImplementsTable->isempty
Declaration: RelTable T1
Action: T1.create; T1.Name:=self.Name;
T1.ImplementsEntity:=T1.ImplementsEntity
->including(self)
```

Rule 3: Performs the transformation of attributes in an entity that has a corresponding table connected to it. The condition ensures that the entity the attribute is contained in has a corresponding table and that the attribute has not already been generated. The action section creates a corresponding relational attribute and connects that attribute to the correct table.

```
Class: ERAttribute
Condition: ParentEntity.NoTable=false and
ImplementsAttr->isempty
Declaration: RelAttribute A1
Action: A1.create; A1.Name:=self.Name;
A1.KeyState:=self.KeyState;
A1.ImplementsAttr := self;
A1.ParentTable:=ParentEntity.ImplementsTable
```

Rule 4: Performs the slightly more complex task of creating the attributes that are connected to entities that have no directly corresponding table. The condition and action for this rule are basically the same as in the third rule. The difference is that the entity may have several dependants. Iteration is thus necessary so that the attributes are added to all of the dependants.

```
Class: ERAttribute
Condition: ParentTable.NoTable=true and
ImplementsAttr->isempty
Declaration: RelAttribute A1
Action: ParentEntity.ToDependency->iterate(DP |
DP.ToEntity->reject(NoTable=true)->iterate(E1 |
A1.create; A1.Name:=self.Name;
A1.ImplementsAttr :=self;
A1.ParentTable:= E1.ImplementsTable)
```

Rule 5: Performs the task of creating a dependency that specifies that the key in the corresponding table is dependent on the key in some other table. The condition guarantees that only relationships of the correct type, which have not previously been transformed, are transformed. Since different actions are performed depending on which of the connected entities have corresponding tables and which do not, this condition also specifies the correct condition to guarantee that the correct action is performed. The action then creates one key dependency for each of the dependants of the affected entities.

```
Class: ERRelationship
Condition: Type="I" and FromCardinality="1" and
ToCardinality="N" and ImplDep->isempty and
FromEntity.NoTable=true and ToEntity.NoTable = false
Declaration: PrimaryKeyDep PK1
Action: FromEntity.ToDependency->iterate( DP |
DP.ToEntity->reject (NoTable=true)->iterate( E1 |
PK1.create; PK1.ImplementsRel:=self;
PK1.ToTable:=E1.ImplementsTable;
PK1.FromTable:=ToEntity.ImplementsTable ))
```

Rule 6: Functionally very similar to the fifth rule, with the difference that the rule only affects relationships that have many-to-many cardinality. The action is more complex since one table and two dependencies have to be created.

```
Class: ERRelationship
Condition: FromCardinality="N" and ToCardinality="N"
and ImplementsFK->isempty and FromEntity.NoTable=false
and ToEntity.NoTable=true
Declaration: ForeignKey FK1, RelTable R1, ForeignKey
FK2
Action: FromEntity.ToDependency->iterate( DP |
DP.ToEntity-> reject (NoTable=true)->iterate( E1 |
R1.create; R1.Name:= FromEntity.Name.concat
(ERRelationship.Name).concat(E1.Name);
self.ImplementsTable:=R1; FK1.create;
FK1.ImplementsRel:=self; FK1.ToTable:=
FromEntity.ImplementsTable; FK1.FromTable:=R1;
FK2.create; FK2.ImplementsRel:=self;
FK2.ToTable:=E1.ImplementsTable; FK2.FromTable:=R1))
```

Rule 7: Performs a cascade of primary keys, required by primary key dependencies. The condition guarantees that the same primary key dependency will not be transformed several times and that the source table of the dependency does not have any dependency that is not transformed. The action statement iterates through the keys and creates a foreign key between the tables.

```
Class: PrimaryKeyDep
Condition: FromTable.FromPKDep->forall(ImplementsAttr-
>notempty)
Declaration: RelAttribute A1, ForeignKey FK1
Action: FK1.create; FK1.FromTable:=FromTable;
FK1.ToTable:=ToTable; FromTable.ChildAttribute->
reject(KeyState=false)->iterate( RA1 | A1.create;
A1.ImplementedbyFK:=FK1; A1.Name:=RA1.Name;
A1.KeyState:=RA1.KeyState; A1.ImplementedbyDep:= self;
A1.ParentTable:=ToTable)
```

Rule 8: Creates foreign keys and the attributes needed to represent each foreign key. The condition guarantees that the foreign key dependency has not already been generated. The action iterates through all of the key attributes in the source table and creates corresponding attributes in the destination table.

```
Class: Foreignkey
Condition: ImplementedbyFK->notempty
Declaration: RelAttribute A1
Action: FromTable.ChildAttribute->
reject(KeyState=false)->iterate( RA1 | A1.create;
A1.Name:=RA1.Name; A1.KeyState:=RA1.KeyState;
A1.ImplementedbyFK :=self; A1.ParentTable:=ToTable)
```

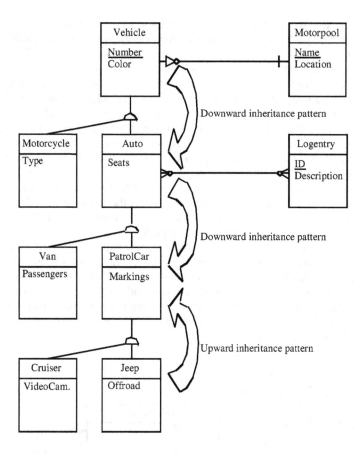

Fig. 3. The example ER diagram

Example Schema

The example schema consists of an inheritance hierarchy that represents a number of different categories of vehicle used by a fictitious police department, described using the information engineering enhanced entity relationship notation (reference here!). The highest level entity (*vehicle*) contains the attributes that are common to all of the different types of vehicles. The vehicle entity has two subtypes, *motorcycle* and *auto*. The motorcycle entity has an attribute which describes the type of motorcycle. All of the different types of auto have an attribute which lists the number of police officers that can be seated. *Van* has an attribute that describes the number of people other than police officers that can be seated in the vehicle. *PatrolCar* has an attribute that describes which type of marking the car has. The two final types of patrol car are the *cruiser*, which may have the capability to record video from the dashboard, and *jeep*, which may have extensive off-road capabilities. The vehicles do not, however, have any attribute that is unique for each vehicle. Each vehicle is identified by the number of the vehicle together with the name of the motor pool of which it is a part. There is thus an identifying relationship going from the *motorpool* entity to the *vehicle* entity. A motor pool has two attributes, the name of the motor pool and an attribute describing the location of the motor pool. Each of the autos may have a set of log entries corresponding to it, containing information about some event pertaining to that vehicle. Each log entry may be connected to several vehicles, and one vehicle may be connected to several log entries. Each log entry is identified by its unique identification number, and each log entry also contains a description of the log entry. In order to demonstrate different types of transformation patterns it has been decided that the vehicle and auto types will use a downward inheritance transformation, and the patrol car types will use upward inheritance.

The resulting schema (figure 4) consists of seven tables, and a number of columns. The tables are represented by rectangles containing the name of the table in the top partition of the rectangle. Primary key columns are underlined, and foreign keys are represented by arrows connecting the various tables.

The recursive inheritance hierarchies have successfully been transformed so that, for instance, the colour attribute is contained in several of the different tables. The transformation rules have also appropriately created multiple instances of the identifying relationships so that *patrolcar*, *van* and *motorcycle* each has the name attribute as part of its primary key. Instances of the many to many relationship have also been created, to both the *patrolcar* and *van* tables, while retaining the composite primary keys of those tables.

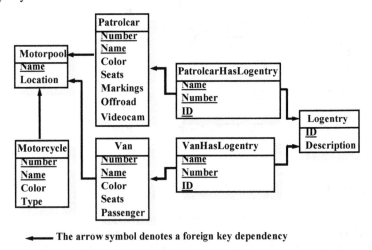

——— The arrow symbol denotes a foreign key dependency

Fig. 4. The resulting relational tables

6 Conclusions and Future Work

In this paper we have presented an extension of the standardised declarative language OCL which, together with an extended meta-model also presented, allows for fuller interchange of models between CASE tools. In particular, it caters for the exchange of transformation information in multi-model situations. In such situations, transformations express constraints between models based on the systematic transformation of one into the other. Such transformations are not only made transparent, but expressed in OCL in such a way as to allow co-operative design using heterogeneous tools. Hence, iterative design can be achieved with repeated exchange backwards and forwards between tools.

From the work presented it can be concluded that complex transformations that are present in modern CASE tools can be achieved using a modest extension of OCL. OCL is already used to express constraints in UML models, and can be used to express basic transformation constraints without extension. The extended language can be used to represent the actions used to transform a model, thus supporting iterative design in a context of model interchange. The transformations are represented in a UML-based meta-model, allowing for arbitrary extension of the transformation options available. Through the use of UML, transformations can easily be interchanged between different tools or tool sets using the standardised interchange language, XMI, which provides mechanisms to allow UML-compliant models to be interchanged using the XML language.

The example rules used in this paper have all been entered into the prototype repository and used for the transformations shown. However, there is not yet user support for the extension. Whilst every effort has been made to represent these rules accurately in OCL, this does present a margin for error. An early goal is to provide a user support for the implementation to save the many hours of work currently necessary to construct each test.

Even though the example meta-model presented in this paper contains many advanced concepts, many more advanced extended ER models exist. For example, the current meta-model does not support models with n-ary relationships and attributed relationships without modification. A further step towards verification of the approach would be to extend the model to support more of these features. Another step would be to examine whether the approach can be utilised for other types of models, such as process models, user interface models and object-oriented models.

The OCL extension was implemented only for a single environment, and to verify that this extension can easily be made to other implementations of OCL interpreters, porting of it could be performed to other environments and languages.

The XMI meta-data interchange standard provides a set of rules to facilitate the mapping of UML models to XML documents. The task of actually creating XML documents from the UML models created for this paper could be considered trivial, but should be undertaken.

In order to create an even more powerful interchange environment, work is underway to create a complete repository environment with support for the extended OCL language, allowing several different tools to share the same set of transformations and model constraints at the storage level.

References

1. Brinkkemper, S. „Integrating diagrams in CASE tools through modelling trans-parency", Information and Software Technology, Vol 35 No. 2, pp. 101-105, 1993

2. C. J. Date, 2000, *„An introduction to database systems – 7ᵗʰ ed. "*, Addison Wesley Longman Inc., 2000
3. Elmasri, R., Navathe S. B., *„Fundamentals of Database Systems – 3ʳᵈ ed. "*, Addison Wesley Longman Inc., 2000
4. Gray, J.P., Liu, A., Scott, L., *„Issues in software engineering tool construction"*, *Information and Software Technology Vol. 42 (2000), pp. 73-77, 2000*
5. Hainaut, J. L. *„Specification preservation in schema transformations – application to semantics and statistics"*, Data & Knowledge engineering 19,pp. 99-134, 1996
6. Hainaut, J. L., Englebert, V., Henrard, J., Hick J. M., Roland D., *„Database reverse engineering: From Requirements to CARE tools"*, Automated Software Engineering 3, 9-45 1996, Kluwer Academic Publishers, 1996
7. IBM, „The Object Constraint Language", http://www.software.ibm.com/ad/ocl
8. ISO/IEC JTC1/SC7/WG11, „Information Technology – CDIF Framework – Part 1: Overview", 2000
9. Kleppe, A., Warmer, J., „Extending OCL to include actions", 3ʳᵈ International Conference on the Unified Modelling Language, UML 2000
10. Mc Brien, P., Poulovassilis, A., „A Uniform Approach to Inter-Model Transformations", CaiSE'99, LNCS 1626, pp. 333-348, Springer-Verlag, 1999
11. Object Management Group, *„XML Metadata Interchange (XMI) "*, Document ad/98-10-06, http://www.omg.org/docs/ad98-10-05.pdf
12. Object Management Group, *„OMG Unified Modeling Language Specification"*, Version 1.3, June 1999, 1999
13. Object Management Group, „Formal MOF 1.3 Specification" formal/00-04-04, http://cgi.omg.org/cgi-bin/doc?formal/00-04-03.pdf

The Real Benefits of Object-Relational DB-Technology for Object-Oriented Software Development

Weiping Zhang and Norbert Ritter

University of Kaiserslautern, Germany
P.O. Box 3049, 67653 Kaiserslautern
{wpzhang, ritter}@informatik.uni-kl.de

Abstract. Object-oriented programming languages (OOPLs like C++, Java, etc.) have established themselves in the development of complex software systems for more than a decade. With the integration of object-oriented concepts, object-relational database management systems (ORDBMSs) aim at supporting new generation software systems better and more efficiently. Facing the situation that nowadays more and more software development teams use OOPLs 'on top of' (O)RDBMSs, i. e., access (object-)relational databases from applications developed in OOPLs, this paper reports on our investigations on assessing the contribution of object-relational database technology to object-oriented software development. First, a conceptual examination shows that there is still a considerable gap between the object-relational paradigm (as represented by the SQL:1999 standard) and the object-oriented paradigm. Second, empirical studies (performed by using our new benchmark approach) point at mechanisms, which are not part of SQL:1999 but would allow to reduce the mentioned gap. Thus, we encourage the integration of such mechanisms, e. g., support for navigation and complex objects (structured query results), into ORDBMSs in order to be really beneficial for new generation software systems.

1 Motivation

Object-oriented programming languages (OOPLs), such as C++, Java, SmallTalk, etc., have established themselves in the development of complex software system for more than a decade. Both, the structure of these systems as well as the structure of objects managed by these systems have become very complex. Object-oriented concepts offered by OOPLs are well suited for managing complex structured objects. However, there are additional requirements, such as persistence and transaction-protected manipulation, which can only be fulfilled efficiently by integrating a database management system (DBMS). Consequently, database technology becomes one of the core technologies of modern software systems. In times of the 'breakthrough' of object- oriented system development, two kinds of DBMSs were of practical relevance: relational DBMSs (RDBMSs) and object-oriented DBMSs (OODBMSs). Using OODBMSs has proved inefficient/inflexible for reasons we cannot go into in this paper. Consequently, OODBMS did not gain wide acceptance [5], and, therefore, will not be further considered in this paper.

B. Read (Ed.): BNCOD 2001, LNCS 2097, pp. 89-104, 2001.
© Springer-Verlag Berlin Heidelberg 2001

Using an RDBMS, on one hand, requires to overcome the well known impedance mismatch [5, 13], i. e., performing the non-trivial task of mapping complex object structures and navigational data processing (at the OOPL layer) to the set-oriented, descriptive query language (SQL92), which supports just a simple, flat data model. Despite this considerable mapping overhead, mature RDBMS technology (index structures, optimization, integrity control, etc.), on the other hand, contributes to keep the overall system performance acceptable. Several commercial systems [2, 12, 14, 15, 17, 19] mapping object-oriented structures onto the relational data model are currently available. Such systems are often referred to as *Persistent Object System built on Relation* (shortly: POS).

The object-relational wave [22] in database technology has decisively reduced the gap between RDBMSs and OOPLs. Although object-relational DBMSs (ORDBMSs) are able to (internally) manage object-oriented structures (see data definition part in [20, 21]), the required seamless coupling of OOPLs and ORDBMSs is not yet possible, because (as in SQL92) results of SQL:1999 queries (see data manipulation part in [20, 21]) are rather (sets of data) tuples than (desired sets of) objects. In summary, the gap between OOPLs and ORDBMSs can be traced back to a whole bunch of modeling and operational aspects, as we will detail in the following sections. Furthermore, the SQL:1999 standard and the commercially available ORDBMSs differ very much in their object-oriented features. Thus, it is by no means clear, how a given object-oriented design can be mapped to a given ORDBMS (most) efficiently, or which features should be offered by ORDBMSs in general in order to enable an efficient mapping of object-oriented structures, respectively.

Our long-term objective is to influence the further development of ORDBMSs towards a better support of object-oriented software development (minimal mapping overhead). Thus, we have proposed a new benchmark approach in [26] allowing to assess a given ORDBMS by taking into account both, its own performance as well as the required mapping overhead. Furthermore, [26] presents basic comparisons of purely relational and object-relational mappings. This paper goes beyond [26] in that the focus is to point up new directions of ORDBMS development, which, as is proved by corresponding empirical examinations, object-oriented software development can leverage from and, therefore, should be further pursued. Thus, this paper is structured as follows. A conceptual examination (section 2) outlines how the object-relational data model (standardized by SQL:1999) corresponds to OOPLs. Section 3 discusses corresponding mapping rules. Afterwards, section 4 gives a brief introduction into our benchmark approach needed to interpret the measurement results detailed in section 5. These results show that object-oriented software development can leverage from object-relational technology (in comparison to purely relational technology), but that further improvements can be reached by a better support of navigational access (retrieving objects by object identifiers) and appropriate mechanisms for retrieving complex structured sets of objects. We propose to admit corresponding mechanisms for navigation and complex object support to future versions of the SQL:1999 standard as concluded in section 6.

2   Conceptual Consideration

There is a multiplicity of object data models, for example ODMG [9], UML [24], COM [2], C++ and Java. All these models support the basic concepts of the OO paradigm, however, there are certain differences. Independently from the modelling language used in the OO software development (e. g., UML), SQL:1999 must be coupled with a concrete OOPL. In accordance to their overall relevance and conceptual vicinity, we concentrate on the object model of C++ and ODMG and compare it with the SQL:1999 standard [11, 20, 21].

2.1   Modelling Aspects

Object Orientation in OOPL. The concept *object* represents the foundation of the OO paradigm. An object is the encapsulation of data representing a semantic unit w. r. t. its structures/values and its behaviour. It conforms to a particular class [16]. In fact, a class implements an object type (*classification*) which is characterized by a name as well as a set of attributes and methods. Each attribute conforms to a certain data type and is either single-valued or set-valued (*collection types*). Furthermore, a data type can be scalar (e. g., integer, boolean, string, etc.) or complex. In the latter case corresponding values can be references (*association*) or objects of other classes (*aggregation*) so that complex structures can be modelled. A class may implement methods (*behaviour*) which can be invoked in order to change the object's state. Classes may be arranged within class hierarchies. A class inherits structures and behaviour from its superclasses (*inheritance*), but may refine these definitions (*specialization*). Due to space restrictions we do not give a more detailed description of the OO paradigm, but discuss how the OR data model conforms to OO concepts.

Object Orientation in SQL:1999. While the relational data model (SQL2) did not support semantic modelling concepts sufficiently, in SQL:1999 the fundamental exten-sion supporting object-orientation is the structured *user-defined data type* (UDT, [11]). UDTs, which can be considered as object types, can be treated in the same way as pre-defined data types (*built-in data types*). Consequently, similarly to the type system of OOPLs the type system of SQL:1999 is extensible. UDTs may be complex structured and, therefore, may not only contain predefined data types but also set-valued attributes (*collection types*) and even other UDTs (*aggregation*) or references (*associations*). Obviously, UDTs are comparable to the classes of the OO paradigm. However, according to the SQL:1999 standard a UDT must be associated with a table. The notion of *typed table*, also referred to as *object table*, allows to persistently manage instances of a certain UDT within a table. Each tuple of such a table represents an instance (*object*) of a particular UDT and is identified by a unique object identifier (*OID*) which can be system-generated or user-defined. Besides instantiable UDTs, SQL:1999 also supports non-instantiable UDTs, which conforms to the notion of abstract classes in OOPLs. In addition, UDTs may have methods (*behaviour*) which are either system-generated or implemented by users. They may participate in type hierarchies, in which more specialized types (*subtypes*) inherit structure and behaviour from more general types (*supertypes*), but may specialize corresponding definitions. Thus, SQL:1999 supports polymorphism and substitutability, however, multiple-inheritance is not supported. Due to the association of UDTs with tables (see above) SQL:1999 does not support encapsulation and, consequently, there is nothing like the degree of encapsulation known from OOPL (*public, protected, private*).

2.2   Operational Aspects

Beside the fundamental modelling aspects discussed so far, we also have to examine operational aspects in order to figure out the *conceptual distance* adequately. The following aspects are most relevant to our consideration:

Descriptive Queries vs. Navigational Processing. While OOPL processing is inherently navigational, SQL supports a set-oriented, descriptive query language. Both navigational and set-oriented query processing are important to modern software systems. Therefore, ORDBMSs should also directly facilitate navigational processing to fulfill this requirement of OO applications. *Direct support of navigational access* by the DBMS would mean that a database object referred to by its OID can be provided as instance of an OOPL class. However, to the best of our knowledge none of the currently available ORDBMSs directly supports this notion of navigation.

A naive coupling of OOPLs with descriptive SQL requires to issue one or several corresponding SQL queries (see Fig. 1) to the database for processing a dereferencing operation, e. g., *GetObject(Ref)*, and retrieving the requested object from the database server. Such a processing scheme will surely lead to

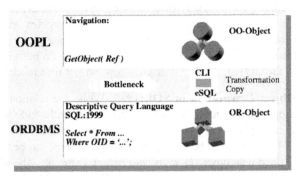

Fig. 1: Bottleneck between OOPL and ORDBMS

a bad runtime behavior of the entire system, since the costs of transforming a navigational operation to SQL queries, of evaluating these queries in the DBS, and of the client/server communication can be very high. Obviously, the lack of DB APIs in directly supporting navigational access impairs the system efficiency badly. Thus, either direct support for navigation[1] must be provided or efficient prefetching mechanisms exploiting set-oriented database access and, thereby, reducing the number

---

1   In section 5 we will see that one of the commercially available ORDBMS provides some basic means for a direct access to objects by OIDs. Measurement results show that this is at least a step into the right direction.

of database roundtrips must be applied in order to effectively couple OOPLs with ORDBMSs.

Structured Query Results. As already mentioned several times before, OOPLs support complex structured object types, especially by the possibility of nesting complex data types as well as using collection types and references. We have also mentioned previously that these facilities of modeling complex structured objects have been integrated into SQL by the SQL:1999 standard. Unfortunately, because of the traditional basic concepts of SQL, complex structures (actually supported both in OOPL and ORDBMS) get lost at the DBMS interface, since only (sets of) simply structured, flat data tuples can be retrieved. Therefore, if we want to couple an OOPL with an (O)RDBMS, it is necessary to separately retrieve simple fragments of complex objects by issuing several SQL queries, and then rebuild complex object structures at the programming language level (see Fig. 1). The mentioned problem even gets worse, if not individual complex objects, but complex structures (object graphs) containing numerous related objects interconnected by object references are to be selected as units. Obviously, the lack of direct support for complex structured objects at the DB API reveals a *bottleneck* between the two paradigms (see Fig. 1), and prevents new generation software systems from exploiting the potential power of ORDBMSs most effectively.

Object Behaviour. Of course, the operational aspects also encompass the object behaviour implemented in the database. Because of special implementation aspects these methods (UDFs) can almost exclusively be executed at the server side, or, if these UDFs or special client-invokable pendants are executed at the client side, it cannot be guaranteed that these pendants perform the original semantics. For example, there may be complex dependencies between UDFs and integrity constraints, e. g., referential integrity constraints and triggers, which are implemented by using SQL and are automatically ensured by the DBMS. Thus, it is almost impossible to support calling UDFs at the OOPL level in the same ('natural') way as usually object methods can be called. Therefore, we do not consider a mapping of object methods in this paper and restrict our considerations to navigational and set-oriented access.[2]

3   Mapping Rules

In the previous section, we outlined the conceptual distance between the OO paradigm and SQL:1999. Considering an individual ORDBMS, its OO features determine the overhead which has at least to be spent in order to bridge this distance. Nevertheless, in theory there is an entire spectrum of possibilities to design the required mapping layer. On one hand, it depends on how 'natural' coding in the OOPL has to remain,

---

2   At this point, we want to mention that there are some more aspects of ORDBMSs, which OO applications may benefit from, but which cannot be captured in this paper, e. g., facilities for integrating external data sources into database processing.

and, on the other hand, on how far the OO features are to be exploited. Regarding the first point ('natural' coding), we demand that the programmer must not be burdened by having to take data management aspects into account. Thus, programming must be independent of the database as well as the mapping layer design. Regarding the second point (degree of exploiting OO features), we want to outline the two extremes of the mentioned spectrum, i. e., pure relational mapping and full exploitation of the OO features offered by the considered ORDBMS[3].

Pure Relational Mapping. As mentioned before, there are several commercial POSs mapping OO structures to relational tables. Objects are represented by table rows. Since RDBMSs do not support set-valued attributes, user-defined data types, and object references, additional tables are required to store corresponding data and to connect them with the corresponding class tables via foreign keys [1]. Thus, several tables, may be required to map a given class. Principally, there are several ways of representing a class hierarchy in the relational model, comprehensively discussed in [8]. After studying pros and cons, we decided to use the horizontal partitioning approach (see [8] for details), since it provides good performance in most cases, and is also used in most commercial POSs [2, 12].

Object-Relational Mapping. Exploiting the OO features of ORDBMSs is commonly argued to be more promising [3], but the real benefits in comparison to the pure relational mapping are not very well studied yet. This paper will give some performance evaluations later on.

Before outlining general mapping rules exploiting OO features of ORDBMSs, we have to re-emphasize the following point. Our benchmark approach, which will be outlined in the subsequent section, assesses a certain ORDBMS by taking the required mapping overhead into account. In order to be fair, the mapping layer used throughout the measurements must be designed in an optimal way w. r. t. the capabilities of the ORDBMS considered. Therefore, the design of the mapping layer may differ with the ORDBMSs to be assessed. In the following, we just outline general mapping rules, which are based on the SQL:1999 concepts, in order to provide some basic understanding on how a mapping layer can be designed.

A C++ class maps to a UDT in SQL:1999. Non-instantiable UDTs correspond to abstract C++ classes. A UDT is associated with exactly one table (*typed table*) to initialize its instances. Each tuple in this table represents a persistent instance (*object*) of a particular class and is associated with a system-generated OID. Embedded objects (*aggregation*) entirely belong to their top-level object and, therefore, do not own an OID. Extents are mapped to the list constructor of C++ STL. Keys are managed at the mapping layer by applying the map constructor of C++ STL. A C++ class hierarchy maps to a hierarchy of structured UDTs. However, SQL:1999 only supports single-

---

3   Note, SQL:1999 and the commercially available ORDBMSs differ very much in their OO features, as we will see in the subsequent sections of this paper.

inheritance so that multi-inheritance has to be simulated at the mapping layer. SQL references are mapped to C++ pointers. Since SQL:1999 does not support diametric references, a relationship type is broken down into two separate primary-key/foreign-key connections and the mapping layer maintains the referential integrity. Except for mutator and observer methods, which are generated by the mapping layer w. r. t. the constraints defined in the user database schema, object behaviour is not yet considered in our performance investigation. Navigation is supported by offering the function *GetObject(Ref)* which, in the case that the DB API does not directly support OID-based object fetching, is implicitly transformed into an SQL query.

After having discussed (modelling and operational) discrepancies between ORDBMSs and OOPLs as well as the mapping rules needed to bridge the gap, we proceed with our performance evaluations.

4   Performance Evaluation

Our discussion in section 2 shows that there is only a small difference between the OO and OR paradigms w. r. t. modeling aspects, but a considerable distance w. r. t. the operational aspects and the application semantics. In order to further evaluate this distance as well as to quantify the overhead required for bridging this gap, we propose a configurable benchmark approach [18, 26].

Remind, we do not consider OODBMSs, but ORDBMSs, because we more and more have to face the situation that people are using OOPLs for software development and (O)RDBMSs for data management purposes so that there is a need for a more detailed examination of the efficiency of possible coupling mechanisms. Consequently, the OO7-Benchmark [5] representing an important standard for benchmarking OO systems, is not appropriate for our purposes. The performance of RDBMSs or ORDBMSs has traditionally been evaluated in isolation by applying a standard benchmark directly at the DBMS interface. Sample benchmarks [8] are the Wisconsin benchmark [3], the TPC benchmark [23] as well as the Bucky benchmark [6]. These benchmarks are very suitable for comparing different DBMSs with each other [8]. However, none of these benchmarks helps to assess the contributions of a DBMS to OO software development. Consequently, these other approaches do not take the typical application server architecture and the fact that the DBMS capabilities determine the overhead of the required application/mapping layer into account. Furthermore, data types as well as operations of the applications we consider may differ significantly (double-edged sword [6, 22]), so that a standard benchmark can not cover the entire spectrum. Therefore, we propose an open, configurable benchmark system allowing to examine the entire system (incl. mapping layer) w. r. t. to its typical applications. Such a system will also help us to get results transcending those reported on in this paper (see succeeding sections), e. g., more detailed examinations of navigational support. In the following, we outline our first prototype. Further details can be found in [1, 26].

4.1 Benchmark System

An open, configurable benchmark system is not necessarily difficult to be applied, as our approach proves. Indeed, our current prototype offers 3 predefined configurations, which w. r. t. database size are *small, medium* and *large* in order to be sufficiently scalable. Both, structures (data type and type hierarchies) as well as complexity of data in the 3 standard configurations are determined in cooperation with one of the leading software vendors for business standard software and, thus, represent a wide spectrum of typical application domains. In addition, our benchmark

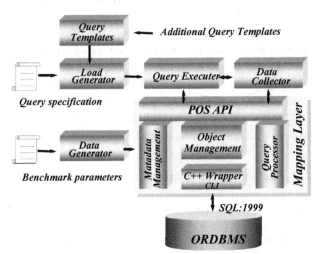

Fig. 2: Architecture of the benchmark system

system can be simply configured according to the particular properties of a concrete application. Fig. 2 gives an overview of the architecture of our prototype. Among other possibilities, users can directly control the generation process of the benchmark database, e. g., specify the database size, the complexity of the class hierarchy and the complexity of the individual objects, in order to take care that the special requirements of the application in mind are taken into account. After having generated the benchmark database the user may select from a given set of query templates (see section 4.2 for further details) and indicate how many times each template is to be instantiated. New query templates can be easily added, if the existing templates do not reflect application characteristics sufficiently. Based on these user selections/specifications the load generator creates a set of queries which is passed to the query executor, which, in turn, serves as a kind of driver for measurements. Users can also specify which kinds of measurement data are to be collected by the system, i. e., amount of time spent at the DB or the mapping layer for query transformation, or the time spent for SQL query evaluation, data loading, and/or result set construction. Corresponding values are collected by the data collector during execution of the query set and afterwards stored in the DBS for further evaluations.

As explained in more detail in [1, 26], the special challenges of this benchmark approach are, on one hand, to properly take into account the requirements of OO system development, and, on the other hand, to guarantee an optimal mapping w.r.t. the particular capabilities of an individual ORDBMS.

4.2   Benchmark and Measurements

In order to get a complete performance evaluation, we concentrate on answering the following questions:

1. Which performance gains offer ORDBMSs in comparison to RDBMSs regarding their usage in OO software development?
2. Which additional overhead has to be spent at the mapping layer in order to bridge the gap between the OO and OR paradigms and how does it behave facing different query types?
3. To which extent is the system performance influenced by the capabilities of the (O)RDBMS API?

In order to be able to answer the first two questions, we have selected a set of typical benchmarking queries according to a long-term study of a leading software company. These queries represent a wide spectrum of typical operations in the target applications of ORDBMSs. We have compared a purely relational mapping with an object-relational one (by means of exploiting its OO modelling power) by using a currently available commercial ORDBMS. This way we 'measured' how OO software development can leverage from the OO extensions offered by ORDBMSs (e. g., structured UDTs, references, etc.). The operations considered for that purpose are implemented as query templates and grouped in following categories:

Navigation operations: Navigation operations, such as *GetObject(OID)*, are not directly supported by almost all currently available ORDBMSs. Considering such operations helps us to assess the performance of ORDBMSs in supporting navigational processing. We hope that corresponding results 'help' ORDBMS vendors to make ORDBMSs as efficient as OODBMSs are in this concern.

Queries with simple predicates on scalar attributes: Queries of this category have simple predicates just containing a single comparison operation on a scalar attribute. This group mainly serves to provide a performance baseline that can be helpful when interpreting results of more complex queries.

Queries with predicates on UDTs: This group contains queries with simple predicates (a single comparison operation) on attributes of structured, non-atomic data types. Thus, it mainly serves for assessing the efficiency of mapping UDTs to (O)RDBMSs.

Queries with predicates on set-valued attributes: This group contains queries with simple predicates (a single IN operation) on nested sets. ORDBMSs directly support set-valued data types. In the relational mapping, several tables (according to the degree of nesting), which are connected by primary/foreign-keys, are necessary.

Queries with path predicates: This group contains queries evaluating simple predicates after path traversals. These queries allow to evaluate the efficiency of processing dereferencing operations (path traversals) in ORDBMSs.

Queries with complex predicates: Queries of this group contain complex predicates challenging both query transformation as well as query optimization.

Queries on the class hierarchy: While all other queries exclusively deliver direct instances of a single queried class, queries of this group deliver transitive instances as well. Predicates conform to those of the second category. This group of queries allows to evaluate the efficiency of the ORDBMS in handling class hierarchies (inheritance). The comparison with the relational mapping has been expected to demonstrate the advantages of ORDBMSs.

The third question posed at the beginning of this section deals with the capabilities of the DB interface especially w. r. t. support for complex structured objects and navigational access. In order to examine these aspects, we performed measurements on two different (commercially successful) ORDBMSs. One of these systems offers the more traditional interface, whereas the second one provides some basic means of supporting complex structures objects.

We performed our measurements[4] on a benchmarking database with 100 classes and 250000 instances (configuration *medium*). In order to use a representatively structured class hierarchy, we studied typical application scenarios of a renowned vendor of business standard software and parameterized our population algorithm accordingly. We measured the database time (DB time) and the total system time (TS time). The DB time of SQL queries is the time elapsed between delegating the queries to the DBMS and receiving back the results (open cursors, traverse iterators). It includes the time for client/server communication, the time for evaluating the queries within the DBS and the time for loading the complete result sets. This has to be taken into account, when analysing the measurement results. The TS time is defined as the total elapsed time from issuing a query operation at the OOPL level until having received the complete result set. It contains the time spent within the mapping layer as well as the DB time.

We think that these 3 questions have to be answered before we can think about, how OR technology can be improved in order to support OOPLs better and more efficiently. In the following section, we report on our measurement results.

5   Measurement Results and Observations

5.1   ORDBMS vs. RDBMS

In the first test series, we have compared a purely relational mapping with an OR mapping by using one of the leading currently available commercial ORDBMSs. This investigation aims at quantifying the benefits of OO extensions offered by ORDBMSs in more detail.

Fig. 3 illustrates the measurement results. Due to space restrictions, it is not possible to analyze all results in detail. It can be observed that the OR mapping outperforms the purely relational mapping in all query categories.

---

4   All experiments in this paper use commodity software. The hardware and the software configurations are left unspecified, to avoid the usual legal and competitive problems with publishing performance numbers for commercial products. All performance measurements are averages of multiple trials, with more trials for higher variance measurements. For each DBMS tested, we put much effort in optimization (e.g., indexes) and mapping layer design in order to achieve the best performance possible.

Although the OR mapping shows only tiny advantages in retrieving small result sets, it provides performance gains of up to 40% in retrieving large result sets, or processing queries on class hierarchies. The reasons are twofold. First, the OO features provided by the ORDBMS contribute to keep the complexity of the mapping layer low (better query evaluation strategy, less overhead for synthesizing the result set) and to reduce client/server communication (less queries). Second, the implementation of the ORDBMS (we used) enables performance improvements, (even) if using OO extensions.

In the purely relational case, it is not possible to map a (complex) class to exactly one table. Mapping set-valued attributes, aggregations and (m:n)-relationships

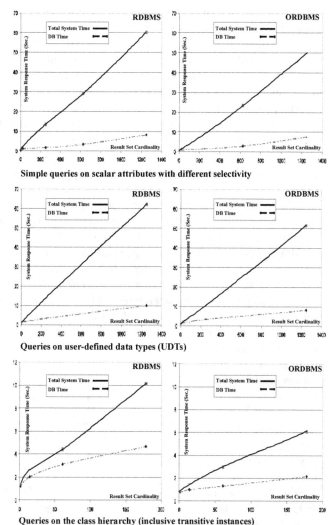

Simple queries on scalar attributes with different selectivity

Queries on user-defined data types (UDTs)

Queries on the class hierarchy (inclusive transitive instances)

Fig. 3: Measurement Results I

properly demands several tables interconnected by primary/foreign keys. This, in turn, requires to pose several SQL queries in order to perform one query at the OOPL level implying a higher DB time and higher communication costs. Compared to a semantically equivalent OR mapping, the more expensive query transformation and the necessary reconstruction of object structures in the pure relational mapping reduce the system efficiency additionally. This effect can even be reinforced if further OR features such as function-based indexing or index structures over class hierarchies, which can be tailored to OO applications, are used in order to further improve the OR mapping.

Since in our measurements both client and server ran on the same machine, the costs of communication between the database server and the mapping layer are relatively small. It is to be expected that a distributed client/server architecture will considerably enlarge the difference between these measurement results. Furthermore, the more complex the data structures, the more additional overhead is to be expected in the relational mapping. As reported in former measurements [6, 25], some OR systems performed in some cases even worse than semantically equivalent relational systems. Due to our examinations, we think that this statement has to be revised and ORDBMSs, in the meantime, have obviously become more and more mature.

5.2   Performance Characteristics of the Mapping Layer

In order to characterize the performance of the mapping layer adequately, we have investigated simple queries with different selectivity. The results are presented in Fig. 4. As already mentioned in section 2, the DB APIs of almost all currently available ORDBMSs do not support navigational access directly. Hence, a navigational operation, such as *GetObject(Ref)*, must be transformed to a database query (SQL:1999), such as *"Select * From... Where OID = Ref"*, by the mapping layer. Such a query strategy, especially when intensively dealing with navigational operations as usually required by most OO applications, obviously leads to high processing overhead spent in the database system as well as very high communication costs (over 70% of the entire system time, Fig. 4, left-hand side). The (probably not very astonishing) observation is that the traditional query strategy is not adequate for supporting navigational access.

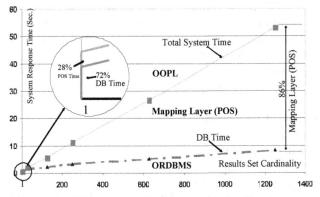

Fig. 4: Measurement Results II

As we can see at the right-hand side of Fig. 4, the DB time of set-oriented queries shows only a slight ascent with increasing result sets, while the additional mapping overhead increases rapidly. When retrieving 1250 objects, the time spent at the mapping layer even exceeds 86% of the total system time (see Fig. 4, right-hand side). This observation can be explained as follows. In the early days of ORDBMSs, these systems comparable to RDBMSs were not very successful in supporting navigational access, but excellent in processing set-oriented access (as they are still today). Unfortunately, OO applications can hardly benefit from this advantage, because the ORDBMS API is 'inherited' from traditional RDBMSs and, therefore, still only supports simple, flat data. In lack of an *extensible* DB API which may generically support complex data types defined by the user, complex objects in an ORDBMS have to be first 'disassembled' into scalar values, and afterwards reconstructed (at the mapping layer) to objects of a certain class in the particular OOPL. This kind of overhead gets dramatic with increasing result set cardinality and impairs the entire system efficiency significantly.

Regarding these measurement results, we can draw the following conclusions. In order to be able to support navigational access better, the ORDB API should directly support navigational operations like *GetObject(Ref)*, so that the costs of transforming navigational operations to SQL queries and for evaluating these queries can be avoided. Furthermore, it should also support the notion of complex objects directly and offer the possibility of retrieving complex objects as units. According to our examinations, such improvements can increase the entire system efficiency by up to 400%.

5.3   Support for Complex Objects

As already mentioned before, the lack of direct support for complex objects and navigational access at the DB API level extremely impairs the overall system efficiency. Fortunately, a leading ORDBMS vendor already offers an extended call level interface, which, as we can see later in this section, directly supports navigational access as well as retrieval of complex objects as units, and, in addition, even retrieval of complex object graphs as units.

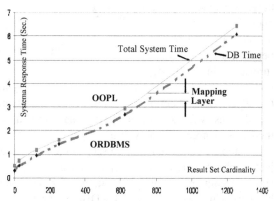

Fig. 5: Measurement Results III

Navigation is enabled by the possibility of autonomously retrieving complex structured objects (by OID) as instances of C structures. This simplifies the mapping to OOPLs, such as C++, considerably and, therefore, is undoubtedly the first step into the right direction, although this mechanism does not yet support the actually wanted seamless coupling (transparent transformation from a database object to an instance of an OOPL class). The mentioned support for complex objects at the level of the DB API allows to directly retrieve a complex object's data from the database into the main memory by specifying its OID or a predicate. Therefore, the expensive query processing strategy described in section 5.2 can be avoided. Remind that the measurements described in section 5.2 have been performed on an ORDBMS that does not possess a DB API as the one described in this section. To show the importance of and the corresponding demand on a suitable support for complex objects at the DB API level, we repeated the measurements described in section 5.2 on the ORDBMS referred to in this section and providing the mentioned complex object support at its API. Fig. 5 illustrates the measurement results. Obviously, the additional overhead spent at the mapping layer is now independent from the cardinality of the query result sets. Thus, the direct support of complex objects at the DB API results in a clear performance gain (up to 400%).

The direct support for navigational access at the DB API level mentioned in this section, allowing to directly access objects by calling a function like *GetObject(Ref)*, avoids expensive processes (query transformation, data types conversion and object reconstruction). This obviously contributes to improve performance significantly. Fig. 6a shows a comparison between a query strategy (transfor-ming a naviga-

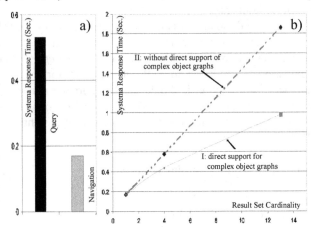

Fig. 6: Measurement Results IV

tional ope-ration to an SQL query) and a navigational strategy (directly calling a *GetObject(OID)* function at the DB API). The advantages of the navigational strategy are obvious. With a direct support of navigational access the entire system efficiency increases by approximately 200%.

OO applications often want a set of objects interconnected by object references (object graph) to be retrieved completely within just a single database interaction. Fig. 6b shows a comparison of two strategies for retrieving complex object graphs. In this measurement, we used the ORDBMS directly supporting navigation as well as retrieval of complex object graphs. It can be seen clearly that strategy I exploiting the ability of retrieving object graphs exhibits a performance gain of about 100% already at a result set cardinality of 13 objects.

The design of a new DB API, which directly supports complex structured objects, is by no means an easy job and requires generic design methods, because user-defined data types can be arbitrarily structured, e. g., contain other complex data types, such as UDTs, references and set-valued attributes. Furthermore, a DB API has always to be multi-lingual requiring to support all common programming languages simultaneously and, therefore, making it very difficult to offer the best of both worlds (DBMSs and OOPLs) without any compromises.

6   Conclusions and Outlook

In this paper, we have emphasized the importance of assessing ORDBMSs w. r. t. their capabilities of supporting OOPLs. We have first qualitatively considered ORDBMSs and OOPLs regarding modelling and operational aspects relevant for object-oriented software development. As the object-relational (SQL:1999) and the object-oriented data model are essentially coming together, the operational distance between these two paradigms is still considerable so that an additional mapping layer is necessary to overcome this gap. Regrettably, such an additional layer impairs the performance of the overall system considerably. Additionally, we performed quantitative examinations (measurements) in order to assess ORDBMSs in their capabilities of supporting OOPLs. Indirectly, these measurements are supposed to contribute to promoting the optimal utilization of currently available ORDBMSs in object-oriented system development and to guide the future development of ORDBMSs in a way that the support for OOPLs is improved.

Regarding our performance examinations, we have motivated the necessity of an open, configurable benchmark approach, because not only the performance of ORDBMSs themselves but also the additional overhead, which is necessary for bridging the conceptual and operational distance between ORDBMSs and OOPLs, have to be taken into account and, therefore, properly characterized. It has been clearly illustrated by our performance measurements that object-relational database technology gets more and more mature, not only conceptually (data model, query processing), but also w. r. t. performance. The model facilities contribute to keep the mapping layer 'thin' in contrast to RDBMSs. This, on one hand, reduces the implementation efforts, and, on the other hand, increases the entire system efficiency. Despite the available object-oriented extensions, which entail an unambiguous gain in comparison to RDBMSs, the potential benefit of object-relational database technology in our opinion is not yet exhausted, since the traditional DB API is so far not capable of successfully supporting object-oriented principles. The DB API of almost all ORDBMSs still can not support navigational operations and complex object structures directly so that new generation software systems can not take advantage of object-relational database technology in an optimal way. It can be called the 'bottleneck' between the object- relational and object-oriented paradigms. Our examinations have shown clearly that a new DB API directly supporting navigational operations and complex objects is necessary. Obviously, it is not easy to equip ORDBMSs with such a new interface. For example, such an interface must be multi-lingual. For answering the question, how user-defined data types can be effectively represented at the OOPL level, further research efforts are required. Altogether, the problem of a seamless and effective mapping of SQL:1999 to OOPLs, such as C++ and Java, has to be worked on further. Our future work will mainly be looking for possible solutions. Furthermore, we plan intensive studies of ORDBMS capabilities for supporting navigational access, because ORDBMSs are still behind OODBMSs in this concern. Generally, after having characterized the performance aspects in more details, our long-term objective is to develop applicable concepts contributing to increase the performance of ORDBMSs.

References

1.   Bernhard, R., Flehmig, M., Mahdoui, A., Ritter, N., Steiert, H.-P., Zhang, W.P.: *"Building a Persistent Class System on top of (O)RDBMS - Concepts and Evaluations"*, Internal Report, University of Kaiserslautern, 1999

2. Bernstein, P.A., Harry, B., Sanders, P.J., Shutt, D., Zander, J.: *"The Microsoft Repository"*, Proc. VLDB Conf., 1997, pp. 3-12
3. Bernstein, P.A., Pal, S., Shutt, D.: *"Context-Based Prefetch for Implementing Objects on Relations"*, Proc. VLDB Conf., 1999, pp. 327-338
4. Bitton, D., DeWitt, D.J., Turbyfill, C.: *"Benchmarking Database Systems: A Systematic Approach"*, Proc. VLDB Conf., 1983, pp. 8-19
5. Carey, M.J., DeWitt, D.J.: *"Of Objects and Databases: A Decade of Turmoil"*, Proc. VLDB Conf., 1996, pp. 3-14
6. Carey, M.J., DeWitt, D.J., Naughton, J.F., Asgarian, M., Brown, P., Gehrke, J.E., Shah, D.N.: *"The Bucky Object-Relational Benchmark"*, Proc. VLDB Conf., 1996, pp. 135-146
7. Carey, M.J., DeWitt, D.J., Kant, C., Naughton, J.F.: *"A Status Report on the OO7 OODBMS Benchmarking Effort"*, Proc. ACM OOPSLA, 1994, pp. 414-426
8. Carey, M.J., Doole, D., Mattos, N.M.: *"O-O, What Have They Done to DB2?"*, Proc. 1999 25th. VLDB Conf., pp. 542-553
9. Cattell, R.G.G., Barry, D., Bartels, D., et al: *"The Object Database Standard:ODMG 2.0"*, Morgan-Kaufman Publishers, San Mateo, 1997
10. Gray, J.: *"The Benchmark Handbook for Database and Transaction Processing Systems"*, Morgen Kaufmann Publishers, San Mateo, CA, USA, 2nd Ed., 1993
11. Gulutzan, P., Pelzer, T.: *"SQL-99 Complete, Really"*, R&D Publications, 1999
12. Keller, A., Jensen, R., Agrawal, S.: *"Persistence Software: Bridging Object- Oriented Programming and Relational Database"*, Proc. ACM SIGMOD Conf., 1993, pp. 523-528
13. Mahnke, W., Steiert, H.-P.: *"The Application Protential of ORDBMS in the Design Environments"*, Proc. CAD 2000, Berlin, pp. 219-239 (in German)
14. Ontos Business Data Server, *http://www.ontos.com*
15. Poet Object Server, POET Software, POET SQL Object Factory, *http://poet.com/*
16. Rao, B.R.: *"Object-oriented Databases: Technology, Applications, and Products"*, McGraw-Hill, New York, 1994
17. RogueWave Software, DBTools.h++, *http://www.roguewav3e.com/products/dbtools/*
18. Schreiber, H.: *"JUSTITIA: A Generic Benchmark for the OODBMS Selection"*, Int. Conference on Data and Knowledge Systems in Manufacturing and Engineering, Tokyio, 1994
19. Scheller, T.: *"Functionality of the Class System in System R/3"*, Function Description, Version 0.9, SAP, Dec. 1997
20. SQL99: ANSI/ISO/IEC 9075-1-1999 Database Launguages SQL Part 1 Framework
21. SQL99: ANSI/ISO/IEC 9075-2-1999 Database Languages SQL Part 2 Foundation
22. Stonebraker, M., Brown, P., Moor, D.: *"Object-relational DBMSs - The Next Wave"*, Morgan Kaufmann, 2nd Ed., 1998
23. TPC: Transaction Processing Performance Council, Standard Specification 1.0, May 1995, *http://www.tpc.org*
24. UML, Rational Software Corp. Unified Modeling Language, *http://www.rational.com/*
25. Zhang, W.P.: *"Evaluation of the First Generation ORDBMSs by Using Bucky Benchmark"* Internal Report, University of Kaiserslautern, 1998
26. Zhang, W.P., Ritter, N.: *"Measuring the Contribution of (O)RDBMS to Object- Oriented Software Development"*, Proc. IDEAS 2000, pp. 243-249

Object-Oriented Versioning in a Concurrent Engineering Design Environment

A. Al-Khudair[1], W.A. Gray[1], and J.C. Miles[2]

[1] Department of Computer Science, Cardiff University , UK
{A.I.Khudair | W.A.Gray}@cs.cf.ac.uk

[2] Cardiff School of Engineering, Cardiff University, UK
MilesJC@cf.ac.uk

Abstract. This paper is concerned with tracking the evolution of design component versions and their related design configuration versions in a concurrent engineering design environment. An important aspect is the capability to determine if a dynamically bound configuration version is consistent with its design goals and its assembly has no design conflicts between its components' versions. We present a generalized object-oriented model which captures the evolution of design configurations and their components by supporting versioning at all levels. The dynamics and consistency of multiversion configurations are also addressed.

1 Introduction

A complex design artefact may be configured from a large number of components each of which may evolve over time. A configuration is a set of component designs which combine to form a version of the design artefact. A configuration itself may evolve over time. This requires that a record of the multiple versions of a configuration needs to be maintained to support the Concurrent Engineering (CE) design activities which are performed *concurrently* rather than *sequentially* in an iterative and tentative fashion. Consequently, configuration versioning enables the designers to work concurrently on different versions of a configuration as well as to *rollback* to a previous stable state of the design configuration whenever changes introduce problems. The binding of a configuration version to its versioned component can be *static* to a specific version of the component or *dynamic* to a default setting that can be resolved at run time. Dynamic evolution of a configuration is the process of allowing a configuration to evolve while at the same time its components are dynamically bound. Furthermore, the consistency in a dynamically bound configuration needs to be maintained. A consistent configuration is a configuration which is composed from a set of components that satisfies design constraints and can be grouped together without causing design conflicts. Hence, a multiversion configuration has to preserve the consistency in each version of the configuration.

B. Read (Ed.): BNCOD 2001, LNCS 2097, pp. 105-125, 2001.

Keeping track of multiple versions of a complex configuration composed of a large number of complex components which are also versioned due to their own evolution, is a challenging task. This complexity increases in a multidisciplinary CE design environment where a large number of participants may be involved in the design process and the design is continually changing due to their interactions.

In a *CE* design, the design activities are normally performed using design tools (i.e. CAD systems). Although these tools can manipulate the geometrical aspects of the design artefact, they lack the support of a powerful management system that can integrate and keep track of all the phases and states of a large and complex design artefact [15,16]. Therefore, a management tool is essential to keep track of the evolution and change in the design artefact and its components.

The basic requirements of a CE design environment supporting configuration version management are the representation of the complex hierarchy of its design objects and their relationships, aggregation of primitive design objects to form a higher level design object,   design concurrency support, version management, configuration management, and design consistency management. In this paper, we are concentrating on these requirements as they form the basis for a design environment supporting design configuration versioning. Conventional database systems, with their emphasis on record-based applications, are unable to satisfy these requirements of engineering applications. For this reason, advanced database systems that can handle such requirements are needed. Object-Oriented Database (OODB) systems are considered capable of satisfying most of these requirements since they possess rich modelling and manipulation features such as Generalization, Classification, Inheritance and Aggregation [1,8,9,10,12,14]. A very important semantic extension in OODB systems is version management. The notion of versions is a widely accepted mechanism for recording design evolution which enables design reuse as well as supporting concurrency [1,3,9,10,11,13,14,15,16,23]. Hence, CAD systems are used to manipulate the geometrical aspects of the design object whereas the database system is used as a *kernel* to keep track of the overall hierarchy of design objects (or structures), design evolution (or versioning), and the relationships between design objects (in this paper, the terms *object* and *design object* will be used interchangeably).

An OODB schema is used to define the design classes which are connected by the superclass/subclass (or is-a) relationships that is called *class hierarchy*. A configuration class is connected to its components' classes by Part-Of relationships that is called a *composite class hierarchy*. We will show an example of a Bridge configuration where the composition of the Bridge components along with constraints on them are represented using a composite class hierarchy. The OODB is subdivided into design workspaces which are used to store and manipulate designs and their versions at different levels of authorization and maturity [7]. A workspace can be *private* or *shared.* A private workspace is owned by a specific designer who is utilizing it for the development of a design. Only the owner of a private workspace can read, modify, or delete its contents. A shared workspace, on the other hand, is common among different designers who can read or deposit their designs in it. However, there should be a verification mechanism which allows only mature (or complete) designs to be deposited in a shared workspace [16]. A shared workspace represents an interaction area between the designers of a specific project and only accessible by the designers in that project and access is granted by a project manager. The *checkin* and *checkout* operations are used to deposit and retrieve design objects to/from workspaces. Some commercial OODB products support private and shared workspaces such as ITASCA and VERSANT [3].

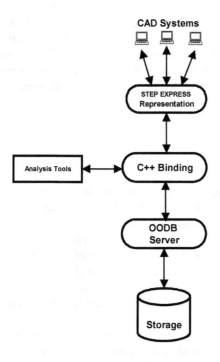

Fig. 1. The architecture of CE design support environment

Fig. 1 shows the architecture of the support environment for the versioning of a CE design. In the Figure, the design artefact is translated from the CAD system into a STEP EXPRESS language representation. EXPRESS is a modelling language of the STEP (Standard for the Exchange of Product data) which is used to model engineering data. This setup is used to establish a uniform interface to heterogeneous CAD systems which may be used in the CE design process. The design constraints are defined in EXPRESS language using a set of rules and other primitive constraints such as value uniqueness of an attribute. These constraints along with the design artefact representation are translated into a C++ binding which maps them into the corresponding design classes in the OODB where the constraints can be triggered by the database events [2]. Hence, the design constraints are defined in the STEP EXPRESS layer and not in the database. Analysis tools, such as a structural analysis tool, are also interfaced with the OODB system using C++ binding and automatically update the calculations defining the properties of the design object if its geometrical properties are changed (e.g. load bearing of a beam). In [7] we showed how a STEP representation of a CAD object along with its analysis data are stored and manipulated in an OODB system. We have shown also how versions of a simple design object and their simple (or non-versioned) design configurations are stored and manipulated in an OODB system which is subdivided into private and shared workspaces. However, dynamic configuration versioning is not supported in that limited model.

In this paper, we discuss design evolution, dynamics, and consistency in a CE design environment supporting configuration versioning. The remainder of this paper is organized as follows. In Section 2, the related work is reviewed. In Section 3, version management in OODBs is discussed. In Section 4, an object-oriented model for configuration versioning is presented. In Section 5, the dynamic and consistency issues in configuration versioning are addressed. In Section 6, concluding remarks and future work are given.

2   Related Work

Version management has received considerable attention in the literature with the aim to maintain a record of the evolution of an object. The deriving motivation for this interest is to match the requirements of engineering and software environments that have an iterative and tentative nature [1,4,9,12,14,16]. The version management of individual objects is covered adequately in the literature [9,18,16,19]. However, less attention has been directed to the versioning aspects of an object that has other objects as components (i.e., a configuration or composite object version management [9,16]). In this section, we review the work which addresses configuration version management within an engineering design context.

Kim et al. [22] presented a model of versions of a composite object or configurations. A set of rules was introduced to capture the semantics of versions of a configuration. Although the model shows the derivation of versions, it does not address explicitly how the version set is organized (i.e. linear, tree, graph). A limited discussion of the dynamic aspects in configuration versions is presented, but the consistency of the versions of a configuration is not discussed. Ahmed and Navathe [11] proposed an approach for the management of configuration versions which are classified into intrinsic interface and non-intrinsic internal assembly. Although disconnected version graphs are used to organize the version set of simple objects, the organization of the version set of a configuration is not clearly addressed. The dynamics in configuration versions is not clearly addressed and the consistency of versions of a configuration is also not discussed. Cellary and Jomier [18] proposed an approach to maintain the consistency of versions by allowing multiple versions of the whole database to co-exist. That is, each logical database version maintains a record of object versions that "go together" (i.e. are consistent with each other). To minimize redundancy, database versions may share similar versions of an object. *Version stamps* (a unique version identifier) are used to link each object and configuration version with the database versions it belongs to. Although a tree structure is used to organize the set of database versions, the model shows flat object versions and no clear relationship between these versions is identified. The maintenance of these multiple database versions will cause substantial overheads particularly in a change-intensive design environment. The dynamic aspects in configuration versions are not thoroughly discussed.

Some proposals such as [10,20] discuss version control for complex artefacts in engineering design but a concrete underlying data model is not clearly specified, and identifying the capabilities of a database system in the design environment is not addressed. Other proposals, such as [12], have a limited discussion on configuration versioning aspects or do not address configurations, concentrating only on simple object versioning [23]. Thus, most of the proposals reviewed concentrate on the basic versioning aspects of a simple object which is not composed of components and then extend the basic versioning to include versions of a configuration. However, this is not adequate in an engineering environment where the versioning system is expected to support the overall engineering design process. Hence, the emphasis on the whole artefact's (or configuration) versions is essential.

Our literature review supports our contention that support for design configuration version management is embryonic and pays little attention to the problem of consistent configuration management. Furthermore, the mechanisms for maintaining the dynamics in configurations are not thoroughly discussed and the concurrency support between designers using configuration versions is not addressed. In the following sections, we will show how these aspects can be addressed.

3   Version Management in Object-Oriented Databases

3.1 Simple Object Versioning

A simple object is an object which does not contain other objects as components. *Simple object versioning* is the creation of a new version of a simple object by amending it in some way. That is, the object state before the change is retained as well as the new state, allowing multiple versions of object states to co-exist. In general, the mechanism for object updates in a system with version management support can be shown as follows:

$$V_i \xrightarrow{\quad} V_{i+1} \xrightarrow{\quad} V_{i+2}$$

Where V_i is an object version, i is a version number, and α and β are changes to the object. Note that α and β are user actions in the CAD interface on a version of object data (or object state) which lead to the creation of a successor version of this object. The process of version derivation can be *linear* or *non-linear*. The linear version management scheme is a very simple scheme as it only allows change to the current version of the design object. This scheme keeps a history of changes to a version in a sequential order as shown in Fig. 2. In the Figure, V_0 is the original version which is created at time instance t_0. The first change occurs at time instance t_1 and version V_1 is created as a result of the change. The most recent change has occurred to the version at time instance t_n, when the current version V_n is created to store the change to the design object. The set $\{ t_0, t_1, t_2, \ldots, t_n \}$ of time instances is a temporally ordered set, i.e., $t_i \leq t_{i+1}$ for all $0 \leq i < n$.

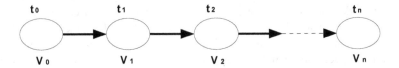

Fig. 2. Linear version management scheme

The non-linear version management scheme, on the other hand, is more general and flexible than the linear version management scheme. This scheme allows a designer to change any previous version to create a new version. A tree data structure is suitable for this scheme as from any node of the tree a new node can be generated. A tree data structure is also used in [16] to manage versions of an object. In our model, this structure is extended to a graph to allow version merging (i.e. more than one parent of a version). Hence, a versioned object consists of a hierarchy of versions called a *version-derivation graph* (VDG) connected by the Derived-From (or Parent/Child) relationships. If a new version of an object introduces cycles in the VDG, then the version is rejected as the new version already exists. New versions of an object need not be generated in a strict linear time sequence. It is possible that two or more versions (*alternative versions*) of an object are derived from the same parent version. This can be used to experiment with different designs of an artefact. It is also possible to have an object version derived from two or more existing versions of an object (*version merging*). This can be used to produce a version of a design artefact that integrates different features from its parent versions, possibly developed by different designers. In our system, this is achieved by the designer combining the required features from the versions in the CAD interface workspace. Fig. 3 shows an example of alternative versions v2 and v3 which are derived from version v1, whereas version v4 is derived from merging versions v2 and v3. Every version of an object has its own *unique* identifier that distinguishes it from other versions of this object. Since object versioning allows multiple states of an object to co-exist, a mechanism is needed to represent an abstract object which is the versioned object. This is facilitated by the notion of a *generic object*. The generic object maintains information about the versioned object which includes version counter, default version, and the VDG. Each version in the object versions set is connected to the generic object by the Version-Of relationship.

Object versioning is supported in many commercial OODB systems such as GemStone, ITASCA, O_2, Objectivity, and VERSANT [3].

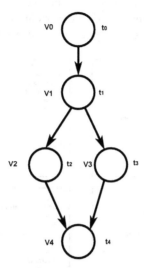

Fig. 3. A graph of version derivation

3.2 Configuration Versioning

A complex design artefact is normally decomposed into subcomponents to facilitate
the design activities. Each subcomponent may, in turn, be subject to further
decomposition recursively. To map this requirement into the object-oriented model, a
composite object may be used. A composite object is an object which is composed of
a set of other objects rather than only primitive domains. A PART-OF relationship is
defined to link a composite object with its component objects. A *configuration* is a set
of component designs which combine to form a version of the design artefact. Hence,
a configuration may be considered as reflecting a particular state of a composite object and , therefore, can be treated as a versioned object. A configuration is normally
represented as a *Composite Class Hierarchy* (CCH) whose nodes, other than the root,
are the classes of components of the configuration and whose arcs represent the Part-
Of relationships [5,9]. Fig. 4 and Fig. 5 show class definitions and a CCH of a simple Bridge configuration. The Bridge is composed of three components: Foundations, Substructure, and Deck. Each component is composed from other components
recursively. This is shown by dotted arrows. The constraints imposed on the Bridge
and its components are shown in each class definition. For example, the maximum
load on the Bridge is 42 tonnes. These constraints are defined in the STEP EXPRESS
layer, as mentioned in Section 1, and mapped into the corresponding classes of the
configuration in the OODB using C++ binding. If a design artefact introduces a constraint violation when grouping its components to form a configuration, the designer
is warned about the conflict and the configuration components are identified as being
inconsistent with that configuration version. Consequently, the consistency descriptor,
which is attached to the configuration and each of its components, is updated accordingly in order to identify whether the component is consistent with a configuration.

The consistency descriptor will be explained in more detail in Section 5. When a designer needs to manipulate a Bridge data, he creates an instance of the Bridge class. This instance represents the Bridge configuration together with its components.

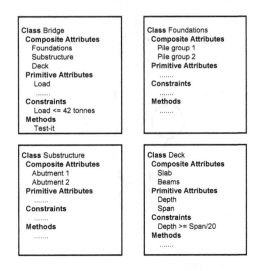

Fig. 4. Class definition of a bridge configuration

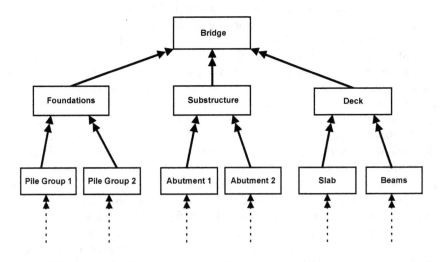

Fig. 5. A CCH of a bridge configuration

The notion of configuration in some commercial OODB systems, such as O_2, refers normally to a collection (or set) of versions of the same simple object. This is different from the present discussion of configuration. However, we have shown that introduction of new classes can be used in these systems to model design configurations [8].

Configuration versioning is the creation of a new version of the configuration. That is, the configuration state before the change is retained as well as the new state, allowing multiple versions of a configuration to co-exist. The evolution of a   configuration is represented as a hierarchy called a *configuration-derivation graph* (CDG). A *generic configuration* represents an abstract configuration which is associated with the versioned configuration. The generic configuration contains the   configuration counter, default configuration version, and a CDG. Configuration versioning allows the instance of each class in the standard CCH to have multiple versions which will be explored in more detail in Section 4. The binding of a configuration to its versioned components can be *static*, i.e. to a specific version of the component, or *dynamic* , i.e. to a default setting that can be resolved at run time.

The concepts discussed for simple object versioning may be extended to the versioning of a configuration. However, keeping track of multiple versions of a configuration is more complex than the versioning of a simple object. Therefore, without careful management of the evolution of a configuration and its components, conflicts may arise between the components of a design artefact. Hence, it is essential to identify which component version is compatible with which configuration version [13] (i.e. consistent configuration). We will discuss in more detail the consistency in dynamically bound configurations in Section 5.

Fig. 6 shows a generalized example of a configuration called CF which has three components A, B and C, each of which may have different versions denoted as $a_{1..k}$, $b_{1..m}$, and $c_{1..n}$ where k, m, and n are the latest version numbers and t_i represents the timestamp at which the version of a configuration or component is derived. At a time instance t_1, the configuration is represented as $CF_1(a_5,b_7,c_{15})$. The number associated with a component version represents which version of the component is bound to this configuration. A static binding is assumed here. Later, at a time instance t_9 the configuration structure becomes $CF_2(a_5,b_{10},c_{18})$. If no configuration versioning is supported CF_2 will replace CF_1, and CF_1 is lost. However, it represents a state of the design which may in the future be consulted or reinstantiated as a new version. If configuration versions are supported, then CF_1 and CF_2 co-exist and they can be return to at any time.

4 An Object-Oriented Model for Configuration Versioning

4.1 The Model

In this section, we present an object-oriented model which supports the semantic extension of versions to cope with configuration versions as shown in Fig. 7. This model is independent of the content of the design object and can represent a totally-versioned configuration (i.e. both the configuration and its components are versioned). This enables the version model to be sufficiently *generic* [16] so that it can be applied to a variety of engineering domains such as the design of automobile, aircraft, buildings, electronic products, VLSI, ... , etc. A basic overview of this model follows. Note that some aspects of the model may appear to be rather complex. This is due to the inherent complexity of the CE design environment.

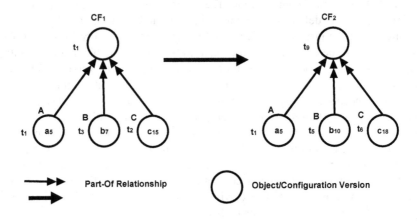

Fig. 6. Configuration versions

4.1.1 Model Elements

The model elements represent both versioned and non-versioned design objects. This means that not only the individual components can evolve but also the whole configuration can evolve and bind its components in a dynamic fashion. To capture the evolution of a CE design, the version sets of both the configuration and its components are represented in a compact form using derivation graphs. The model also supports non-component objects which may be referenced by a configuration and/or its components.

A versioned configuration contains a set of components and a set of references to a non-component objects. The component can be simple or composite. The composite component is called *subconfiguration* which is composed from other components. Hence, a configuration may contain subconfigurations recursively. Moreover, the simple and composite components can be versioned or non-versioned. The model at all levels of the configuration composition captures this setup.

Now each element of the model will be looked at in a top-down fashion. The set of versions of a configuration is represented as a CDG. A CDG is a DAG which shows the evolution of a particular configuration in a compact form. The nodes in a CDG represent a configuration version and the arcs represent the Derived-From relationship between a pair of consecutive configuration versions.

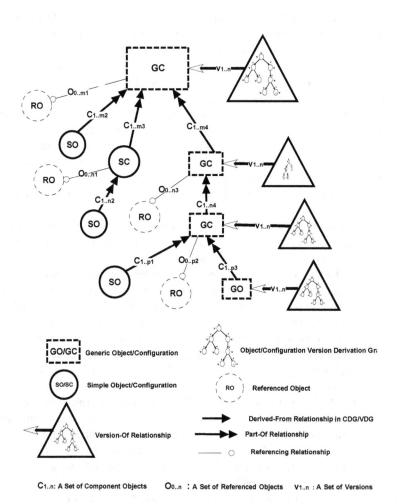

Fig. 7. An object-oriented model of configuration versions

A *Generic Configuration* (GC) is associated with each versioned configuration and maintains a record of the versions of a design configuration. A GC is shown by dotted box in Fig. 7. The set of versions of a configuration in a CDG is shown inside a tri-angle. A non-versioned configuration is called a *Simple Configuration* (SC). It is a design object which contains other design objects as components. This is equivalent to a composite object and only the latest version is kept (i.e. no versioning). A *Simple Object* (SO) is a design object that is self contained and does not include other design objects as components and it can be versioned or non-versioned. The non-versioned simple object and configuration are shown as circles in Fig. 7. If the simple object is versioned, its set of versions are   represented as a VDG. A VDG is a DAG which shows the evolution of a particular object in a compact form. The nodes in a VDG

represent a version of the simple object and the arcs represent the Derived-From relationship between a pair of   consecutive simple object versions. The set of versions of
a simple object is shown inside a triangle. A *Generic Object* (GO) is associated with
each versioned object which is shown as dotted box in Fig. 7. A *Referenced Object*
(RO) is a non-component object that is referenced by a configuration and/or component. It is shown as a dotted circle in Fig. 7.

In our model, a versioned component can be further composed from other
components. In this case, it is considered as a subconfiguration and the mechanism
used in configuration versioning is applied to it. If a versioned component, on the
other hand, does not contain components, then it is considered as a simple object and
the mechanism used in simple object versioning is applied to it.

The model identifies four basic relationships. The cardinality of the relationship is
shown on each link:

1. **Configuration-to-Component relationship**: This relationship links a configuration to its components via a Part-Of relationship. This relationship is
   shown in Fig. 7 as double-headed arrows.

2. **Object-to-Versions relationship**: This relationship links a design object (i.e.
   configuration/component) to each version in its version set via a Version-Of
   relationship. This relationship is shown in Fig. 7 as single-headed arrow followed by a triangle that contains the version set of the object.

3. **Version-to-Version relationship**: A pair of versions are linked using this
   relationship which links an object or a configuration version to its immediate
   successor version in the CDG/VDG via a Derived-From relationship. This
   relationship is shown in Fig. 7 as single-headed arrows inside the triangle.

4. **Configuration/Component-to-Non-Component relationship**: This relationship Links a configuration or its components to a non-component object.
   This relationship is shown as dotted circle-headed lines in Fig. 7.

Note that a version of a component may be part of more than one configuration
version. Hence, a referencing mechanism is required to indicate in each component
version the corresponding configuration version it belongs to. This is facilitated by a
reverse reference in each version of a component showing to which configuration
version it belongs. Furthermore, a component may be part of more than one configuration, other than the versioned configuration. Again, the reverse reference can be
used to facilitate component sharing.

4.1.2 Model Basic Operations

A design object can be versioned or non-versioned. The following is an overview of
the basic operations for manipulating design objects identified by their names. The
object id (OID) is automatically generated by the system which maintains the mapping
between the OID and the object name. The designer issues these operations using
CAD system extended tool set which enables him to interact with the OODB server as
we showed in detail in [7]:

- Simple object
- **CREATE**   \<object name> OF \<class name>
                  {list of \<attribute name, value>}
- **MODIFY**   \<object name> WITH
                  {list of \<attribute name, value>}
- **DELETE**   \< object name >

- Configuration

- **CREATE**   \< configuration name> OF \<composite class name>
                  {list of \<attribute name, value>}
                  COMPONENT {list of \<components> }
- **MODIFY**   \< configuration name> WITH
                  {list of \<attribute name, value>}
                  COMPONENT {list of \<components> }
- **DELETE**   \< configuration name>

The operations specific to versioned objects/configurations are:
- Simple object

- **DERIVE**   \<object name>.\<version number>
                  FROM {list of parents}
- **DELETE**   \<object name>.\<version number>
- **SET DEFAULT**   \<object name > TO \<version number>

- Configuration
- **DERIVE**   \<configuration name>.\<version number >
                  FROM
                  {list of parents (\<component name>.\<version number>)}
- **DELETE**   \<configuration name>.\<version number >
- **SET DEFAULT**   \<configuration name > TO
                     \<configuration version number >

The **CREATE** operation of a simple object is used prior to that of the configuration. That is, the list of attribute values in the **CREATE** operation of a configuration is used to assign values to the primitive attributes of the configuration such as the load of a Bridge. To assign values to the attributes of the components, the CREATE operation must be issued to the component. Furthermore, It is important to differentiate between the creation of an object itself and the creation of a version of this object. The creation of an object is the process of establishing new knowledge in the database and adding a new object as an instance of a specific class. The creation of a version of an object is the process of *augmenting* an existing object (or an object version) and hence creating a new version. Therefore, a versioned object must be created first using the **CREATE** operation. This will establish the first   instance of the object as the root of the VDG. Further modification to the object can be done using the **DERIVE** operation. When deriving a new version of a configuration, the component name along with the specific version number should be specified. If no version number is specified, then the reference will be to the component's generic object and the component version will be resolved at run time using the default setting in the generic object. Version merging and alternative (or branching) versions are facilitated in the **DERIVE** operation. When merging versions, two or more parent versions are identified in the list of parents. For example, the operation **DERIVE** v7 **FROM** v1, v2, v5 will create version v7 by merging parent versions v1,v2, and v5. The semantics of merging versions is the responsibility of the designer who selects parts of the CAD drawings to create the new version. Alternative versions, on the other hand, are created by using the **DERIVE** operation more than once on the same parent version. For example, the operations **DERIVE** v5 **FROM** v4 and **DERIVE** v6 **FROM** v4 will create two alternative versions v5 and v6 from the same parent version v4. The full mechanisms governing version merging and alternative versions are beyond the scope of this paper.

The deletion of a configuration may involve the deletion of all its components whose existence depend on it whether they are shared or not. If a component is independent (i.e. its existence does not depend on the configuration existence), then it is not deleted because it may be referenced by other configurations and/or objects. Note that the deletion of a configuration becomes more complicated when versioning of a configuration of a design is supported. Moreover, a configuration components may be owned by different designers and a deletion of a particular component of a configuration may lead to a *dangling reference*. Hence, the deletion of a component should be avoided if a configuration still references it. To assist this feature, each component of a configuration may contain a *reverse reference* showing to which configuration it belongs as mentioned earlier. It is preferable in a design database to keep deletions of designs to a minimum. Configuration versioning may be considered as a desirable alternative to deletion, as it introduces a new version of the configuration which does not include the deleted component while preserving the references to the "deleted component" in the previous version. This is called *virtual deletion*.

Fig. 8 shows an example of a Bridge configuration used in an experimental study conducted in [8]. The configuration consists of three components: Foundations, Substructure and Deck. Each component may be composed from other components recursively which is shown as dotted arrows in the figure. The dynamic aspects in this configuration are shown as boxes which means that the Bridge configuration version v9 is *dynamically bound* to the Foundations component. This binding is resolved at run time to the default setting defined in the generic object of the Foundations component. Likewise, the Deck component includes a dynamic binding to the Beams component. The circles, on the other hand, show a static binding to a specific version of the component.

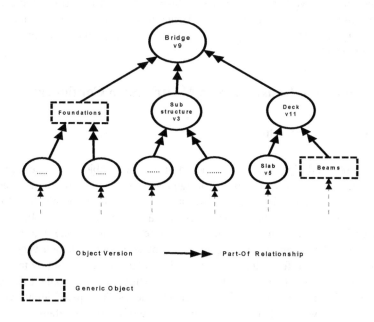

Fig. 8. An example of a Bridge dynamic configuration version

4.2 Configuration Versions in a CE Design

We differentiate between two modes of concurrency in a CE environment which are:

Local Concurrency: The concurrency of tasks within a particular product development phase such as the design phase and the manufacturing phase.

Total Concurrency: The concurrency which involves all the product development phases from the conceptual design to marketing.

In this paper, we concentrate on the local concurrency within the product design phase. The multiversion configuration model facilitates CE design by allowing versions of a configuration and/or its component to be designed simultaneously. Hence, each designer can have a version of the configuration that reflects a design state. This is done by a **DERIVE** operation of the required configuration or component. To this end and according to CE principles, the components of a configuration may be designed concurrently. Sequential engineering, on the other hand, requires that design activities are conducted in a consecutive manner [6]. Therefore, in the example of a Bridge design in Fig. 8, all the components of the Bridge can be designed concurrently by supplying each design group with their own version of a particular component or even the complete configuration (i.e. the complete artefact), provided the authorization to access the corresponding design objects is granted. Obviously, there should be a mechanism for coordination and communication between the concurrent design groups which was discussed in [3]. This allows the Foundation and

Deck designers to work at the same time using their own version of the component/configuration. Later on in the CE design process, the design versions can be grouped/merged together to form a new complete configuration represented as a new version in the CDG.

5 Dynamics and Consistency in Multiversion Configurations

5.1 Default Version Resolution

Since a versioned design object is composed of a generic object and a set of versions each of which represents a state of the design object at a time instance, it is necessary to resolve dynamic binding to a generic object rather than static binding to a particular version in the version set. Furthermore, a versionable design object may be referenced by many design objects, therefore, one needs to include two types of default selection in the generic object. The first type is a *context* default version that is used for a particular referencing resolution. This default version is set by the designer who references the versionable design object. Thus, multiple context default versions may co-exist for a versionable component. The second type of default version is a *generic* default version that is used in the absence of a context default version. This generic default version is set by the designer who creates the component object and only one generic default version can be defined for a component. If no generic default version is specified by the designer, the most recent version will be considered. The advantage of the context default version assigned by the designer is it allows the default selection to be obtained from a set of consistent versions that matches with the referencing configuration version. The SET DEFAULT operation which is shown in Section 4.1.2 is used to set the generic and context default versions. However, the designer who sets the context default version must have an authorization to access the corresponding versioned configuration/component.

5.2 Consistency in Dynamic Configurations

The consistency between a configuration and its components is one of the key issues in a CE design. It refers to the requirement that the design interface between components does not result in conflicts and that the component is within design constraints for its properties. This issue becomes more complex in a dynamic environment where both the configurations and their components are versioned. Hence, a consistent configuration is a configuration which satisfies the consistency constraints imposed on it [2]. These constraints are modelled using STEP EXPRESS language [2], which was addressed in [3]. This implies that a consistent configuration version is a configuration which has a version of each of its components that can be grouped together without causing design conflicts. The number of component versions may grow rapidly. Hence specifying which version of the component is consistent with which configuration version is problematic. Note that enforcing design constraints is not discussed here. The concern in this paper is whether the components of a dynamically bound configuration version are consistent. However, due to the tentative nature of the design process, designers may need to keep inconsistent versions of a component which require further refinement.

To maintain consistency, we introduce the notion of a *consistency descriptor*. A consistency descriptor is an object that is associated with each design object versioned or non-versioned. It contains details about the objects that are related to it in terms of their consistency in the community of design objects. The descriptor contains a set of the following information (one for each referenced object):
1.   Object/version ID of the referenced object.
2.   Consistency state: consistent/inconsistent.
3.   Time stamp: the time of determination of the consistency state.
4.   Relationship: ingoing/outgoing (this indicates whether the design object is part of other design objects or if it references other design objects as its components. This enables bi-directional consistency relationships that can be obtained from either of the related design objects).

Most of the proposals in the literature decouple the consistency representation from the object itself where a static mechanism is used to link consistent objects (e.g. layers, surfaces). Therefore, the maintenance of these links impose overheads [18]. The technique proposed in this paper associates the consistency information with each design object. The advantage of this approach is to dynamically identify the objects in the database that are consistent with each other.

Consistency constraints are automatically checked in multiversion configuration at two levels. The first is at the level of a component version. The second is at the level of a configuration version. Hence, if the resulting configuration version is consistent (i.e. conforms to its design constraint), then the consistency state entry in the consistency descriptor is automatically updated for the configuration version and each of its constituent components to reflect the consistency state (i.e. consistent). If, on the other hand, the configuration is not consistent, then only the consistency descriptor in the configuration version is updated to show that the configuration is inconsistent. The reason for not updating the corresponding consistency descriptor of the components' version to inconsistent state is that when a new component version is derived, then its consistency state entry in the consistency descriptor is always set to inconsistent. Hence, only when constraint checking at the configuration level reveals a consistent configuration is the consistency state of the component version set to consistent. Consequently , the system can automatically determine whether the components of a configuration version are consistent with each other.

The binding of a configuration to its components can be static or dynamic. The problem associated with the dynamic binding is the rule by which the reference resolution of a default setting is made. Some proposals consider the default version to be the *latest* version created [14]. Others distinguish the *current* version from the latest and decouple the default from the latest version[16]. Other proposals leave this choice to the designer who decides on a default setting [3]. None of these previous approaches discusses the consistency issues in dynamic binding. We believe that this is a key issue in resolving dynamic binding. Otherwise, major conflicts between a configuration and its component versions may occur. Note that ultimately static and dynamic schemes will bind a configuration to a particular component version. The question is whether this version is consistent with the configuration. This question is difficult to answer in the case of dynamic binding since the version is not known in advance as is the case in static binding. A solution to this problem is introduced which is based on dividing the space of versions of a component into *consistent* and *inconsistent* version subsets. The next step is to decide on a default version for the consistent subset (i.e the context default). This will ensure that during dynamic binding resolution, the default version is only obtained from the consistent subset of versions. If the designer decides to ignore the consistency factor, the default version of the whole version set (i.e. the generic default) will be considered based on a resolution policy (e.g. latest, current, user defined version). In effect, this default version may be in a consistent or inconsistent state. Note that the default version resolution in the consistent subset of versions may have its own resolution policy which may be different from the policy used in the whole version set. Fig. 9 shows a versioned configuration which has two components, one is versioned and the other is not. The figure shows the VDG of the component versions. *Relative* to that configuration, the consistency state of each version is shown as **C** if the version is consistent with the configuration and **I** if the version is inconsistent with the configuration.

A configuration is said to be consistent if *all* the states of its components are in a consistent state, and inconsistent if *at least* one of the states of its components is in an inconsistent state. Note that a configuration may have components that are in consistent and/or inconsistent states which implies that the whole configuration is inconsistent. This means that an inconsistent configuration may contain consistent subconfigurations. Later on, when all the components reach a stable state and satisfy consistency constraints of the design, the whole configuration becomes consistent which is shown in Fig. 10. This approach enables a flexible design environment to be supported, in which designers are not constrained in their creation of new component versions.

Since the design environment evolves in a continuous manner, the consistency states may be subject to change. Therefore, a notification mechanism is needed to inform the designers who are referencing a design object that its state now may not match the consistency descriptor in their version of the design object. Furthermore, when a design object/version is deleted, all the consistency descriptors in the design objects referencing it, need to be updated. Hence, the consistency descriptor needs continuous maintenance to reflect the actual consistency between design objects accurately. The consistency descriptor facilitates this process by keeping a record of all the design objects/versions that reference an object/version. A lookup/notify mechanism can then be applied for each entry in the consistency descriptor.

6   Conclusions and Future Work

In this paper, we have presented an object-oriented model for design configuration versioning in a CE design environment. The dynamic aspects in multiversion configurations as well as the consistency between a versioned configuration and its versioned components are discussed. We are extending an earlier work [8] which implements the versioning of simple design objects to include configuration versioning and this is currently under implementation in prototype form using the Objectivity OODB system [26] which is distributed on SUN SPARC Ultra stations running Solaris 7 and Windows NT4 stations.

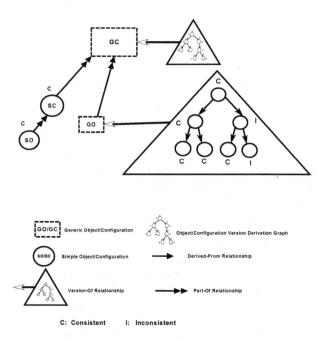

Fig. 9. Configuration consistency

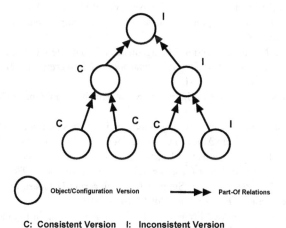

Fig. 10. Configuration consistency states

One of the important aspects in managing configuration versions is the change propagation and its effect in automatically generating new configuration versions. Another important aspect is the authorization which governs the access to a configuration version and its components. The future work includes extending the configuration versions model to incorporate change propagation and authorization.

References

[1]   S. Ahmed, A. Wong, D. Sriram, and R. Logcher, "Object-Oriented Database Management Systems for Engineering: A Comparison," *Journal of Object-Oriented Programming*, Vol. 5, No. 3, 1992.

[2]   S. Yoo and H. Suh, "Integrity Validation of Product Data in a Distributed Concurrent Engineering Environment," *Concurrent Engineering:Research and Applications*, Vol. 7, No. 3, 1999.

[3]   A. Al-Khudair, W. A. Gray and J. C. Miles , "Issues in Management of Distributed Concurrent Engineering Design in Object-Oriented Databases," *7th ISPE International Conference on Concurrent Engineering CE2000*, Lyon, France, July, 2000.

[4]   P. O'Grady and R. Young "Issues in Concurrent Enigineering Systems," *Journal of Design and Manufacturing*, Vol. 1, PP. 27-34, 1991.

[5]   R. Ramakrishnan and D. Ram, "Modeling Design Versions," *Proceedings of the 22nd VLDB Conference,* Bombay, India, 1996.

[6]   B. Prasad, Concurrent Engineering Fundamentals, Prentice Hall,1996.

[7]   T. W. Cardnduff, W. A. Gray, J. C. Miles and A. Al-Khudair, "An Object-Oriented Database System to Support Concurrent Design, " *7th ISPE International Conference on Concurrent Engineering CE2000*, Lyon, France, July, 2000.

[8]   J. C. Miles, W. A. Gray, T. W. Cardnduff, I. Santoyridis, A. Faulconbridge, "Versioning and Configuration Management in Design using CAD and Complex Wrapped Objects," *Artificial Intelligence in Engineering*, Vol. 14, No. 3, pp. 249-260, 2000.

[9]   W. Kim,.Introduction to Object-Oriented Databases, MIT Press,1990.

[10]   R. Fruchter, K. Reiner, L. Leifer and G. Toye, "VisionManager: A Computer Environment for Design Evolution Capture," *Concurrent Engineering: Research and Applications*, Vol. 6, No.1,1998.

[11]   R. Ahmed and S. Navathe, "Version Management of Composite Objects in CAD Databases," *Proc. Of the 1991 ACM SIGMOD International Conference on Management of Data*, Denver, Colorado, USA, 1991.

[12]   E. Sciore, "Versioning and Configuration Management in an Object-Oriented Data Model," *VLDB Journal, vol. 3*, 1994.

[13]   J. Rykowski, and W. Cellary, "Using Multiversion Object-Oriented Databases in CAD/CIM Systems," *Lecture Notes in Computer Science*, No. 1134, pp. 1-10, 1996.

[14]   H. Chou and W. Kim, "Versions and Change Notification in an Object-Oriented Database System," *The 25th ACM/IEEE Design Automation Conference*, 1988.

[15]   K. Dittrich and R. Lorie, "Version Support for Engineering Database Systems," *IEEE Transactions on Software Engineering*, Vol.14, No. 4, 1988.

[16]   R. Katz, R., "Toward a Unified Framework for Version Modeling in Engineering Databases," *ACM Computing Surveys*, Vol. 22, No. 4,1990.

[17]   M. özsu and P. Valduriez, Principles of Distributed Database Systems, Prentice-Hall, 1999.

[18]   W. Cellary and G. Jomier, "Consistency of Versions in Object-Oriented Databases,"
       Proceedings of the 16th VLDB Conference, Brisbane, Australia, 1990.
[19]   G. Talens, C. Oussalah and, M. Colinas, " Versions of Simple and Composite Objects",
       Proceedings of the 19th VLDB Conference, Dublin, Ireland, 1993.
[20]   K. Krishnamurthy and K. Law, "Configuration Management in a CAD Paradigm," *Proc.
       Of 1995 Int'l Mechanical Engineering Congress,* 1995
[21]   G. Kaiser, "Coopertive Transactions for Multiuser Environment," *In: Modern Database
       Systems: The Object Model, Interoperability and Beyond* (W. Kim ed.), ACM Press,
       NewYork, USA, 1995.
[22]   W. Kim, E. Bertino, and J. Gavza, "Composite Object Revisted," *Proc. Of the 1989
       ACM SIGMOD International Conference on Management of Data,* Portland, USA,
       1989.
[23]   T. Harder, W. Mahnke, N. Ritter and H. Steiert, "Generating Versioning Facilities for a
       Design-Data Repository Supporting Cooperative Applications," *International Journal of
       Cooperative Information Systems,* Vol. 9, Nos. 1&2, pp. 117-146, 2000.
[24]   M. Hague, and A. Taleb-Bendiab, "Tool for the Management of Concurrent Conceptual
       Engineering Design," *Concurrent Engineering: Research and Applications,* Vol. 6, No.
       1. 1998.
[25]   O₂ ODBMS, Release 4.5, Ardent Software, Inc. , 1998.
[26]   Objectivity ODBMS, Release 5.2, Objectivity, Inc., 1999.
[27]   VERSANT ODBMS, Release 5.2, Versant Ltd.,1998.

Experiences with IR TOP N Optimization in a Main Memory DBMS: Applying 'the Database Approach' in New Domains

Henk Ernst Blok[1], Arjen P. de Vries[2], Henk M. Blanken[1], and
Peter M.G. Apers[1]

[1] Computer Science Department, University of Twente,
PO BOX 217, NL 7500 AE, Enschede, The Netherlands
tel. +31 53 489 3690, fax. +31 53 489 2927
{blok, blanken, apers}@cs.utwente.nl
[2] CWI, Amsterdam, The Netherlands
arjen@acm.org

Abstract. Data abstraction and query processing techniques are usually studied in the domain of administrative applications. We present a case-study in the non-standard domain of (multimedia) information retrieval, mainly intended as a feasibility study in favor of the 'database approach' to data management.

Top-N queries form a natural query class when dealing with content retrieval. In the IR field, a lot of research has been done on processing top-N queries efficiently. Unfortunately, these results cannot directly be ported to the database environment, because their tuple-oriented nature would seriously limit the freedom of the query optimizer to select appropriate query plans.

By horizontally fragmenting our database containing document statistics, we are able to combine some of the best of the IR and database optimization principles, providing good retrieval quality as well as database 'goodies' like flexibility, scalability, efficiency, and generality. Key issues we address in this paper concern the effects of our fragmentation approach on speed and quality of the answers, opportunities for scalability, supported by experimental results.

Keywords: top-N, indexing, query optimization, content based retrieval, multimedia, databases

1 Introduction

Data abstraction is the essence of the 'database approach' to data management. Specifying the manipulation and definition of data at a high level of abstraction provides not only data independence, but also enables a database management system to facilitate a wide variety of additional 'goodies', including *efficiency*, *scalability*, and *flexibility*.

B. Read (Ed.): BNCOD 2001, LNCS 2097, pp. 126–151, 2001.
© Springer-Verlag Berlin Heidelberg 2001

The importance of services such as *transaction management* and *concurrency control* in administrative applications – and their excellent support in commercial relational database management systems – has resulted in the database approach being the norm in the domain of business applications. Unfortunately, the benefits of the database approach to data management are not so well established in most other application domains.

This paper demonstrates how two key elements of the database approach (i.e. data abstraction and query optimization) can play a similarly important role in the domain of information retrieval (IR). In general, IR systems are not very flexible, in the sense that e.g. changing the retrieval model (ranking algorithm) is far from trivial. Also, the physical access and storage structures, although often quite sophisticated, are 'hard-coded' into the system. As a result, it is not so easy to turn an existing stand-alone IR system into a parallel and/or distributed system. Neither is generality a common property among IR systems; most systems support document retrieval by content only, and not by other attributes such as author, category, or publication date. In any case, it will be very difficult to add extra attributes in a later stage.

In contrast to the conventional approaches in the IR field, we do not tie our IR retrieval model onto a physical data structure like inverted files, but specify the model declaratively at a high level (allowing flexibility in the choice for retrieval model) as described in [15,11]. The particular advantage of this approach is that it allows us to extend our research DBMS with IR techniques, *without breaking the set-oriented nature of query processing*. Such a combination of IR techniques with traditional database technology is an important ingredient for the development of search engines for large collections of XML documents that allow queries on the combination of structural properties and field values (traditional *data retrieval*) as well as their content (requiring the *information retrieval* techniques). Also, as motivated in [9], and demonstrated in [10] at VLDB'99, the same techniques provide a strong foundation for the implementation of multimedia retrieval systems.

The main objective of our paper is to (1) present a case-study demonstrating how data abstraction is equally useful in non-traditional application domains as in the administrative domain, and (2) motivate why a novel DBMS architecture is required to facilitate such broadening of core database technology for new domains. We start with a state-of-the-art IR retrieval model, that performs very well on retrieval evaluation experiments (see [16]). We then present the integration of these algorithms in our research DBMS, which resulted in a system sufficiently powerful to participate in TREC[1] [19]. This paper discusses the development of new query processing techniques at the logical level of the DBMS, improving its efficiency and scalability on IR query loads. These techniques are applied transparently in the mapping from abstract specification to implementa-

---

[1] The TREC, Text Retrieval and Evaluation Conference, is a well known IR conference, organized annually by NIST in the US (http://trec.nist.gov/). A key part of the conference submissions involve the benchmarking results of retrieval systems. To support this, standardized sets of documents and queries are provided by the conference organization.

tion, thus retaining the flexibility to combine queries on content with the usual data retrieval, and/or experiment with novel IR models at a declarative level.

The remainder of the paper is organized as follows. First, we outline the intuition underlying our optimization strategy in Section 2, and introduce the MirrorDBMS prototype in Section 3. Next, we describe the proposed query processing techniques in Section 4. Section 5 outlines the experimental setup to evaluate these techniques, and Section 6 presents and analyzes the results of our experimental evaluation. Section 7 presents the conclusions and future work.

2   Problem Statement

In IR systems, users express their information needs using a small number of keywords and relevance judgments on previously retrieved documents (called **relevance feedback**). Similarly, querying multimedia objects requires the user to specify characteristics of the content, e.g. by describing a color histogram of desired images. However, for sake of clarity, we limit the scope of our discussion to the ranked retrieval of text documents. Using the query and relevance feedback as an approximation of the real information need, the system then selects objects with characteristics 'similar' to those specified in the query. Notice that this comparison between objects is usually based on metadata extracted from the original documents, such as words occurring in the texts.

In the straightforward implementation of this process, each interaction step between user and system involves ranking all objects based on their similarity to the query, although only the N 'most' similar objects are presented to the user (the top-N objects). Obviously, top-N query optimization (attempting to compute only the similarity for the top-N documents to be presented) is a natural step to improve the efficiency of (multimedia) information retrieval.

As mentioned briefly, content querying is interactive and iterative: after reviewing, a user gives an indication of the quality of the answer (relevance feedback) which is used to modify the original query. Processing the modified query generates new answers, and so on. Thus, it seems particularly interesting to cut off query processing at a *reasonable* stage, and show the results computed till then to the user for relevance feedback. Although the quality of the answer may be impeded, this may allow for great reductions in computations, possibly without diminishing the effectiveness of the relevance feedback process. Our intuition is that incomplete answers can still provide a good basis for relevance feedback: a quick approximate response may still provide sufficient information to refine the estimate of the user's information need, and consequently improve the effectiveness of retrieval. For each iteration, the users may decide for themselves whether they prefer quicker responses of (generally) lower quality, or slower responses of (hopefully) higher quality.

In handling top-N queries more efficiently, implementations of IR systems have drawn on a combination of domain knowledge – exploiting the Zipfian [20] distribution of terms found in documents (see e.g. [17]) – with smart element-at-a-time cut-off operations derived from the ranking function, like in the implementation of the well-known INQUERY retrieval system [7,6]. Exploiting the element-at-a-time manner of processing, highly accurate cut-off conditions can be updated after evaluating each element, allowing for efficient reduction of obsolete intermediate results being computed. This algorithm and comparable ones (e.g. [8]) exploit a carefully designed ordering of the data, mathematically well-founded by the work of Fagin [14,12,13].

Obviously, the element-at-a-time nature of these native IR algorithms for top-N query processing reduces significantly the number of possible query plans under consideration in the query processor of a DBMS combining IR techniques with data retrieval; which is unacceptable in many cases. So, the goal in this paper is to devise a database approach that is able to satisfy the following goals:

- Improving the efficiency and scalability using (a) domain knowledge and (b) new techniques inspired by the (element-at-a-time) cut-off operations, and,
- Maintaining the flexibility and generality of the database approach to IR.

Summarizing, we have identified two potential approaches to improve efficiency in information retrieval query processing in a database environment: on the one hand, we may reduce the amount of work by ranking fewer documents, and on the other hand, we may take advantage of computing only partial answers in the first iterations of the retrieval process. In the remainder of this paper, we will demonstrate how the database approach allows us to exploit **fragmentation** of the metadata to achieve these ideas in a simple yet effective manner, requiring only minimal changes to the original, declarative specification of the IR retrieval model.

3   IR Query Processing in the **MirrorDBMS**

The architecture of the MirrorDBMS, our research prototype, consists of two layers: the logical layer, based on Moa object algebra [4], and a physical layer, realized by the binary relational main-memory DBMS Monet [2,3]. The query processor transforms the algebraic query expressions specified in Moa into the – highly efficient – physical operators offered by Monet. The distinguishing feature of the MirrorDBMS is that it is extensible at all levels of its architecture: enabling the encoding of domain knowledge and advanced query processing techniques at the logical level as well as the physical level (please refer to [9, Chapter 2] for more information). Also, the prototype DBMS is well prepared for scalability, as Moa supports shared-nothing parallelism, and shared-memory parallel computing is supported by Monet at the physical level.

3.1   The IR Retrieval Model

A retrieval model specifies how the similarity between a document and the query is computed, given the query and the relevance feedback from one or more previous iterations. Most probabilistic IR models rank the documents based on two parameters:

term frequency: For each pair of term and document, *tf* is the number of times the term occurs in the document.

$$TF(term, document, tf) \hspace{4cm} (1)$$
$$IDF(term, idf) \hspace{4.5cm} (2)$$
$$Q(term) \hspace{5.5cm} (3)$$

Fig. 1. Relations

inverse document frequency: For each term, *idf* is the inverse number of documents in which the term occurs.

In a more database like notation we can describe these two statistics as the relations 1 and 2, respectively, as shown in Figure 1.

Furthermore, we introduce the set of query terms, i.e. the unary relation 3 shown in Figure 1.

In most probabilistic retrieval models, the ranking of a document given a query is almost completely determined by the sum of the product between the *tf* and *idf* of the query terms occurring in the document, sometimes normalized with the document length in one way or another. See [19] for more detailed information about our specific ranking formula and retrieval model.

3.2   Query Processing in an IR System

The algorithm shown in Figure 2 in pseudo-code, consisting of three parts, sketches how a typical IR system computes its query results from these tables in a nested-loop manner, thus determining precisely the physical execution order. We will assume that IDF is ordered descending on *idf*.

It may be clear that this algorithm allows a very efficient cut-off, but also is highly inflexible with respect to execution order.

3.3   Set-Oriented IR Query Processing

To reduce this inflexibility of the IR retrieval process, and thus enable smooth integration with traditional DBMS query processing, we reformulate this algorithm at a higher, declarative level.[2]

In the implementation, the information retrieval techniques are supported by extensions at both levels of the MirrorDBMS. While the exact ranking formula requires some minimal extensions at the physical level, the set-oriented formulation of IR query processing is almost completely modeled at the logical level as a Moa extension. Although the real algorithm is specified using the powerful but relatively low-level Monet Interface Language (MIL), we prefer an SQL-flavored syntax for didactic reasons.

Again, the algorithm, as shown in Figure 3, consists of three parts.

---

[2] For the impatient: the usefulness of this seemingly minor step will become more clear when we present our optimization techniques based on data fragmentation in Section 4.

Part A Limit the TF and IDF to match the terms in query Q:

```
foreach t1 in TF do
  if (t1.term in Q) then
     INSERT t1 INTO TFQ
  endif
end

foreach t1 in IDF do
  if (t1.term in Q) then
     INSERT t1 INTO IDFQ
  endif
end
```

where t1 denotes the tuple-variable associated to the relations.

Part B Loop over the terms to compute the ranking contribution per document-term pair, and update the document ranking incrementally each time a new ranking contribution for that document becomes available. Stop as soon as a test (based on the processed IDFQ and TFQ values, knowing that IDFQ can only decrease, cf. [13]) shows that no document could obtain a ranking better than the current top-N.

Like before, t1 and t2 are tuple-variables. Furthermore we assume the existence of a table RANK that has two columns: document and rank.

```
foreach t1 in IDFQ do
  # Find the matching tf values
  TFQsel = findrecords(TFQ, t1.term)

  foreach t2 in TFQsel do
    tfidf = t1.idf * t2.tf;
    if (t2.document in RANK) then
       updateranking(RANK,
         t2.document, tfidf)
    else
       addranking(RANK,
         t2.document, tfidf)
    endif
    # topN test criterium
    if (!topNcanimprove) then
       exitloops
    endif
  end
end
```

Part C Return the top ranking documents:

```
i = 0
foreach t1 in RANK
do
   if (i < N)
   then
      INSERT t1 INTO TOPRANK
   else
      exitloops
   endif
   i = i + 1
end
```

Fig. 2. IR query evaluation algorithm

Part A Do some initialization given query Q.

Part B Limit the TF and IDF to match the terms in query Q:

$$TF_Q = TF \bowtie Q$$

and

$$IDF_Q = IDF \bowtie Q.$$

Next, place the IDF_Q values next to the corresponding entries in TF_Q:

$$TFIDF_{lineup} = TF_Q \bowtie IDF_Q.$$

Now, compute the $tf \cdot idf$ value per term-document pair, aggregating the last two columns into one:

$$TFIDF = SELECT\ term, document, tf * idf$$
$$FROM\ TFIDF_{lineup}.$$

Finally, compute the ranking per document by aggregating all term contributions per document:

$$RANK = SELECT\ document, AGGR(tfidf)$$
$$FROM\ TFIDF$$
$$GROUP\ BY\ document.$$

Please note that in the actual code, the AGGR()-operator does not exist as one operator, but denotes a combination of several functions that together compute the ranking. We abbreviated it here for reasons of simplicity.

Part C Normalize RANK and select the top-N documents:

$$TOPRANK = TOP(RANK, N).$$

Fig. 3. Set-oriented IR query processing

3.4 Discussion

The main performance bottle-neck lies in handling the TF table[3]: TF contains over 26 million entries in the experiments performed for this paper – which is only about a quarter of the complete TREC data set. Only **Part B**[4] in the algorithm described above handles a very large amount of data. At a first glance, the pre-selection on query terms, $TF_Q = TF \bowtie Q$, at the beginning of **Part B**, may potentially reduce the remaining dataset to a manageable size. But, it is a well-known fact in IR experiments that for the average query, roughly about half of the database remains after that pre-selection: still a very large dataset as input for the subsequent computations.

Since, $N = 1000$ or (often) less, pushing the top-N operator into the query could be very profitable. However, pushing it down the query plan implies pushing it through the AGGR()-operator, and therefore through the $tf \cdot idf$ product.

---

[3] Since we work on a binary model, several tables represent together the columns of TF. However, for didactic reasons we will stick to the normal table approach since this has no significant consequences for the core of our idea.

[4] From now on, when we refer to **Part A**, **Part B**, or **Part C**, we mean the ones described in the database approach and not in the IR approach as described in Subsection 3.3.

A generic (set-oriented) mathematical solution for this top-N query optimization problem is not a trivial one, despite its innocent look. In the next Section, we therefore propose data fragmentation as another means to prune the search, while keeping (the declarative specification of) the algorithm practically untouched.

4   Data Fragmentation and the Top-N Query Optimization Problem

Since Monet is a main-memory DBMS, the data used in the hot set should always fit in main-memory (to avoid performance degradation due to swapping, or even worse, a crash caused by running out of memory). The natural way to meet this requirement is to horizontally fragment the TF table into a small (yet to be determined) number of suitably sized parts. Such a fragmentation strategy is orthogonal to the actual retrieval algorithm, and can be managed in the mapping from Moa to MIL.

In this paper, we elaborate on the use of additional knowledge for choosing the fragmentation scheme, *specific for query processing in the IR domain.* We show how this enables us to achieve both proposed strategies to improve the efficiency of IR query processing: (1) computing partial answers, and (2) top-N query optimization. Furthermore, the implementation of the fragmentation strategy remains almost entirely orthogonal to the IR retrieval algorithm outlined before. Remark that we will focus on optimization techniques at the logical level of the MirrorDBMS.

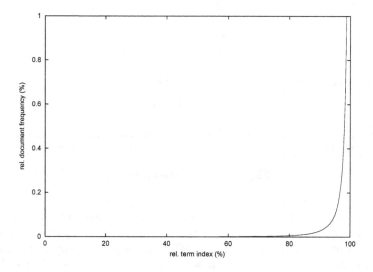

Fig. 4. Relative document frequency (zoomed on y-axis to show lower values)

Restricting query processing to a smaller portion of the metadata is a well-known approach to increase the efficiency of IR system implementations by computing approximate answers. Obviously, this implies that the effectiveness of the answer (measured using precision/recall) will degrade: we trade quality for speed. To minimize the loss on quality, we exploit the properties of the afore-mentioned Zipfian term distribution. The hyperbolic curvature of the document frequency plot, shown in Figure 4, confirms that the data in our test database (see also Section 5.1) indeed behaves as predicted by Zipf, validating the underlying reasoning behind our approach.

4.1   The Fragmentation Algorithm

Now, Figure 5 shows the simplified basics of our fragmentation algorithm for splitting the data up in two fragments using the additional information about the term distribution. To keep the example simple, we take the first fragment such that it contains $s_1 \cdot |IDF|$ of the terms and the second one the other $s_2 \cdot |IDF|$ terms, where $s_2 = (1 - s_1)$ and $0 < s_i < 1$, $i \in \{1, 2\}$.

Step 1 Sort the IDF descending on the *idf* values, i.e., terms that occur in many documents get lower in the list compared to terms that occur in less documents.

$$IDF_{sorted} = \text{SELECT} *$$
$$\text{FROM IDF}$$
$$\text{ORDER BY idf DESC}$$

Step 2 Create two fragments IDF_1 and IDF_2 such that

$$\text{SELECT COUNT}(*)$$
$$\text{FROM } IDF_i$$
$$=$$
$$\text{SELECT } s_i \cdot \text{COUNT}(*)$$
$$\text{FROM } IDF_{sorted}$$

for $i \in \{1, 2\}$.

Step 3 Create two fragments TF_1 and TF_2 such that

$$TF_i = TF \bowtie IDF_i$$

for $i \in \{1, 2\}$.

Notice that, for $s_1 = 0.95$, TF_1 would now contain approximately 5% (not 95%!) of the tuples of TF, and TF_2 the rest, due to the high skewedness of the data.

Fig. 5. Fragmentation algorithm

Since the terms in IDF_1 have a high *idf* their contribution to the ranking of a document is likely to be higher than for terms in IDF_2 (having lower *idf* values). In other words, the terms in IDF_1 are *a priori* more promising than the terms in IDF_2. Fortunately, these *interesting* terms only use about 5% of the data (in case $s_1 = 0.95$). So, in case all query terms are stored in the first fragment, we only need to compute the results using IDF_1 and TF_1. This would mean that the following semijoin $TF_Q = TF \bowtie Q$ in **Part B** of the algorithm would become $\text{TF}_\text{Q} = \text{TF}_1 \bowtie \text{Q}$, which will be significantly faster due to the much smaller first operand.

In case not all query terms are contained in the first fragment, one might decide to still compute the results on the first fragment only. This could of course result in a different top when too much significant information is ignored that way. Some experiments described later in this paper try to determine the effects of ignoring the second fragment on the quality of the answer.

Finally, notice that the fragmentation algorithm described above can easily be used to handle different fragmentations, for instance for different relative sizes (just choose a different s_i) and/or more than two fragments (have $i \in S$, with $S \subset \{1, 2, 3, \ldots, M\}$, $|S| > 2$, $M = |\text{IDF}|$). For reasons of simplicity, it is sometimes more practical to join TF and IDF before fragmenting the data, and propagate the fragmentation into TF and IDF fragments subsequently. This other method is particularly handy to obtain fragments of (almost) equal data size.[5]

4.2   Fragment-Based IR Query Processing with Top-N Cut-off

The algorithm in Figure 6 shows the top-N cut-off idea in a similar manner like the set-based description of the retrieval algorithm as described in Subsection 3.3 exploiting the fragmentation idea described above.

This algorithm in fact is a sub-set-at-time version of the element-at-a-time version described in Subsection 3.2.

Unsafe Top-N Optimization. Note that this algorithm is a so called *unsafe* top-N cut-off algorithm [6]. Top-N query optimization relies on the cut-off of the query evaluation at a certain stage when certain characteristics concerning the still remaining work[6] provide sufficient evidence that the top-N cannot be improved anymore. However, this also means that at the cut-off moment certain information, e.g. ranking contributions, have not been taken into account. This usually results in a top-N containing the correct documents but with an incomplete ranking. In turn, this can result in a different ordering of the top-N. Unsafe top-N query optimization stops at this 'incorrectly' ordered top-N.

Safe Top-N Optimization. The *safe* alternative to the unsafe method does indeed return the top-N with the correct ranking values and inherently can deliver them in the correct order. To obtain these final ranking values the ranking contribution for the documents in the unsafe top-N needs to be computed for all fragments that have not been taken into account, yet. This of course will (slightly) reduce the profit of top-N cut-off due to the extra work that has to be done.

---

[5] The fragmentation process itself is part of the physical design of the database, and therefore its performance is not really an issue, at least for mostly static collections.

[6] In the algorithm described here the topNcanimprove variable represents the information needed to make the cut-off decision.

Part A Similar to **Part A** in Subsection 3.3. Set i to the first fragment that contains a query term.

Part B Similar to **Part B** in Subsection 3.3, but this time using fragment i instead of the unfragmented TF and IDF. Let's call the resulting ranking RANK_i.

Part B' Merge RANK_i into any existing RANK or otherwise set $\text{RANK} = \text{RANK}_i$.

Part C Normalize RANK and select the top-N documents:

$$\text{TOPRANK} = \text{TOP}(\text{RANK, N}).$$

Part C' Compute the lowest ranking in the current intermediate top-N:

$$\text{topLB} = \text{MIN}(\text{TOPRANK})$$

and the highest ranking in the remaining intermediate results:

$$\text{restUB} = \text{MAX}(\text{RANK} - \text{TOPRANK}).$$

Furthermore, compute the highest possible ranking contributions over all fragments $j > i$:

$$\text{contribUB} = \text{MAXRCONTRIB}(\text{TFIDF}_j, \dots, \text{TFIDF}_{25})$$

and the lowest possible ranking contribution

$$\text{contribLB} = \text{MINRCONTRIB}(\text{TFIDF}_j, \dots, \text{TFIDF}_{25}).$$

Part C'' Test whether the top-N still can be improved:

$$\text{topNcanimprove} = (\text{restUB} + \text{contribUB} \geq \text{topLB} + \text{contribLB})$$

and limit RANK to those documents that still can move up into the top-N:

$$\text{RANK} = \text{SELECT} * \text{FROM RANK}$$
$$\text{WHERE rank} \geq \text{topLB} + \text{contribLB} - \text{contribUB}$$

as soon as:

$$\text{MIN}(\text{RANK}) \leq \text{topLB} + \text{contribLB} - \text{contribUB}$$

and $\text{COUNT}(\text{TOPRANK}) > \text{N}$ and limit all fragments $j > i$ to match this new intermediate ranking.

Part C''' If topNcanimprove is true, then find the next fragment i containing a query term and return to **Part B** (in this algorithm) . Otherwise, return TOPRANK and quit.

Fig. 6. Fragment-based IR query processing with top-N cut-off

Heuristic Unsafe Top-N Optimization. Going even further on the unsafe principle, we can drop the requirement in **Part C''** that the intermediate rank only can be restricted when

$$\text{MIN}(\text{RANK}) \leq \text{topLB} + \text{contribLB} - \text{contribUB}.$$

The algorithm then becomes even 'more' unsafe: as soon as COUNT (TOPRANK) > N, documents that have no ranking yet are ignored, even when they would have received a high ranking otherwise. In turn, this *heuristic unsafe* method is very likely to achieve a much better performance due to the earlier and more restrictive limitation imposed on RANK and all fragments $j > i$. The 'level of unsafe-ness' can be controlled by adding some documents (with initial ranking 0.0) to RANK already during **Part A** using an a priori notion of ranking between the documents. These documents cannot be forgotten anymore, but will keep their 0.0 ranking when they do not contain any query terms, thus not disrupting the ranking process in case they were wrongly added in advance.

In our case we control the level of unsafe-ness using a factor l (where $0.0 < l < 1.0$) to select the $l \times$ no. of documents with the highest document length to be added in advance. The document length appeared to be an interesting, natural measure of a priori document relevance for the IR model we used. However, one can think of many other other means to 'pre-select' documents that should not be ignored (i.e. the documents that are most referenced in a digital library case, or most linked to in the web case). Also note that a too high l will cause the performance to drop rapidly because of the then extremely high number of documents that are forced to be ranked.

5   Experimental Setup

In the experimental evaluation of the ideas put forward in the previous section, we focus on the following three concrete research questions:

1. How can fragmentation improve efficiency for top-N query execution?
   a) What are the consequences for the speed?
   b) What are the consequences for the quality of the query results, also taking into account the impact of safe/unsafe top-N optimization?
2. How can fragmentation improve scalability, to either manage the same database on smaller hardware (like a notebook), or a larger database on the same hardware (such as a search engine for the WWW).

5.1   Data Set and Evaluation Measures

The experiments are performed on the *Financial Times* (FT), a major subset of the TREC data set, using the 50 topics (i.e. queries) and relevance judgments used in TREC-6. Since we want to investigate the trade-off between quality and speed we need a good benchmark for the precision and recall. The used TREC relevance judgments are the most widely accepted retrieval quality benchmarks. Also, the FT document collection is sufficiently large to show the important effects.

We defined four series of experiments, which we evaluate using the measures described in Figure 7.

5.2   Overview and Motivation of Experiments

Here, we discuss the four series of experiments that we performed:

Series I: Baseline. The first series of experiments are meant to show the quality and performance of our system without any special tricks: the Monet DBMS determines whether to build any access structures (usually hash tables) to speed up certain operations (for instance: joins). In this version the main focus was on the quality of the retrieval results and flexibility of the retrieval model. The effort to optimize this system for performance did not exceed the typical exploitation of certain typical alignment issues important in main memory computing.

Average Precision We define the average precision (AP) as:

$$AP \equiv avg(p_i)$$

where p_i is the average 11-point-precision for each query i, $i \in \{1, 2, 3, \ldots, 50\}$. So, the AP measure is actually the average average 11-point-precision.

Average Retrieved Relevant We define the average retrieved relevant (ARR) as:

$$ARR \equiv avg(r_i)$$

where r_i is the number of relevant documents retrieved for each query i, $i \in \{1, 2, 3, \ldots, 50\}$. Notice that the well-known *recall* measure is defined as r_i divided by the total number of relevant documents for query i.

Average Execution Time The average execution time (AET) is defined as:

$$AET \equiv avg(t_i)$$

where t_i is the (wall clock) execution time measured for each query i, and $i \in \{1, 2, 3, \ldots, 50\}$.

Fig. 7. Fragmentation algorithm

Series II: Speed/Quality Trade-off. In the second series of experiments, we concentrate on the effects of ignoring data on the trade-off between quality and efficiency. We defined two variants of these series of experiments:

(a) Always use the first fragment (and forget about the second fragment).
(b) Take the first fragment, unless

$$\mathrm{NIDF}_1 \ltimes Q = \emptyset.$$

We used a term-fragment index to allow an efficient choice, instead of using just this semijoin.

Both types of experiments are executed for several different fragmentations, where the relative size in terms of the first fragment varies from 90% to 99.9%, using the fragmentation algorithm described above.

Obviously, the (a) series can result in loss of quality; if none of the query terms have a high *idf* value, the answer set has been reduced to a random sample from the collection. The (b) series are meant to reduce this negative effect.

We expect that the speed will decrease in favor of the quality with increasing first fragment size. The second experiment should be slower, since the evaluation of the second fragment triggered by some of the queries will increase the execution time considerably; though resulting in a better quality than for series (a).

Series III: Benefits of Fragmenting. Series II focuses on the trade-off between ignoring data to obtain speed compared to the quality of the resulting answers. However, the second fragment is still quite large in terms of data size, impeding main-memory execution. The experiments in series III are mainly intended to investigate the effects of executing our query algorithm on relatively small fragments. To do so, we fragment our database in 25 smaller fragments of equal data size. The number of fragments was experimentally determined based on two constraints: there should be sufficiently many fragments to demonstrate the expected behavior, but, each fragment should still be reasonably large as to obtain the advantage of set-oriented processing.

Again, we perform a couple of variants of these experiments:

(a) This variant studies the effects of the fragmentation procedure described in Section 4 on execution time and quality of results. As in Series IIb, we use a term-fragment index to efficiently determine whether a fragment should be evaluated or not.

(b) This variant uses the same fragmentation as for (a), but this time we allow query evaluation to be cut-off after each fragment. The choice whether to stop processing the query (and after which fragment) is based on estimates whether the top-N can still be improved by processing of any following fragments. This strategy uses the computed lower and upper bounds to restrict the intermediate ranking to those documents that may still move into the top-N, thus limiting the computational efforts needed for any successive fragments still to be evaluated. We evaluate both the safe and (normal) unsafe cut-off principle in this variant.

(c) As described in Section 4 one can relax certain conditions for the unsafe algorithm, obtaining a, what we call, heuristic unsafe method. This variant performs the heuristic version of the unsafe experiments done for the (b) variant, taking $l \in \{0.00, 0.05, 0.10, 0.25, 1.00\}$. As explained before we used l to pre-select the fraction of a priori most interesting documents[7] that should not be ignored in case of intermediate result restriction in **Part C''**.

Since variant IIIa takes into account all query terms, we expect the AP and ARR to be equal to the figures measured in Series I. The AET will probably be better (e.g. lower) than for Series IIb, since the overhead occurring from using an extra fragment is likely to be lower (since the fragments are smaller).

Of course, the computation of the estimates in series IIIb introduces an overhead in execution costs; this investment only pays off if the profits of the optimization are high enough. The (b) variant of these series are meant to show whether this is still the case when applied to subsets-at-a-time processing rather than the element-at-a-time case studied in [6]. Note that in [6] the results for the safe method showed no real significant performance improvement.

As mentioned before, the quality is likely to be somewhat lower in case of the unsafe variant of the cut-off.

We expect the IIIc variant to outperform IIIa and IIIb (both for safe and unsafe runs) by far for $l = 0.00$ and quality to be lower but not really bad. For growing l we expect the performance to degrade rapidly since the overhead will grow significantly. However, in the case of $l = 1.00$ the quality should reach the same levels as measured for the IIIa variant.

---

[7] We used the document length which appeared as a natural candidate given the IR model we used. As stated before, other measures might be more appropriate in other environments.

Series IV: Influence of Query Length and Top-N Size. Because we calibrate the quality measurements using the relevance judgments of the TREC-6 queries, the experiments in Series III have been performed with fairly long queries: an average length of 27 terms, and the longest query contains over 60 terms. Also, TREC evaluation requires the top 1000 to be produced for each query.

Series IV try to provide insight in (a) the effect of query length on the AET and (b) the effect of the size of required top-N on the AET. The (a) variant repeats the experiments of Series I (unfragmented case), IIIa (25 fragments, no top-N cut-off), IIIb (25 fragments with normal safe/unsafe top-N cut-off), and IIIc (25 fragments with heuristic unsafe top-N cut-off) for limited query lengths. The new queries are constructed by taking the first k terms of each original query (or the entire original query in case it was shorter than k terms). We let k range from 1 to 25. The (b) variant leaves the queries untouched and computes Series I, IIIa, IIIb, and IIIc for several top-N sizes ranging from 10 to the original 1000.

We expect that the (a) variant will show a relative performance advantage in favor of the top-N cut-off for longer queries compared to the cases without top-N cut-off. For shorter queries, fragmentation alone will already result in quite efficient processing whereas top-N cut-off would only cause extra computational costs without much chance to gain a profit. The (b) variant is expected to demonstrate better AET values for lower N. The shorter the required top-N, the higher the lowest ranking value topLB occurring in the top-N; and, the higher topLB, the higher the value of topLB + contribLB − contribUB used to restrict the intermediate result RANK. This means that more elements in RANK are likely to be cut away. Also, the higher ranking values usually tend to be further away from their closest neighbors. So, the higher the topLB, the higher the chances that restUB will be so much further away (i.e. lower) that the gap cannot be bridged anymore: thus allowing for a top-N cut-off. In both cases the execution time is reduced, either due to less computational load per fragment or fewer fragments being evaluated.

6   Experimental Results

The hardware platform used to produce the results presented in this section is a dedicated PC running Linux 2.2.14, with two Pentium™ III 600 MHz CPUs (of which only one was actually used in the experiments), 1 GB of main-memory, and a 100 GB disk array mounted in RAID 0 (striping) mode; no other user processes were allowed on the system while running the experiments.

The remainder of this section is divided in four parts, corresponding with the four series of experiments. For each of these series of experiments, we included some figures/tables to illustrate the results.

6.1   Series I: Baseline

In this subsection we present the AP, ARR, and AET for the baseline run of the retrieval experiments. Table 1 shows the measured values, next to the values provided by TREC as the benchmark. The AET of course is not available for the benchmark.

Table 1. [Series I] Baseline result statistics (TREC benchmark included for comparison)

	AP (%)	ARR	AET (s)
Benchmark	100.0	31.8	-
Series I	31.0	22.9	44.4

The ARR of 22.9 means that the recall of our unfragmented is

$$\frac{ARR_{unfragmented}}{avg.\ actual\ no.\ relevant} = \frac{22.9}{31.8} = 0.72.$$

Taking into consideration the fact that many IR systems stay below the 30% precision next to this fairly high recall, demonstrates that we used a state of the art IR model indeed.

The AET of 44.1 seconds is of course not very competitive. However, note that this is also due to the relatively large (1000), and therefore expensive, top-N we computed, required to legitimate the use of the TREC benchmarks. In Series IV we demonstrate that much better times can be achieved in case of a smaller top-N. Furthermore, the relatively long queries we used (again because of the use of the TREC benchmarks) also are quite costly when evaluated without any special measures like top-N optimization, which we did not exploit in these series, yet.

6.2   Series II: Cut-off Moment

Series II has been designed to develop an intuitive feel for the trade-off between quality and efficiency. Recall that only two fragments are used: a small fragment containing the 'interesting' terms and a much larger fragment containing mainly 'common' terms.

Series IIa: Use First Fragment Only. Figures 8, 9, and 10 plot the AP, the ARR, and the AET of Series IIa, respectively, together with the baseline performance of the unfragmented case. Figure 9 also plots the average number of relevant documents in the collection, averaged over all topics. The x-axis denotes the term count of the first fragment in ‰ (i.e. tens of percentages) with respect to the total number of terms in the dictionary.

The experiments confirm our expectations. The $AP_{fragmented}$ increases with increasing term count of the first fragment, moving towards the $AP_{unfragmented}$. This also holds for the $ARR_{fragmented}$, respectively $ARR_{unfragmented}$. The shape of the plot in Figure 10 is also not surprising; since the data distribution is highly skewed, the data size of the first fragment grows faster and faster with increasing term count of the first fragment; explaining perfectly how the AET increases ever faster as the term count of the first fragment increases, reaching an AET of just over 44 seconds when the first fragment contains all terms (100%).

If the first fragment contains 99% of the terms, the AET is still 3.8 s while the ARR is 16.2 (or, average recall is 0.51) and the AP is 0.27: half of the documents that should have been retrieved are (on average) indeed retrieved, and, the average precision drops only a few percentages (to a level that various custom IR systems would not reach). In other words, a very reasonable quality can be reached in almost 20 seconds, which is more than 2 times faster than the time required to compute the best possible answers (given our retrieval model).

Series IIb: Use Second Fragment when First One is Unable to Handle Query. Even the best known retrieval models don't exceed the 40% AP level. So, although the results shown in the previous case can be considered quite good compared to many other IR systems, the quality degradation still comes down to moving away further from that – already quite poor – upper limit of 40% AP. Series IIb aims to investigate a possible improvement in the quality at the cost of, hopefully, only a minor fall-back in efficiency.

As is clearly demonstrated by the results shown in Figures 8 and 9, the quality of the results has improved significantly thanks to the switching technique. But, the AET has risen significantly (Figure 10). This observation particularly holds for the fragment size ranges below 98.5%. For larger fragments, the AET has stayed the same.

This behavior can be explained by the following argument. The larger the size of the first fragment, the more terms are handled by the first fragment; so, the higher are the chances that at least one of the query terms is contained in the first fragment. But, this also implies that the chances that a switch is needed drop. Conversely, the smaller the first fragment, the system switches more often, to a rather large second fragment; resulting in quite expensive execution costs.

When increasing the number of terms in the first fragment up to approximately 98.5%, the system switches less and less often to the second fragment; and, as the 'data size' of the first fragment is still relatively small, and the second (more 'expensive') fragment is used ever less, the total execution time drops. Up from 98.5%, the first fragment always contains at least one of the query terms. But, from that same point the data size of the first fragment starts to grow faster and faster: causing the AET to rise. Since from the 98.5% point up only the first fragment is used, the quality and performance coincide with the figures obtained at the previous experiments.

As expected, the efficiency of Series IIb is lower than that of the previous experiment, in particular for smaller first fragment ranges. But, the AET is still always 2 times smaller than for the unfragmented case and the quality exceeds, or at least equals (from around the point of 98.5% terms in the first fragment), the levels reached in Series IIa, as we had hoped. The AP never drops below 0.23, and the ARR always stays above 14. Summarizing, the switching procedure does improve the quality, but in more extreme cases also degrades efficiency quite firmly; caused by either switching to an expensive second fragment (sizes smaller than 95%) or always operating on an often too expensive first fragment (up from 99%).

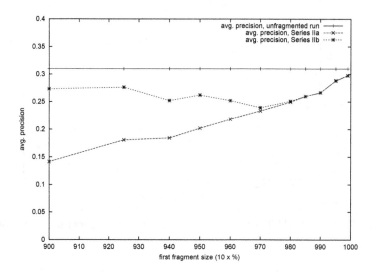

Fig. 8. [Series IIa/b] AP for several relative sizes, one fragment used, preferably the first

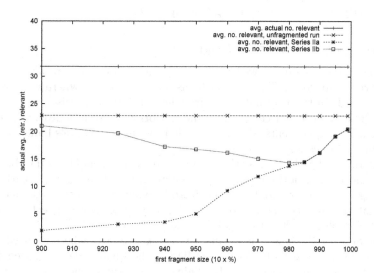

Fig. 9. [Series IIa/b] ARR for several relative sizes, one fragment used, preferably the first

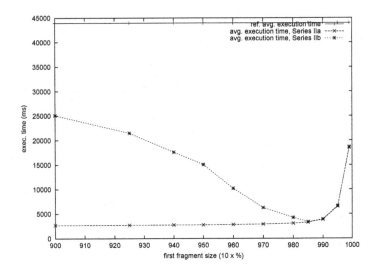

Fig. 10. [Series IIa/b] *AET* for several relative sizes, one fragment used, preferably the first

Concluding Remarks. These series of experiments clearly show the trade-off between speed and quality. They also demonstrated that, while remaining quite competitive quality, the efficiency of the retrieval process can be increased significantly by using this two-fragment approach.

6.3   Series III: Benefits of Fragmenting

In Series I we already showed the quality and performance results of the 'no fancy tricks' approach. These series focus on the situation where we have many equally sized (in terms of data size) fragments (25 to be precise).

In Table 2 we listed the quality and performance results of the Series IIIa, IIIb, and IIIc experiments. We also included the results of Series I and the TREC benchmark values for comparison.

The results for the Series IIIa, where we only fragmented the database in 25 fragments but did nothing else in particular to speed things up, clearly shows that fragmentation by itself does not introduce any extra costs. Also one clearly sees that the quality has not decreased in any way, as we expected, since all information of any relevance has been taken into account.

The Series IIIb shows the results for the experiments where we used normal safe/unsafe top-N cut-off. As we predicted, the quality has degraded for the unsafe top-N technique (but only slightly) and stayed the same for the safe method.

Although we did anticipate on a poor performance gain for the safe method, the drop in performance was rather unexpected. The unsafe method was expected to perform even more better than the safe approach, but also shows disappointing execution times. This performance degrade of course is the opposite of what we intended to happen. A more close review of our log files learned

Table 2. [Series III] Results of experiments with 25 fragments, with and without top-N cut-off (TREC benchmark and Series I results included for comparison)

	AP (%)	ARR	AET (s)
Benchmark	100.0	31.8	-
Series I	31.0	22.9	44.4
Series IIIa	31.0	22.9	44.8
Series IIIb (safe top-N)	31.0	22.9	50.9
Series IIIb (unsafe top-N)	31.0	22.7	51.0
Series IIIc ($l = 0.00$)	30.0	15.1	7.9
Series IIIc ($l = 0.05$)	29.8	15.6	13.5
Series IIIc ($l = 0.10$)	29.7	15.9	18.7
Series IIIc ($l = 0.25$)	30.0	17.6	33.0
Series IIIc ($l = 1.00$)	30.1	22.9	89.1

that the cut-off conditions were too weak, allowing a cut-off in only rare cases. Also the intermediate result restriction technique appeared to suffer from the same weak boundaries resulting in no effective limitation of the computational effort. Due to the extra administrative work needed for the desired but never occurring cut-off this resulted in a performance degrade instead of a performance gain.

However, the reasons for the disappointing results for IIIb also explain the huge performance gain for the IIIc case with low l. For the IIIa (and IIIb) case the computational effort (indeed) appeared to increase for fragments with terms with higher df – e.g. the fragments in the end of the fragment-sequence – due to the Zipfian nature of the data. In case of IIIc the intermediate result restriction did occur with almost no exception, reducing the computational effort per fragment to almost a constant factor. Furthermore, the AP stayed almost the same, while the ARR dropped a bit more. However, the recall still is about 50% in the worst case, which is not really that bad. For the case of $l = 1.00$ the quality indeed equals the values measured for the IIIa case, as expected. However, the performance for this case is very bad, as one can expect of this naive approach to forcefully rank all documents.

6.4   Series IV

Here we describe the measured performance and quality results when we relax the requirements we used to comply with the TREC evaluation standards till now. The (a) variant shows the effects of shorter queries, whereas the (b) series show what happens when a smaller top-N is delivered.

Series IVa: Influence of Query Length. Figures 11, 12, and 13 plot the AP, the ARR, and the AET of Series IVa, respectively, together with the baseline performance of the unfragmented case.

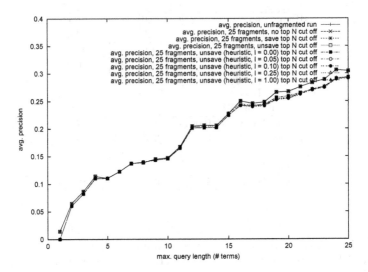

Fig. 11. [Series IVa] *AP* for several max. query lengths, no/safe/unsafe/(heuristic) unsafe top-N cut-off

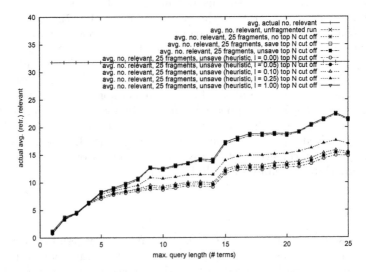

Fig. 12. [Series IVa] *ARR* for several max. query lengths, no/safe/unsafe/(heuristic) unsafe top-N cut-off

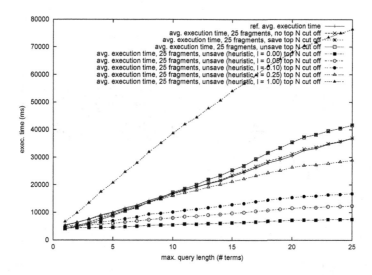

Fig. 13. [Series IVa] *AET* for several max. query lengths, no/unsafe/unsafe/(heuristic) unsafe top-N cut-off

As expected, the smaller the query length the better the performance. And, although not completely compliant with the usual TREC evaluation standards, we also performed the query result quality evaluation, which not surprisingly, shows a degrade for reducing query length. Again, the normal safe and unsafe techniques do not result in a significant performance gain. The heuristic method, in turn, shows very good performance for the lower l values. For $l = 0.00$ the execution times per query only lightly increases for growing query lengths. However, for growing l the performance collapses quickly.

Series IVb: Influence of Top-N Size. Again, we combined all the results of these series into 3 plots, being the Figures 14, 15, and 16.

We expected the performance to increase for decreasing top-N size. This indeed does happen, but it clearly only happens for really small top-N sizes, and then still only in a minimal form, which is less than we hoped for. Apparently the size of the required top-N does not really affect the computational effort that is required. Probably this has to do with the fact that the top-N cut-off did not really work as we expected and that the main performance gain is obtained from reducing the intermediate results/work. This latter observation is supported by the fact that the heuristic unsafe method always results in significantly lower execution times for lower values of l, independent of the size of the top-N. In general, the differences between the results obtained for the used optimization techniques are clearly visible and resemble the figures we already saw for the (a) variant.

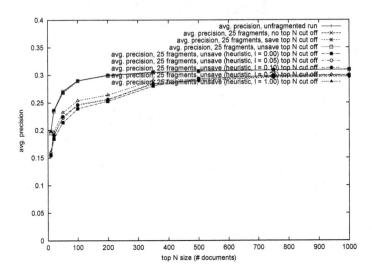

Fig. 14. [Series IVb] AP for several top-N sizes, no/safe/unsafe/(heuristic) unsafe top-N cut-off

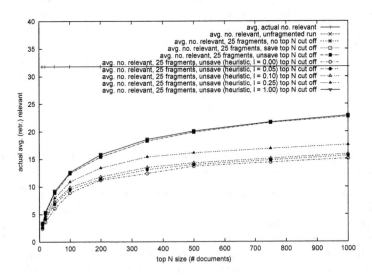

Fig. 15. [Series IVb] ARR for several top-N sizes, no/safe/unsafe/(heuristic) unsafe top-N cut-off

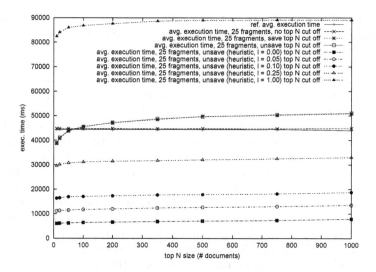

Fig. 16. [Series IVb] AET for several top-N sizes, no/safe/unsafe/(heuristic) unsafe top-N cut-off

Concluding Remarks. The effects we hoped to see for the (a) variant indeed occurred and the heuristic unsafe cut-off technique seems very promising due to its still relatively good quality along with very good performance for low l values. The (b) variant also, in a sense, did show what we expected, but much less significantly than we hoped for. Apparently the size of the top-N is not really an important issue in our case. Future research has to show whether we can improve the top-N cut-off conditions to obtain effective top-N cut-off behavior indeed. Maybe then indeed the size of the top-N will turn out to be of significance.

Fortunately, our heuristic unsafe method does show very interesting performance gain with only minor quality loss.

7   Conclusions and Future Work

This paper presents a convincing case for the suitability of the 'database approach' in the non-standard domain of information retrieval. We first specified the typical IR retrieval process declaratively. This allows the integration of IR techniques in our prototype DBMS, without fixing the physical execution of queries that use these techniques on a predetermined order, which is particularly important for the development of search engines for XML documents, handling queries that refer to a combination of traditional boolean retrieval with retrieval by content.

The experimental validation of our proposed techniques confirm strongly the expected quality versus efficiency trade-off. Series II and III establish the suitability of data fragmentation as an instrument to tailor the physical database design to match the hardware restrictions of the server machines. The final series of experiments demonstrates further evidence in favor of further adaptation of our fragmentation method for top-N optimization techniques.

Summarizing, our results demonstrate convincingly that the smart usage of domain knowledge can significantly improve the retrieval efficiency when operating in a database context. Note that for short queries (i.e. only a couple of terms) the execution times reduce to only a few seconds per query when using our heuristic unsafe top-N cut-off technique. This even outperforms the initial Google of few years ago for uncached short queries [5]. Of course Google then (already) operated on a data collection of about 100 times bigger than the one we used in this paper. Also, such state of the art search engines make use of (query) caching techniques closely related to database optimization techniques like multi query optimization, which we haven't incorporated in our system, yet.

Based on the results of Series II we have already devised a first prototype cost model that seems to predict the execution costs of our fragmented query evaluation approach very accurately (also see [1]). We eventually plan to use this model to optimize the allocation of fragments on a shared nothing parallel system. Next to that we plan to incorporate the cost model in the (physical)optimizer under the logical level of our system (i.e. Moa). This will allow the optimization of the IR part to blend in with the rest of the optimizer, due to the transparent nature of our approach. To evaluate the efficiency gain and opportunities for scalability of this cost based optimizer we are setting up a database with a data collection that is a 100 times larger than the one we used to perform the experiments presented in this paper. We plan to exploit the parallel processing features of our physical (Monet) and logical (Moa) layers to cope with this dataset using a cluster of PCs similar to the one we described in Section 6. Our ultimate goal is to demonstrate that our fragmentation approach indeed does allow seamless integration of multi media information retrieval technology in a DBMS in an efficient, scalable, and flexible manner.

Finally we want to point out that a dedicated IR system most likely always will outperform the best database solution but will lack its flexibility, scalability, and general efficiency. This holds in particular when dealing with both structured and unstructured (like text content) data. Our goal is to find a database solution that at least shows acceptable performance for the unstructured part. We see the results presented in this paper are a first step in the right direction.

References

1. H.E. Blok, S. Choenni, H.M. Blanken, and P.M.G. Apers. A selectivity model for fragmented relations in information retrieval. CTIT Technical Report Series 01-02, CTIT, Enschede, The Netherlands, feb 2001.
2. Peter A. Boncz and Martin L. Kersten. MIL Primitives For Querying A Fragmented World. *VLDB Journal*, 8(2), oct 1999.
3. Peter A. Boncz, Stefan Manegold, and Martin Kersten. Database Architecture Optimized for the new Bottleneck: Memory Access. In Malcolm P. Atkinson, Maria E. Orlowska, Patrick Valduriez, Stanley B. Zdonik, and Michael L. Brodie, editors, *Proceedings of the 25th VLDB Conference*. VLDB, Morgan Kaufmann, sep 1999.

4. Peter A. Boncz, Annita N. Wilschut, and Martin L. Kersten. Flattening an Object Algebra to Provide Performance. In *Proceedings of the 14th International Conference on Data Engineering (ICDE'98)*, IEEE Transactions on Knowledge and Data Engineering. IEEE Computer Society, feb 1998.
5. Sergey Brin and Lawrence Page. The Anatomy of a Large-Scale Hypertextual Web Search Engine. In *Proceedings of the Seventh International World Wide Web Conference (WWW7)*. WWW7 Consortium, apr 1998.
6. Eric W. Brown. Execution Performance Issues in Full-Text Information Retrieval. Ph.D. Thesis/Technical Report 95-81, University of Massachusetts, Amherst, okt 1995.
7. J.P. Callan, W.B. Croft, and S.M. Harding. The INQUERY Retrieval System. In A. Min Tjoa and Isidro Ramos, editors, *3rd International Conference on Database and Expert Systems Applications (DEXA'92)*, pages 78–83, 1992.
8. Douglass R. Cutting and Jan O. Pedersen. Space Optimizations for Total Ranking. In *Proceedings of RAIO'97, Computer-Assisted Information Searching on Internet*, pages 401–412, jun 1997.
9. A.P. de Vries. *Content and multimedia database management systems*. PhD thesis, University of Twente, Enschede, The Netherlands, December 1999.
10. A.P. de Vries, M.G.L.M. van Doorn, H.M. Blanken, and P.M.G. Apers. The Mirror MMDBMS architecture. In *Proceedings of 25th International Conference on Very Large Databases (VLDB '99)*, pages 758–761, Edinburgh, Scotland, UK, September 1999. Technical demo.
11. A.P. de Vries and A.N. Wilschut. On the integration of IR and databases. In *Database issues in multimedia; short paper proceedings, international conference on database semantics (DS-8)*, pages 16–31, Rotorua, New Zealand, January 1999.
12. Ronald Fagin. Fuzzy Queries in Multimedia Database Systems. In *Proceedings of the 1998 ACM SIGMOD International Conference on Principles of Database Systems (PODS'98)*, pages 1–10. ACM Press, 1998.
13. Ronald Fagin. Combining fuzzy information from multiple systems. *Journal on Computer and System Sciences*, 58(1):83–99, feb 1999. Special issue for selected papers from the 1996 ACM SIGMOD PODS Conference.
14. Ronald Fagin and Yoëlle S. Maarek. Allowing users to weight search terms. Retrieved from authors website.
15. David A. Grossman and Ophir Frieder. *Information retrieval: algorithms and heuristics*. The Kluwer international series in engineering and computer science. Kluwer Academic, Boston, 1998.
16. D. Hiemstra and W. Kraaij. Twenty-One at TREC-7: Ad-hoc and cross-language track. In Voorhees and Harman [18].
17. C.J. van Rijsbergen. *Information Retrieval*. Butterworths, London, 2nd. edition, 1979.
18. E.M. Voorhees and D.K. Harman, editors. *Proceedings of the Seventh Text Retrieval Conference (TREC-7)*, NIST Special publications, Gaithersburg, Maryland, nov 1999.
19. A.P. de Vries and D. Hiemstra. The Mirror DBMS at TREC. In Voorhees and Harman [18], pages 725–734.
20. G.K. Zipf. *Human Behavior and the Principle of Least Effort*. Addison-Wesley, Reading, MA, USA, 1949.

Limiting Result Cardinalities for Multidatabase Queries Using Histograms*

Kai-Uwe Sattler[1], Oliver Dunemann[1], Ingolf Geist[1],
Gunter Saake[1], and Stefan Conrad[2]

[1] Department of Computer Science, University of Magdeburg
P.O. Box 4120, D-39016 Magdeburg, Germany
fusion@cs.uni-magdeburg.de
[2] Department of Computer Science, University of Munich
Oettingenstr. 67, D-80538 München, Germany
conrad@dbs.informatik.uni-muenchen.de

Abstract. Integrating, cleaning and analyzing data from heterogeneous sources is often complicated by the large amounts of data and its physical distribution which can result in poor query response time. One approach to speed up the processing is to reduce the cardinality of results – either by querying only the first tuples or by obtaining a sample for further processing. In this paper we address the processing of such queries in a multidatabase environment. We discuss implementations of the query operators, strategies for their placement in a query plan and particularly the usage of histograms for estimating attribute value distributions and result cardinalities in order to parameterize the operators.

Keywords: Result Cardinality, Histograms, Multidatabase, Optimization

1 Introduction

In a large number of application areas integration of data from heterogeneous sources is required, e.g., for building federated information systems or data warehouses. Besides integration of data there is often also a need for cleaning and analyzing the data in order to obtain qualitatively appropriate results.

By means of multidatabase languages (for instance MSQL [GLRS93], SchemaSQL [LSS96], FRAQL [SCS00]) we have the tools at hand which are needed for querying across diverse data sources. Querying using multiple data sources usually produces complete result sets. This requires processing large amounts of data and, thus, results in very poor query response time taking the physical distribution of the data into account.

In data analysis applications such as OLAP, data mining or information fusion we often want to get the 'first' results quickly, e.g., in order to find interesting regions in data or to parameterize the methods and tools. Another example is

---

* Research was supported by the grant FOR 345/1 from the DFG.

B. Read (Ed.): BNCOD 2001, LNCS 2097, pp. 152–167, 2001.

the case of identifying conflicting values for semantically related attributes stored in different databases. In this case, one does not want to obtain all conflicting pairs of values because there might be too many of them for manual inspection. Instead, a certain number of conflicting pairs given as examples can help to understand the basic problem (e.g. different scaling of values in the different data sources). Then, adding a corresponding conflict reconciliation function to the multidatabase query used for detecting this conflict should show whether there are no further conflicts (i.e., the reconciliation function is working for all data) or whether we have to modify the reconciliation function in order to capture more conflicts.

Thus, if multidatabase features are combined with techniques for reducing query response time by limiting result cardinalities, more explorative and interactive data integration and analysis will be possible. Unfortunately, all multidatabase languages so far proposed do not allow requests for a specified number of resulting tuples as examples instead of the complete result set. Therefore, we are seeking suitable extensions of multidatabase languages leading to efficient retrieval of example data. In this paper we will explore two ways of getting such example data:

1. asking for the *first* n results of an integrating multidatabase query and
2. asking for a *sample* containing n tuples of the complete result (or for a certain percentage of resulting tuples).

These two possibilities have already been considered in other contexts. For instance asking for the first n (or the best n) results is typical for information retrieval. Much of the work regarding this subject proposes optimization for evaluating such queries (cf. e.g. [CK97,TGO99]). In contrast to these approaches we have to deal with the problem that in a multidatabase environment there are usually legacy systems acting as local data sources.

These local systems may have their own query processing and optimization engine (in particular, if they are database management systems). If such a system offers the possibility to retrieve the first n tuples or a sample of a result, we obviously should try to use this possibility instead of transferring the complete result set for a query to the multidatabase system and computing the first n tuples or the sample there.

Another aspect that we give detailed consideration to in this paper is the case that statistical data (histograms) about the data stored in a local source is available and can be accessed by the multidatabase system. In this case we develop a global query optimization taking this meta-data into account – focusing on the processing of 'first n' and 'sample' queries.

Our work is based on the object-relational multidatabase language FRAQL which in particular allows the dynamic addition of user-defined conflict reconciliation functions. For this language a query engine has been implemented which is able to access heterogeneous database systems by means of specific database adapters. In our current prototype environment we are using native adapters for Oracle and MySQL and access other data sources via ODBC. So, the main contribution of this paper is the application of histogram-based techniques for optimization and processing of 'first n' and 'sample' queries under the special circumstances of a multidatabase system.

The remainder of this paper is organized as follows. In the next section we briefly present related work. Section 3 gives an overview of basic techniques for limiting result cardinalities and sampling described in the related literature and discusses their suitability in multidatabases. In Section 4 we describe the usage of histograms for estimating query parameters such as intermediate result sizes and attribute value distributions in the FRAQL system, which are essential for optimizing and processing first-n and sample-n queries. Some evaluation results for our approach are presented in Section 5. Finally, we conclude by summarizing the main insights and by pointing out future work.

2   Related Work

Statistical methods have been used in central database systems for twenty years, predominantly in the area of the query optimization and query result size estimation. Recently, strongly associated to data warehouse techniques, several works on this matter investigate how to limit the query results and how to provide approximate answers to user queries. An overview of these data reduction methods is given in [BDF+97]. [CK97,CK98] discuss an approach to restrict the result set by allowing the user to specify the desired result set size. This is accomplished by the SQL extension STOP AFTER. The intermediate results are limited by placing a stop node in the query tree. The authors propose two optimization strategies, namely a conservative and an aggressive. In addition they recommend a restart node in cases in which the original stop node did not produce the desired result size. Several commercial database management systems provide a similar technique to compute the top-n results.

Sampling is another technique for data reduction. The authors of [OR86] describe different kinds of uniform random sampling techniques in a DBMS, because the integration of sampling in a database system can increase the performance of the sample computation. They discuss several techniques for uniform random sampling from base relations or the output of relational operators.

In [CMN99] and [AGPR99] the join sampling problem is pointed out as an example of the problem of commuting the sample operator with relational operators. [AGPR99] uses precomputed join samples, so-called join synopses, to provide approximate answers for join aggregation queries. These synopses are well suited for star or snowflake schemas which are usual in the data warehouse area. This approach is implemented in the AQUA system [AGP99], which works on top of any commercial DBMS and stores its precomputed statistical data in relations within the DBMS. For providing fast approximate answers for user queries, the system rewrites the query using the AQUA relations instead of the base relations and scales the aggregated query in the desired manner.

Using precomputed histograms for determining approximate answers is yet another possibility to reduce the query result size and to achieve short query response times. This technique is among others described in [PGI99]. The authors show that it is possible to execute non-aggregate and aggregate queries using this method. Thereby the queries are executed using the histograms instead of the base relations.

An interactive and iterative way to provide approximate answers for aggregated queries, called online-aggregation, is described in [HHW97]. Here the user starts with a relative imprecise answer provided by a first small random sample of the data. This initial value will be improved during the processing. The user can observe online the value changes and the error bounds in order to decide when the exactness of the answer is sufficient for his needs.

3   Result Cardinality Limitation in Query Processing

As discussed in the previous section there are several approaches to limit the result size of a query in order to improve the response time of query evaluation. In the following we will focus on two approaches which are implemented as part of the multidatabase system FRAQL query processor [SCS00]: LIMIT FIRST and LIMIT SAMPLE. Both are extensions to the standard SQL SELECT statement:

```
SELECT <projection list>
FROM <table expression>
[ WHERE <condition> ]
[ ORDER BY <order spec> ]
LIMIT FIRST|SAMPLE <value expr> [PERCENT]
```

The parameter <value expr> can be any expression which represents a positive integer value including zero. Thus it can be a constant, a functional expression or a sub-query that is not correlated with the main query. If the keyword PERCENT is given, <value expr> denotes the percentage of the desired result size.

3.1   First n Tuples

With LIMIT FIRST at most <value expr> tuples are retrieved from the result set, if they exist. Please note that grouping and ordering have higher priority than cardinality reduction, so these operations are performed before any kind of limitation. Conversely, projection as well as aggregations have lower priority, i.e., the query

```
SELECT avg(balance)
FROM Accounts
ORDER BY balance
LIMIT FIRST 10 PERCENT
```

computes the average of the top 10% of the account balances.

Obviously, the cardinality limitation could be performed on top of the database engine in the application by closing the database cursor when the limit is reached. However, the performance benefits would be rather low. Thus, a special query operator is required which can be placed in the query execution plan and 'cuts' the tuple stream after the desired cardinality. Following the operator introduced in [CK97], we added an operator *stop* to our query engine, which implements the iterator model [Gra93] and passes a given number of tuples from the input stream. At physical level the stop operator has several implementations: a simple pipelined scan-stop operation for unordered limitations and a blocking sort-stop operation, that collects the top or bottom n tuples from the input stream in a sorted heap and produces the result set after processing the whole input.

In order to minimize the costs for query execution the stop operator should placed low in the operator graph. In [CK97] two placement strategies are discussed. With the conservative policy, the stop operator is inserted at a point in the query plan where no tuple is discarded that might be part of the final result. Let Op_i be an operator of a plan $P = Op_1 Op_2 \ldots Op_{i-1} Op_i \ldots Op_r$ with Op_r as root operator and card(Op) the cardinality of the result produced by Op, then Op_i is *cardinality-preserving* if the following condition holds:

$$\text{card}(Op_i) \geq \text{card}(Op_{i-1})$$

The aggressive approach tries to place the stop operator earlier in the plan, i.e., even where it could provide a cardinality reduction. This requires estimating the stop cardinality by using database statistics as well as a restart operator which ensures that the desired number of tuples is produced even if the estimated stop cardinality was too low. In this case, the sub-query below the restart operator has to recompute the missing tuples.

The scenario which we support with our FRAQL system contains some special characteristics. At first, we operate in a multidatabase environment, i.e., parts of the query are performed by the local component databases which are often full-fledged DBMS. Thus, we want to exploit the ability of the sources to limit the result cardinality in order to reduce the communication costs and the query evaluation effort at global level. Restarting a query could be very expensive, so a safe estimation of the cardinality limit is needed. The second specialty of our scenario is a relaxed requirement regarding the exactness of the cardinality limitation. For supporting explorative data analysis tasks it is more important to get results meeting a given criterion very quickly. In addition, if a percental limit was specified, a small discrepancy is often tolerable. Thus, we embark on a strategy for placing the stop operator in the query plan, which is enforced by the following rules:

1. The main goal is to insert stop operators as deep as possible in the query execution tree according to the query's semantics and the capabilities of the component databases.
2. A *safe placement* is possible if the subsequent operators are cardinality-preserving and contain no sorting (cf. the conservative policy mentioned above). In this case the limit parameter need not be modified.
3. If the query contains a sort operator which cannot be performed by the component databases, this operator is replaced by a sort-stop operator.

4. If the remaining operators are not cardinality-preserving an *unsafe placement* can be performed, i.e. the limit parameter has to be recomputed.
5. For unsafe placement an additional stop operator has to be inserted near the root of the global plan respecting the higher priority of grouping operators.
6. For a join operation the stop operator is inserted only in one of the branches, either according to the safe placement policy, i.e., in the branch, for which the join predicate is cardinality-preserving, or – if no advantage can be taken from referential integrity constraints – in an unsafe manner by choosing the branch where it effects the largest decrease of costs.

A plan for a query containing a LIMIT FIRST clause is constructed as follows: after substituting global view definitions, performing the usual transformations (e.g., standardization, simplification [JK84]) and decomposing the query into sub-queries processable by the sources, the optimizer seeks to insert a stop operator according to the rules given above at the root of the sub-query. If the global remaining operations are not cardinality-preserving, the limit parameter has to be adjusted by estimating the cardinality of the sub-query, which is computed from the selectivity of the operations and the histograms of the base relations as well as the intermediate results. Let $card(P_{all})$ be the estimated result size without limitations and n the limit specified in the LIMIT FIRST query. So, the proper cardinality limit for the stop operator above operator Op_i is as follows:

$$L_{stop} = \frac{card(Op_i) * n}{card(P_{all})} \qquad (1)$$

An additional stop operator is placed at the root of the global plan just to ensure that not too many tuples are produced. In case of a LIMIT FIRST ... PERCENT clause the unlimited result size is estimated from the histograms and the percentage needed for parameterizing the stop operator is computed.

3.2   Random Sampling

By using the notation LIMIT SAMPLE <value expr> [PERCENT] the system generates a simple uniform sample of size n of the query result. An efficient computation requires a sample operator, as described in [OR86], being applied as low as possible in the query plan.

As we are in a multi database environment, there are several constraints, which have to be considered. Our system uses virtual integrated relations, so there are no indexes or complete statistics available. Furthermore an efficient random access is not possible. But on the other hand, the different sources can have different features, which have to be exploited. The histogram capabilities of the FRAQL system have to be taken into account for optimizing sampling queries.

Because of missing random access to the data, sequential sampling algorithms have to be utilized. There are two types of scenarios: known and unknown relation sizes. In the first case, algorithms as described in [Vit87] can be used, which have the advantage of not blocking. In the second case sampling with reservoir

[Li94] is necessary. These algorithms do not need the relation size, but provide the first tuples only after the complete scan of the relation.

After the description of our environment and constraints, we now want to show which approaches can be adapted to our scenario. The crucial point is sampling of join and union operations.

Several approaches of random join sampling exists in literature. The objective of such strategies is to push down the sampling operator on one side of the operator tree since it is not possible to use sampling on both relations [CMN99]. Possible strategies are:

- *Naive sampling* includes a first complete computation of the join of R and T followed by the application of the sample operator.
- The second strategy is proposed in [OR86] and includes the following steps. Consider the computation of a join of R and T. First sample uniform randomly one tuple from R and join it with T and getting the result V. Select randomly one tuple from V and accept it with the probability proportional to the cardinality of V. These steps are repeated until the required sample size n is obtained.
- In [CMN99] further join sample strategies were proposed, which only require statistics or partial statistics on one relation. *Group-sample* is one strategy of these and consists of following steps for the join of the relations R and T:
  1. First produce a weighted WR-sample of relation R of the size n. The weight $\omega(t)$ for a tuple t is the number of distinct tuple with value v in join attribute $t.A$. This sample is denoted by S_1.
  2. Join S_1 with T and group the join after the tuples of S_1. The result is S_2.
  3. The last step consists of picking out one tuple from each group of S_2 using a unweighted random sample algorithm.

With the above constraints, the sampling approach according to [OR86] cannot be applied in our environment because it requires an index as well as full statistics. However, the naive sampling algorithm or group-sample is possible. To support the latter strategy the FRAQL system supports a histogram scheme, the application of which is described in section 4.

There are different approaches to obtain samples of the union operation. These techniques require indexes and statistics and from there a materialization. So they cannot be used in our scenario.

4   Using Histograms

In relational database systems, information about cardinalities of the relations and the distributions of attribute values is essential for calculating the costs of query execution plans. Thus, modern systems maintain statistical information mostly in the form of histograms which are particularly well suited to the representation of approximations of non-parametric distributions. Using this information the query optimizer is capable of estimating selectivities of operators and cardinalities of result sets. A histogram consists of a set of buckets representing a subset of values of an attribute. Each bucket contains the number of tuples having the value associated with the bucket. In the following we denote the number of buckets as B and the number of tuples in the i-th bucket as $bucket(i)$ for $i = 1 \ldots B$.

There are various classes of histograms used in database systems nowadays. In *equi-width histograms* the size of the range of values in each bucket is the same, whereas in *equi-height histograms* the frequencies of the attribute values contained in each bucket are equal. Typically, equi-height histograms are used in database systems because of the lower worst case error [PSC84]. In [IP95] serial and end-biased histograms are proposed as optimal solution in many cases, but they are currently not very common. However, using histograms in a heterogeneous database environment entails several difficulties:

- the representation of histograms in system catalogs differs for the various available database systems,
- the availability and efficient access to histograms are crucial factors for processing global queries,
- there are data sources which do not maintain histograms or for which histograms cannot be calculated due to limited query capabilities.

Thus, for our FRAQL system we have chosen an approach for histogram maintenance where histograms of global visible relations, i.e., the integrated relations, are kept in the global layer of the multidatabase. When a relation is 'imported' from a source, i.e., a global virtual view is defined in FRAQL on this relation, the histograms for these relations are retrieved. The adapters for the individual database systems participating on the multidatabase are responsible for a uniform access to the system-specific histograms. So, each adapter provides a method for obtaining a histogram which can be implemented in one of the following ways:

- get the histogram directly from the database catalog of the source,
- trigger the computation of the histogram in the source (e.g., 'compute statistics' in Oracle),
- compute the histogram in the adapter itself,
- construct a trivial histogram representing an equipartition if neither a histogram is available nor can it be computed.

Obviously, caching histograms in the federation layer is a compromise between efficient access as well as availability and the actuality of statistics on data. However, for our intended application scenario – data analysis in heterogeneous databases – this approach seems to be practical.

In the following subsection we describe the usage of histograms for supporting result cardinality limitation techniques introduced in Section 3. In particular we discuss the calculation of estimations for intermediate result cardinalities and distributions as implemented in the FRAQL query processor.

4.1   Using Histograms for Estimating Stop Cardinalities

In Section 3 we have identified cardinality estimation as an important task for parameterizing the stop operator, if only an unsafe placement is possible. For this purpose histograms are very helpful. Based on histograms of the base relations, the distribution and cardinality of the intermediate results after applying the particular operators of the query plan can be estimated by the global query optimizer. Finally, the limit parameter for the stop operator can be derived according to equation (1). This approach is implemented in FRAQL system by means of the following three steps:

1. Traversing the operator tree top-down, all attributes are determined for which histograms are needed, i.e., attributes referenced in expressions of join or selection conditions for example.
2. For each operator node the attribute value distribution in form of the histogram, the cardinality of the result set as well as the selectivity of the operator are calculated. This is performed bottom-up for all attributes identified in Step 1.
3. The limit parameter for the stop operator is calculated using equation (1).

Fig. 1 illustrates these steps for the operator tree of the query:

```
SELECT *
FROM customers c, insurances i, accounts a
WHERE c.cust_id = i.cust_id AND
      c.cust_id = a.account_no AND
      a.balance > 6000
LIMIT FIRST 10 PERCENT;
```

Assuming that coincided histograms are available for the attributes c.cust_id and i.cust_id (denoted as $hist_1(cust\_id)$ and $hist_2(cust\_id)$) of the base relations the buckets of the histogram $hist_5(cust\_id)$ for the join $c \bowtie i$ can be calculated using the following formula [SS94]:

$$\forall j = 1 \ldots B : bucket_{c\bowtie i}(j) = \frac{bucket_c(j) * bucket_i(j)}{\max(d_c, d_i)}$$

Here, d_c and d_i are the numbers of distinct values present in the join column from c or i respectively. If the histograms do not coincide a preceding normalization step has to be performed.

For the selection operator on relation accounts the histogram can only be derived indirectly by calculating the selectivity of the operator. According to the formulas presented in [PSC84] we can estimate the selectivity sel for the expression balance > 6000. Let $sel_{\theta c}$ be the estimated selectivity of comparison $attr \ \theta \ c$ for $\theta = \{<, >, \leq, \geq, =\}$. Since

$$sel_{>c} = 1 - sel_{\leq c} \quad \text{and}$$
$$sel_{\leq c} = sel_{<c} + sel_{=c}$$

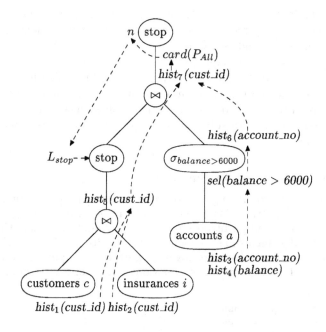

Fig. 1. Histogram estimation for a LIMIT FIRST-query

we have only to estimate $sel_{<c}$ and $sel_{=c}$. In [PSC84] the following formulas are given for the case where the value c is in the k-th bucket:

$$sel_{<c} = \frac{k - 1 + 1/3}{B + 1}$$

$$sel_{=c} = \frac{1/3}{B + 1}$$

Based on these formulas the selectivity of the expression can be computed using the histogram of a.balance. This value is used to adjust the histogram for a.account_no (denoted as $hist_6(account\_no)$) by reducing the height of each bucket assuming independence of the attributes:

$$\forall j = 1 \ldots B : bucket(j) \leftarrow bucket(j) * sel_{>6000}$$

Next, the histogram $hist_7(cust\_id)$ for $(c \bowtie i) \bowtie a$ is calculated as shown above, whereas the stop operator is ignored for the moment. The cardinality of the final result set at the root of the operator tree is equal to the sum of the heights of all buckets of this histogram:

$$card = \sum_{j=1}^{B} bucket(j)$$

Finally, the limit parameter for the stop operator is calculated. This requires firstly estimating the percentage of the cardinality of the whole relation. This value then can be inserted as parameter n in equation (1).

A special treatment is required for histograms of relations containing attributes which are transformed by applying so-called mapping functions [SCS00] as part of the view definition. Because the mapping is implemented as a special query operator in the query plan the involved histogram also has to be mapped. A straightforward solution is to apply the mapping function to each bucket boundary value.

4.2   Using Histograms for Sampling

In this section the use of histograms to support the sample operation is discussed. As shown in section 3 there is a need to apply a weighted sampling algorithm to overcome data skew and problems with join sampling. Calculating these weights requires knowledge regarding frequencies of the distinct values which can be provided by histograms. The following example query computes a random sample of size 1,000 of the join between the relations `customers` and `insurances`.

```
SELECT *
FROM customers c, insurances i
WHERE c.cust_id = i.cust_id
LIMIT SAMPLE 1000
```

In order to improve the performance the sample operator has to be moved towards the leaves in the operator tree. One strategy, the group sample mentioned above, is introduced in [CMN99]. Figure 2 shows how we support this strategy with histograms.

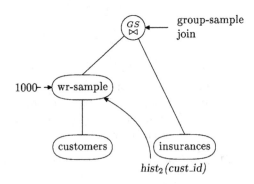

Fig. 2. Histogram estimation for a `LIMIT SAMPLE`-query

We want to sample the join of `customers` and `insurances` on the attribute `cust_id`. According to the group-sample strategy we therefore need frequency information about the distinct values of cust_id in relation insurances as provided by a histogram. A weight $w(t)$ of a tuple t of the relation c is calculated as follows:

$$w(t) = card(P_{all}) * sel_{=t.cust\_id}(i).$$

The expression $sel_{=t.cust\_id}(i)$ denotes the selectivity of the value in relation insurances and is computed by the statistical data in the histogram for the column insurances.cust_id. So the first step of the group-sample strategy is accomplished. The second step is performed in the group-sample-join operator, whose output is a sample of the join of the relations customers and insurances.

5 Evaluation

The main focus of the following empirical evaluation is not on the possible performance gains, because these depend strongly on the characteristics of the involved data sources. Instead, we evaluate the quality of estimations and results, which rely on statistical information contained in histograms as previously described. For this purpose the following schema is used:
db#1: customers (cust_id, income)
        insurances (insurance_id, cust_id)
db#2: accounts (account_id, account_no, balance)
Database db#1 consists of two relations customers and insurances. It stores information about 250,000 customers, each one having one, two or no insurances with the average of one. No special distribution describes the attribute cust_id, but there is a foreign key constraint from insurances to customers. The second database db#2 to be integrated to a global view consists of a table of about 325,000 accounts. The attribute account_no matches to customers.cust_id and for about 57% of all customers at least one account can be found. The balances are normally distributed with a mean of 10,000 and a standard deviation of 5,000. For all involved attributes equi-height histograms consisting of 10 buckets are calculated.

The example query executed on this constellation leads to the access plan shown in table 1. Here, x in step 7 stands for the requested cardinality in percent. Because in the average case there exists one insurance per customer, the cardinality of the index scan in step 2 is approximately the same as the number of tuples in customers. The limit L_{sub} for the subplan depends on the choice of the percentage of data sets to be retrieved. It is calculated with support of the histogram. To verify, whether this calculation step leads to a correct limitation, the desired and the actual generated result sizes for estimated L_{sub}, computed as illustrated in section 4.1, are compared in Fig. 3(a). The number of tuples of the exact calculated percentage is compared with the number of tuples retrieved using the estimation techniques in Fig. 3(b). It can be seen that the histogram supported estimation leads to a result size which is near to the requested cardinality. The difference increases with higher limit values. For the considered query, the number of retrieved tuples is underestimated in all cases, so that at least the desired cardinality is provided.

Table 1. Access plan: verification of cardinality estimation

Step (i)	Operator(Op_i)	Cardinality($card(Op_i)$)
7	Select	$\approx L = card(P_{all}) \cdot \frac{x}{100}$
6	Join results from Step 4 and 5	see section 4.1
5	Table access [accounts]	$card(\texttt{accounts})$
4	Stop L_{sub}	$\leq L_{sub}$
3	Join [customers] and [insurances] using index on [insurances]	$\approx card(\texttt{customers})$
2	Unique index range scan [Primary key of insurances]	$\approx card(\texttt{customers})$ $\approx card(\texttt{insurances})$
1	Table access [customers]	$card(\texttt{customers})$

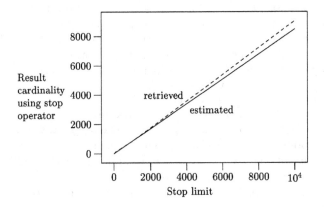

(a) Comparison between estimated and retrieved size

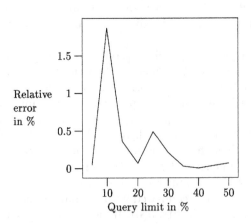

(b) Relative estimation error

Fig. 3. Evaluation results

The quality of the sample operation is verified by testing, whether the existing data distributions are maintained or not. For this test a sample of 1,000 tuples of the joined relations customers and insurances is generated. The access plan is shown in table 2. The methodology of at first generating a weighted sample and applying the modified join operation on the result is described in detail in [CMN99] as stream-sample strategy. The attribute income is in the base

Table 2. Access plan: verification of maintaining of distribution

Step (i)	Operator(Op_i)
5	Select
4	Join
3	Weighted sample with replacement of [customers] Weights are frequencies from Step 2
2	Histogram access (frequency of cust_id [insurances]
1	Table access [customers]

relation [customers] approximately normally distributed with a mean of 5,000 and a standard deviation of 1,000. Using a goodness-of-fit χ^2 statistic we test the hypothesis that this distribution is maintained by the join operation on a sample of $n_1 = 100$ and $n_2 = 1000$ tuples. Let the level of significance be $\alpha = 0.05$ and the test intervals $A_1 = (-\infty; 1000], A_2 = (1000; 2000); \cdots ; A_{10} = (9000; \infty]$. Further, let $freq_j$ be the observed frequency of a value of the sample in interval j and p_j the theoretical expected count. Then, the value of the test function

$$v = \frac{1}{n} \cdot \sum_{j=1}^{10} \frac{freq_j^2}{p_j} - n \qquad (2)$$

calculates to 8.69 in the case of the sample size n_1 and to 6.31 in the case of 1000 data sets to be retrieved. Because the value of the $x_{1-\alpha}$ fractile of the distribution $\chi^2(k-1) = \chi^2(9) = 16.92$ is larger than these values, we cannot reject the hypothesis that the original distribution is maintained. Consequently, sampling constitutes an adequate way to reduce the data for analysis purposes.

References

[AGP99]   S. Acharya, P.B. Gibbons, and V. Poosala. Aqua: A Fast Decision Support Systems Using Approximate Query Answers. In M.P. Atkinson, M.E. Orlowska, P. Valduriez, S.B. Zdonik, and M.L. Brodie, editors, *VLDB'99, Proceedings of 25th International Conference on Very Large Data Bases, September 7-10, 1999, Edinburgh, Scotland, UK*, pages 754–757. Morgan Kaufmann, 1999.

[AGPR99]   S. Acharya, P.B. Gibbons, V. Poosala, and S. Ramaswamy. Join Synopses
           for Approximate Query Answering. In A. Delis, C. Faloutsos, and S. Ghan-
           deharizadeh, editors, *SIGMOD 1999, Proceedings ACM SIGMOD Interna-
           tional Conference on Management of Data, June 1-3, 1999, Philadephia,
           Pennsylvania, USA*, pages 275–286. ACM Press, 1999.

[BDF+97]   D. Barbará, W. DuMouchel, C. Faloutsos, P.J. Haas, J.M. Hellerstein, Y.E.
           Ioannidis, H.V. Jagadish, T. Johnson, R.T. Ng, V. Poosala, K.A. Ross, and
           K.C. Sevcik. The New Jersey Data Reduction Report. *Data Engineering
           Bulletin*, 20(4):3–45, 1997.

[CK97]   M.J. Carey and D. Kossmann. On Saying "Enough Already!" in SQL. In
           J. Peckham, editor, *SIGMOD 1997, Proceedings of Annual Meeting, May
           13-15, 1997, Tucson, Arizona, USA*, pages 219–230. ACM Press, 1997.

[CK98]   M.J. Carey and D. Kossmann. Reducing the Braking Distance of an SQL
           Query Engine. In A. Gupta, O. Shmueli, and J. Widom, editors, *VLDB'98,
           August 24-27, 1998, New York City, New York, USA*, pages 158–169. Mor-
           gan Kaufmann, 1998.

[CMN99]   S. Chaudhuri, R. Motwani, and V.R. Narasayya. On Random Sampling
           over Joins. In A. Delis, C. Faloutsos, and S. Ghandeharizadeh, editors,
           *SIGMOD 1999, Proceedings ACM SIGMOD International Conference on
           Management of Data, June 1-3, 1999, Philadephia, Pennsylvania, USA*,
           pages 263–274. ACM Press, 1999.

[GLRS93]   J. Grant, W. Litwin, N. Roussopoulos, and T. Sellis. Query Languages for
           Relational Multidatabases. *The VLDB Journal*, 2(2):153–171, April 1993.

[Gra93]   G. Graefe. Query Evaluation Techniques For Large Databases. *ACM
           Computing Surveys*, 25(2):73–170, 1993.

[HHW97]   J.M. Hellerstein, P.J. Haas, and H. Wang. Online Aggregation. In J. Peck-
           ham, editor, *SIGMOD 1997, Proceedings ACM SIGMOD International
           Conference on Management of Data, May 13-15, 1997, Tucson, Arizona,
           USA*, pages 171–182. ACM Press, 1997.

[IP95]   Y.E. Ioannidis and V. Poosala. Balancing Histogram Optimality and Prac-
           ticality for Query Result Size Estimation. In M.J. Carey and D.A. Schnei-
           der, editors, *ACM SIGMOD '95, Proceedings of Annual Meeting, San Jose,
           California, May 22-25, 1995*, pages 233–244. ACM Press, 1995.

[JK84]   M. Jarke and J. Koch. Query Optimization in Database Systems. *ACM
           Computing Surveys*, 16(2):111–152, 1984.

[Li94]   K.-H. Li. Reservoir-sampling algorithms of time complexity $O(n(1 +
           \log(N/n)))$. *ACM Transactions on Mathematical Software*, 20(4):481–493,
           December 1994.

[LSS96]   L. V. S. Lakshmanan, F. Sadri, and I. N. Subramanian. SchemaSQL - A
           Language for Interoperability in Relational Multi-database Systems. In
           T. M. Vijayaraman, A. P. Buchmann, C. Mohan, and N. L. Sarda, editors,
           *Proc. of the 22nd Int. Conf. on Very Large Data Bases, VLDB'96, Bom-
           bay, India, September 3-6, 1996*, pages 239–250, San Francisco, CA, 1996.
           Morgan Kaufmann Publishers.

[OR86]   F. Olken and D. Rotem. Simple Random Sampling from Relational
           Databases. In W.W. Chu, G. Gardarin, S. Ohsuga, and Y. Kambayashi,
           editors, *VLDB'86 Twelfth International Conference on Very Large Data
           Bases, August 25-28, 1986, Kyoto, Japan, Proceedings*, pages 160–169. Mor-
           gan Kaufmann, 1986.

[PGI99]   V. Poosala, V. Ganti, and Y.E. Ioannidis. Approximate Query Answering
           using Histograms. *IEEE Data Engineering Bulletin*, 22(4):5–14, 1999.

[PSC84]   G. Piatetsky-Shapiro and C. Connell. Accurate Estimation of the Number of Tuples Satisfying a Condition. In B. Yormark, editor, *SIGMOD'84, Proceedings of Annual Meeting, Boston, Massachusetts, June 18-21, 1984*, pages 256–276. ACM Press, 1984.

[SCS00]   K. Sattler, S. Conrad, and G. Saake. Adding Conflict Resolution Features to a Query Language for Database Federations. In M. Roantree, W. Hasselbring, and S. Conrad, editors, *Proc. 3nd Int. Workshop on Engineering Federated Information Systems, EFIS'00, Dublin, Ireland, June*, pages 41–52, Berlin, 2000. Akadem. Verlagsgesellschaft.

[SS94]   A.N. Swami and K.B. Schiefer. On the Estimation of Join Result Sizes. In M. Jarke, J.A. Bubenko Jr., and K.G. Jeffery, editors, *Advances in Database Technology - EDBT'94. 4th International Conference on Extending Database Technology, Cambridge, United Kingdom, March 28-31, 1994, Proceedings*, volume 779 of *Lecture Notes in Computer Science*, pages 287–300. Springer, 1994.

[TGO99]   K.-L. Tan, C. H. Goh, and B. C. Ooi. On Getting Some Answers Quickly, and Perhaps More Later. In *Proceedings of the 15th International Conference on Data Engineering, 23-26 March 1999, Sydney, Austrialia*, pages 32–39. IEEE Computer Society, 1999.

[Vit87]   J.S. Vitter. An Efficient Algorithm for Sequential Random Sampling. *ACM Transactions on Mathematical Software*, 13(1):58–67, March 1987.

Memory Aware Query Routing in Interactive Web-Based Information Systems

Florian Waas[1] and Martin L. Kersten[2]

[1] Microsoft Corp., One Microsoft Way, Redmond, WA 98052, USA, flw@mx4.org
[2] CWI, Kruislaan 413, 1098 SJ Amsterdam, The Netherlands, mk@cwi.nl

Abstract. Query throughput is one of the primary optimization goals in interactive web-based information systems in order to achieve the performance necessary to serve large user communities. Queries in this application domain differ significantly from those in traditional database applications: they are of lower complexity and almost exclusively read-only. The architecture we propose here is specifically tailored to take advantage of the query characteristics. It is based on a large parallel shared-nothing database cluster where each node runs a separate server with a fully replicated copy of the database. A query is assigned and entirely executed on one single node avoiding network contention or synchronization effects. However, the actual key to enhanced throughput is a resource efficient scheduling of the arriving queries. We develop a simple and robust scheduling scheme that takes the currently memory resident data at each server into account and trades off memory re-use and execution time, reordering queries as necessary.
Our experimental evaluation demonstrates the effectiveness when scaling the system beyond hundreds of nodes showing super-linear speedup.

1 Introduction

A significant number of web-based information systems rely on database technology to serve large user communities which makes scalability a key issue for the design of web-enabled database systems. Parallel processing and data replication, are necessary to deal with the peak loads encountered. Likewise, an effective query dispatching scheme is needed to level the system load as well as to guarantee quality-of-service in terms of response time.

In this paper we are concerned with initial experiences with a multi-media portal under construction based on the Monet database system [BK99]. The system is intended to provide efficient access to a large collection of indexed multi-media objects. It is endemic to this kind of information system that user interaction is dominated by read accesses. A number of systems with similar requirements regarding the deployed database backend have been developed and many more are currently under construction.

With each user interaction, the interface emits a number of queries to the database that ideally lead to an answer set of a few tens of candidate results. Involving accesses to different multi-dimensional indexes, the evaluation of such

B. Read (Ed.): BNCOD 2001, LNCS 2097, pp. 168–184, 2001.

queries is usually in the order of few seconds. Still, the queries are of distinctly low complexity compared to queries in classical database applications. Moreover, the deviation of running time among the queries is limited, not least to ensure acceptable response times.

The primary challenge in this setting is to develop processing techniques to optimize the query throughput. Parallel processing is an essential element to achieve this, however, a straight forward recasting of methods developed for parallel databases does not apply here since most solutions devised in this area are almost exclusively geared to tackle highly complex and long running queries. There, queries are usually parallelized on a granularity of partial plans or even single operators, i.e. single operators like the join of two tables are executed in parallel on different nodes involving exchange of partial results among the single nodes. However, these techniques are ineffective for the kind of query we are considering since communication and coordination overheads would outweigh the actual benefits.

In this paper, we propose a parallel query processing architecture that can take advantage of the query characteristic by its physical design, suitable query scheduling, and the way queries are executed.

The platform of operation is a shared-nothing environment—i.e. a cluster of inexpensive PCs—where each node runs a Monet server with a fully replicated copy of the database. One machine is distinguished as coordinator node that dispatches the arriving queries to the servers according to a scheduling strategy. The scheduling schema we develop in this paper differs radically from previous work as we do not try to model various system parameters in order to exploit primarily idle system resources, but take into account what data is memory-resident at the servers, i.e. cached by the servers. The algorithm is based on a metric that determines the *distance* between a server and a query—the less this distance, the more similar the state of the memory at this server and what is required to process this query. Moreover, we investigate possibilities of re-ordering and deferred execution of queries to further reduce execution costs. Once a query is assigned to a server it is executed in isolation on this server, so no synchronization or communication within the cluster is needed freeing interconnection bandwidth for shipping of both queries and results.

Since we are dealing with read-only accesses, we do not have to consider transaction mechanisms to keep the replicated data consistent across the database cluster. Rather, the databases are periodically updated by mirroring a master database.

The experimental evaluation of the techniques proposed show substantial savings over conventional greedy scheduling that takes only the machines' workload into account. In a large number of experiments we investigate the impact of individual parameters closely. Our results confirm the architectural decisions showing excellent scaling behavior.

The remainder of this paper is organized as follows. We review related work in Section 2. In Section 3 we present the architecture and describe the query model in Section 4. Section 5 discusses the modeling of the server pool and the scheduling algorithm. In Section 6, we present a comprehensive performance analysis. Section 7 contains a discussion of the design decisions. We conclude the paper with Section 8.

2   Related Work

Parallel query processing has been studied in a large variety of facets, see e.g. [PMC+90,DG92,HS93,WFA95,Gra95]. Most of related work in this field concentrated on possibilities to speedup highly complex queries with long running times. Approaches as taken in [HM94] and [GI96] suggest a decomposition of the query plans into sub-plans which are then executed in parallel on different nodes of the parallel processing environment. The granularity of this decomposition varies and can be as fine as parallelizing single operator as studied for example in [SD89,SD90,WFA95] but is often chosen coarser [HM95,CHM95,GI96,GI97].

These approaches have in common that they require communication between single nodes for shipping or exchanging partial results. This causes network contention and synchronization effects where nodes have to wait for others to complete their tasks first. As a result, a parallelization along these lines only pays if the query is of sufficiently high complexity. Otherwise communication overhead and synchronization effects outweigh performance gains.

Moreover, parallel processing as outlined above scales only for small numbers of nodes effectively. In shared-nothing architectures, network contention becomes increasingly a bottleneck; in the case of shared-everything, the high degree of resource sharing limits the scaling [Sto86,NZT96].

What makes most of these approaches, however, questionable is the fact that during the optimization a number of highly sensitive parameter—which are hard to model mathematically and impossible to maintain accurately during running time—have to be taken into account. Parameters like network load, page faults etc. are assumed constant during the query execution and estimate errors, which may have severe impact on the performance, can not be corrected (see e.g. [GI97]).

General memory allocation issues have been explored extensively with respect to various aspects of query processing. In [MD93], authors proposed dynamic memory allocation schemes for multi-query workload to level memory allocation without sharing resident data among different queries. By analyzing queries and their common sub-expressions the re-use of memory resident data is often a by-effect [SSN94]. In [MSD93], authors consider batch scheduling for parallel processing. However, main-memory is in both cases transparently viewed as a central resource and data location within distributed memory has not been considered.

In the context of transaction processing, several query routing schemas for database clusters have been investigated (see e.g. [Tho87,FGND93,RBS00]). This field of application differs from the problem at hand in its preliminaries: queries are usually of complex nature and updates to the database need to be propagated over the complete cluster. One of the major goals is for instance to schedule queries so that locking conflicts are avoided. For a comprehensive overview on this subject see e.g. [Rah92].

3 Architecture

Figure 1 shows the architecture of our system. It consists of a cluster of database servers managed by a central scheduler node. All machines have separate main-memory, CPU, and disks not sharing any resources other than network bandwidth. We use Monet, the main-memory database system developed at CWI, as database server [BK95,BK99]. Besides its vertical fragmented data model, Monet is distinguished by its memory awareness, i.e. it solely uses operating system primitives for its memory management, mapping database tables directly to virtual memory, to avoid the overhead of a proprietary buffer manager simulating a virtual memory layer. Moreover it provides specifically cache aware operator implementations [BMK99] to maximize system utilization on running queries.

Additionally, a pool of web-servers forms the front-end of the system which clients interact with. The web-servers receive either parameterized queries using text-based forms, or they interact with visual query formulation tools.

Processing of a client query is done in 7 steps: Users formulate their query using the web-interface (Fig. 1,(1)). At the web-server, the query is re-formulated using the internal procedural query representation of the database system—in our case MIL, the query language of Monet—and submitted to the query scheduler (2). The scheduler maintains a queue of queries that are to be executed. By analyzing the data requirements for the execution of a query and the data resident in main-memory at the servers, the scheduler determines a favorable assignment of queries to servers (4). The query is executed on the assigned node (5) and the result is returned to the front-end host (6).[1] After formatting the result, it is shipped to the user (7).

This architecture directly aims at the throughput optimization of compact queries where an execution on a single node is the most efficient kind of processing. But this architecture also exploits the second query characteristic: the impreciseness of the data. For example, data gathered by robots from the Internet to build up a multi-media index is updated only at low frequency. Thus, the server cluster do not have to be kept in sync as would be the case if updates by users were allowed. Instead, the databases are updated periodically replicating the master database (U). The frequency of updates depends naturally on the application domain.

---

[1] For simplicity of presentation arrows (6) follow the routing of the query (2–4), however, the query result can be sent directly to the front-end and does not have to pass the query scheduler.

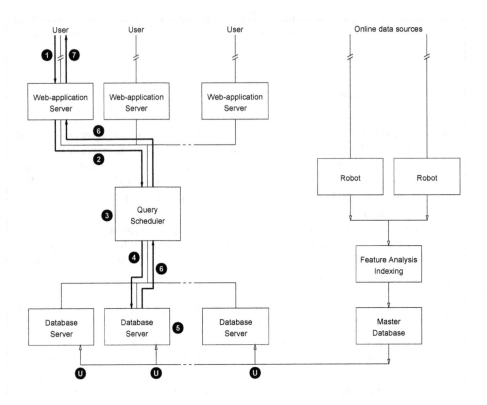

Fig. 1. Query processing architecture

4   Query Model

The choice of Monet as database software for the back-end cluster implies a specific model for the query execution. The vertical fragmentation of the tables in Monet causes bulk-processing to be more efficient than pipelining techniques. As a consequence, there are no more than two tables processed on a single CPU at a time. Note, this execution model does not impose any restrictions on the shape of the execution plans—both linear and bushy plans are feasible. Access to a table can be either of type LOAD or SCAN. LOAD reads a table from disk into memory to make it part of the hot set, e.g. used with inner relations of nested-loop joins. SCAN reads the table, but does not keep the data in memory after the actual operation is performed, e.g. used in selections or for the probe relation of a hash join. The building of a hash table can be seen as special type of load as the result is only accessible via the hash attribute.

The costs for executing a relation algebra operator consists of the costs of loading/scanning of the table plus the actual costs for the operation. Fitting the pieces together, we can describe a query as a sequence

$$Q = \langle (t_1, a_1, l_1, w_1), \ldots, (t_n, a_n, l_n, w_n) \rangle$$

where each quadruple corresponds to an operator or—as in case of a join—to a partial operator. t_i specifies the table necessary for the operation. a_i denotes the hash attribute, i.e. the operator accesses t_i via this attribute; $a_i = \epsilon$ if not applicable.

The associated *loading costs*, if the table is not already resident in main-memory, are given by l_i. We denote the *total loading costs* of a query as

$$L(Q) = \sum_i l_i.$$

The costs to execute the operator, the *operator costs*, are denoted by w_i. We denote the *total operator costs* of a query as

$$W(Q) = \sum_i w_i.$$

Note, both l_i and w_i are expressed in terms of the same unit to achieve a proper comparison.

A queries execution time on a "cold" server, i.e. no data is loaded yet, is

$$\chi(Q) = L(Q) + W(Q).$$

If all tables needed by Q are already in memory—and in case of hash tables, are hashed by the proper attribute—the execution costs of the query amounts to $W(Q)$ only.

Examples

Here are some examples to illustrate this modeling based on Monet performance characteristics. The two tables A and B used in this example are of size 8.8MB and 4.95MB, respectively. Our test platform achieved a bandwidth of 5.5MB/s for disk access.

– Nested-Loop Join, $A \bowtie B$

$$Q = \langle (A, \epsilon, 1.6, 0), (B, \epsilon, 0.9, 2.6) \rangle$$

Table A takes 1.6s to load, no operator costs occur. Table B takes 0.9s to load; performing the join requires 2.6s.

– Hash Join, $A \bowtie B$

$$Q = \langle (A, a, 2.7, 0), (B, \epsilon, 0.9, 1.1) \rangle$$

Similar to previous but now, A must be a hash table with hash attribute a. Hence loading A is more expensive as it includes building the hash table.

5   Query Scheduling

The query scheduling comprises several elements. Besides a model for the servers we define a *server-query distance* which captures the potential re-use of memory resident data. Additionally, we also introduce deadlines.

5.1   Servers

For the scheduling, a server of the database cluster is modeled by its state of memory and the workload. The state of memory is the set of tables resident together with a replacement strategy. We are considering base tables only and discard intermediate results of the processing as soon as they are no longer used. As a replacement strategy we use LRU as it exhibits the best average performance. The loading and dropping of tables is done via the memory mapping functionality of the operating system. To maintain sufficient control over the memory allocation throughout the complete cluster we load and drop only complete tables. This way, the scheduler can rely on the information which tables are memory-resident, i.e. accessing them will not cause additional costs for swapping. Swapping may only occur when all unused tables are already dropped but the memory requirements of the current operation are still not met.

For the workload, we distinguish the two states *idle* and *busy*, i.e. we assign one query to one server at a time. This is not just a simplification to facilitate the scheduling but a necessity in main-memory databases where cache awareness and concurrent memory access are of distinctly higher importance than in I/O-dominated database models [MBK00]. We model the workload as function $J(S)$ which returns the expected time of job completion at server S, given its current workload, i.e. the expected time from now when S will become idle. If the server is idle, $J(S)$ evaluates to 0. J will be used in the scheduler to find the node that will finish its job next. J is computed by conventional cost formulae known from sequential query processing: Given the time x_0 the currently running query has been assigned to server S, x the time J is evaluated, and e the expected running time of the query, the time of job completion computes to $J(S) = x_0 + e - x$. See also Section 7 for a discussion on the accuracy of J.

5.2   Distance Metric

We define the *server-query distance* as the costs to load the tables for a given query Q on a server S:

$$d(Q, S) = \sum_i R(t_i, a_i) \cdot l_i$$

where

$$R(t_i, a_i) = \begin{cases} 0, & \text{if } t_i \text{ is memory-resident at } S \text{ and hashed by attribute } a_i \\ 1, & \text{else} \end{cases}$$

indicates whether table t_i is resident in memory at S. In case t_i is required as hash table, R also checks whether the table is hashed by attribute a_i.

Scheduling a batch of queries optimally on k servers is finding a division into k batches $B_1, \dots, B_k$, each of which are executed sequentially on one server, such that the running time of the batch with the longest completion time

$$\max_i \left\{ \sum_j (d(Q_j, S) + W(Q_j)), \quad Q_j \in B_i \right\}$$

is minimal.

5.3   Scheduling Algorithm

We use the distance measure to develop a greedy scheduling algorithm that establishes an acceptable trade-off between workload- and memory-focused scheduling. Figure 2 shows an outline of our algorithm called *Memory Aware Scheduling* (MAS). It iterates over the queue of arriving queries, selecting one at a time, and determines the best ad-hoc assignment.

In detail, we examine the first n elements of the queue—or less if the queue does not contain n queries. We investigate the impact of n and suitable values for it in the next section. For each of the n queries, we compute c which consists of the distance to all servers S_i plus the operator cost of the query and the expected time at which server S_i becomes available, $J(S_i)$. We record the pair $(\widehat{Q}, \widehat{S})$ with the lowest value for c. After examination of all n queries, we assign $\widehat{Q}$ to $\widehat{S}$ which means that $\widehat{Q}$ will be executed on $\widehat{S}$ as soon as this server gets idle.

The algorithm is in $O(N \cdot n \cdot s)$ where N is the number of queries in total, n is the number of queries considered in each run, and s is the number of servers available, i.e. the algorithm is linear in the number of queries. To give any meaningful bounds on the performance is particularly difficult because of the LRU replacement of tables.

5.4   Deadlines

In order to give the user a guarantee of service, we tag every query with a deadline. This deadline refers to the latest point in time the query has to be assigned to a server for execution, i.e. as soon as the deadline of a query expires, the scheduler has no other choice than assigning this very query to a server.

We tag all queries with a time stamp according to their arrival. In other words queries are not forced by deadlines to overtake others, though it is often beneficial. As a result, we need only check the first query of the current top n batch for deadline expiration. If the first query's deadline is expired, we do not need to examine any other query in the batch but have to assign the first immediately to a server. Otherwise, if the first query's deadline is *not yet* expired,

Algorithm MAS

while queue not empty **do**

$c_{min} \leftarrow \infty$

foreach query Q in top_n(queue) **do**

for $i = 1$ to number of servers **do**

$$c = d(Q, S_i) + W(Q) + J(S_i)$$

if $c < c_{min}$ **do**

$$\widehat{Q} \leftarrow Q$$
$$\widehat{S} \leftarrow S_i$$
$$c_{min} \leftarrow c$$

done

done

if $expired(Q)$ **then break**

done

assign query $\widehat{Q}$ to server $\widehat{S}$

remove $\widehat{Q}$ from queue

done

Fig. 2. Scheduling Algorithm MAS

no other deadline can be due. Testing for expiration after the first query has been checked against all servers ensures the best assignment in case the deadline expired.

6   Experimental Results

In this section, we describe experimental results obtained with a simulator. We chose to simulate the system in order to experiment with parameters that are strictly limited by an actual hardware configuration, such as size of the database cluster or main-memory available at the individual servers.

6.1   Preliminaries

Since the full multi-media Acoi demonstrator database is still under construction, we had to confine the experiments to the part already operational. The part chosen is the index system of the ACM Anthology, which is included in the demonstrator to assess its capabilities in the area of XML-based database processing. We used statistical data available from an actual Monet database instance which contains the complete XML code of the Anthology decomposed into the vertically fragmented data model [SKWW00]. Including indexes, the database contains 376 tables with up to nearly 60000 rows. The numbers of tables according to their sizes are given in Table 1. Typical queries use some 5

Table 1. Sizes and numbers of base tables

Size	≤ 20MB	≤ 30MB	≤ 40MB	≤ 50MB	> 50MB
#Tables	233	87	24	15	17

tables or less, seldom up to 10 or more. We generated batches of 10,000 and 100,000 queries of exponentially distributed sizes accessing 5 tables on average.

We do not consider mechanisms to reject user queries due to overload since this can be done already at the front-end level. Modeling arrival rates probabilistically is not necessary as queries do not significantly differ in running time, thus information about the queries does not need to be considered to make a choice which queries to accept and which to reject. For our experiments, we assume the maximal expected query arrival rate to model the worst case behavior with maximum load. Moreover, we assume all hosts within the database cluster are of identical configuration regarding the cost relevant parameters.

Since the replacement of tables along an LRU strategy makes analytical modeling of the algorithm hard, we implemented *Graham's list scheduling* (GLS), which is based on workload figures [Gra69], for comparison. We chose Graham's algorithm instead of seemingly more advanced techniques, like [GI96], as it is the only algorithm that does not make assumptions concerning parameters like network load etc., which are impossible to maintain accurately at reasonable costs (see also Sections 2 and 7).

We adapted the original algorithm to fit the online arrival of queries, i.e. to use the kind of look-ahead we introduced in MAS above. Graham's algorithm is known to be highly effective despite its simplicity overcoming some characteristic disturbances also known as *scheduling anomalies*. These anomalies occur with jobs that differ significantly in completion time. Please note, we run Graham's algorithm in exactly the same setting, i.e. with LRU replacement of tables as necessary. As a result, Graham's algorithm also profits from re-use of memory resident data.

The main parameters we want to investigate are, foremost, the number of servers, the look-ahead during the scheduling, and the amount of memory available at each server. Note, there are two principal ways of comparison: a one-on-one comparison of both algorithms run on identic configurations of the platform (relative performance), or a comparison of the scaling characteristics. Typical examples for the latter are speedup and scale-up. We will compare the two algorithms using both principles where adequate.

6.2   Warm/Cold Processing

In this first experiment we investigate the differences between warm and cold servers. We refer to a server as *cold* if no other tables than system tables have

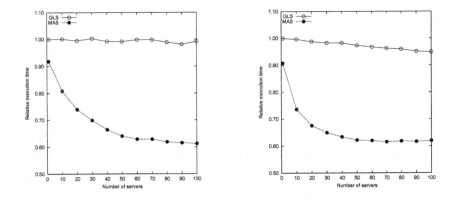

Fig. 3. Relative performance of warm over cold servers

been loaded. If more than 80% of the available memory are allocated we call a server *warm*.[2] This is not only relevant for later experiments but also for the real application scenario when the system has to be shutdown and re-started for technical reasons like maintenance etc. We can expect different effects if the amount of memory per server is varied. For small server configurations the warm up is completed earlier than for large ones. However, more important is the amount of memory in total, i.e. the number of servers. Figure 3 shows the relative execution times of batches of 10,000 queries as function of the number servers. For example the leftmost data point for MAS reflects the ratio of execution times for MAS on a cold to that on a warm server. The left graph shows times for a server configuration of 64, the right for 256MB.

For GLS, cold and warm execution times are almost the same. Warm processing is only up to 5% quicker. For MAS the ratio differs significantly showing gains of more than 35%. Especially for the range up to 50 servers, the larger configuration (right) achieves better performance, i.e. the curve is steeper. For more servers, the impact of the larger amount of memory decreases: for 100 servers and more, results are virtually equal. We address the issue of memory sizes in more detail in 6.5.

All further results presented in this section are obtained from warm servers.

6.3   Reordering of Queries

The next experiment investigates the impact of the look-ahead during scheduling, i.e. the maximal number of queries that may be re-ordered between each assignment.

Figure 4 shows execution times for a single server (left) and a cluster of 100 servers (right). In both cases the server(s) had 64MB of memory. The execution

---

[2] We determined the value 80 in preliminary experiments. Execution times on servers with more than 80% allocated memory did not differ significantly.

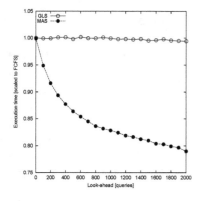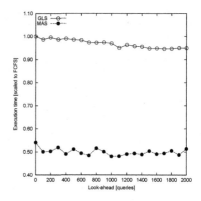

Fig. 4. Impact of look-ahead; Single server (left) and cluster of 100 servers (right)

time is shown as a function of the look-ahead, scaled to GLS's first data point, which corresponds to a first-come-first-serve (FCFS) scheduling. The size of the complete query batch was 10,000. In the case of one server, the look-ahead is of high importance for MAS and savings can amount up to 20% of the execution time. GLS, however, does not significantly profit from look-ahead.

In the case of 100 servers, the situation changes. GLS relatively improves more with increasing look-ahead but for MAS hardly any improvement is noticeable, though its execution time is substantially below the one of GLS. This is due to the fact that in a pool of 100 servers many server offer a very low server-query distance and differences are often very small. As a consequence re-ordering cannot help finding a significantly lower server-query distance as it did in the sequential case.

In all further experiments we use a look-ahead of 100 queries unless stated otherwise.

6.4   Speedup and Scale-Up

The two fundamental measures when investigating the performance of parallel systems are speedup and scale-up. The previous quantifies the gains when scaling up the platform but keeping the problem size constant, the latter describes the system's ability to cope with problem sizes growing proportionally with the platform (cf. e.g. [DG92]).

Figure 5 shows the speedup for a query batch of 100,000 queries evaluated on up to 4096 servers with 64MB memory each. As the plot shows, GLS achieves slightly sub-linear speedup whereas MAS achieves even super-linear speedup which translates to effective re-use of memory resident data. To better illustrate this phenomenon, consider a very basic example using 4 tables A,B,C and D of same size such that only two table fit into memory at the same time, and a batch of 4 queries:

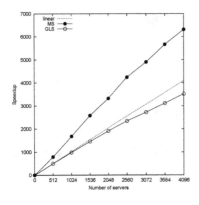

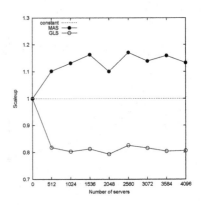

Fig. 5. Speedup

Fig. 6. Scaleup

$$Q_1 = \langle (A, 2, 2), (B, 2, 2) \rangle$$
$$Q_2 = \langle (C, 2, 2), (D, 2, 2) \rangle$$
$$Q_3 = \langle (D, 2, 2) \rangle$$
$$Q_4 = \langle (A, 2, 2) \rangle$$

On a single machine, the total costs amount to $8 + 8 + 4 + 4 = 24$. With linear speedup, we would expect 12 cost units for a parallelization on two hosts. MAS assigns queries Q_1 and Q_4 to one, Q_2 and Q_3 to the other machine which amounts to $8 + 2 = 10$ costs at each node. Hence, the total execution time is 10 compared to 24 on a single node which gives a speedup of 2.4.

Figure 6 shows the scale-up for the same server pool configuration. MAS maintains a scale-up of about 1.1 even for large configurations whereas GLS drops quickly to about 0.8.

6.5 Direct Comparison

In our last experiment, we compare the algorithms directly, i.e. we determine the ratio of MAS's execution time to the one of GLS for each individual parameter setting. Values below 1.0 indicate that MAS outperforms GLS. As parameter of the experiment we vary number of servers, memory available, and look-ahead.

Figure 7 shows the relative execution time as a function of the number of servers and the amount of memory per server. The number of servers varies between 5 and 100, memory between 32 and 640MB. As the diagram displays, MAS outperformed GLS in all 400 individual experiments achieving execution times as short as 40% of those of GLS. However, as the diagram reveals, this is no monotonic process, rather, with increasing memory sizes, GLS manages to "catch up", though only to a certain degree. See for example the front row where, after MAS increases its lead (0.4 at ca. 160MB) it cannot further improve on the running time whereas GLS becomes increasingly better. For more than ca. 320MB neither algorithm can achieve any improvement, thus the plateaux.

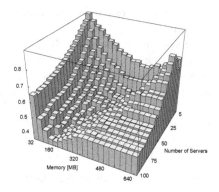

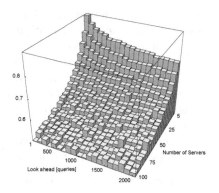

Fig. 7. Relative performance; memory available and number of servers varied

Fig. 8. Relative performance; look-ahead and number of servers varied

Figure 8 shows the relative performance as function of the number of servers and the look-ahead. All servers had 64MB of memory. The plot shows results that affirm the previously found ones now also in the direct comparison: For small number of servers look-ahead plays an important role (see last row), which fades as the number of server increases (see front row).

7 Discussion

While implementing and testing different versions of MAS we made several design decisions which are not self-evident at first sight and deserve to be discussed more elaborately in the following.

The most important question in the design process was whether to include more system information about the servers or not. Typically, cost models in parallel databases try to model the system—particularly the shared resources like network or shared disks—as detailed as possible. We chose not to incorporate this kind of information for three reasons: Firstly, the type of query we are dealing with cannot profit much from the kind of parallel processing these cost models have been developed for. Secondly, a cost computation that takes details at this fine granularity into account is computationally too expensive to deliver cost estimates for hundreds of servers when an online arrival of queries needs to be scheduled in real-time. Lastly, this detailed system information is hard to maintain. To keep it accurately up-to-date during the processing would require a substantial share of both network and processing resources and is thus unfeasible.

In contrast to that the cost values used by MAS are of simpler nature. The cost estimates for the query execution time (see Section 5.1) can be assembled from sequential cost estimates. Since the queries are emitted by a fixed interface, there is the possibility to pre-compile queries which are then instantiated with a few parameters. In that case highly accurate cost estimates can be pre-computed and—like the queries—instantiated with parameters.

The information necessary to describe the system for the scheduling is in so far easy to maintain as it consists only of a feedback indicating that processing of the last query has terminated, i.e. the result has been shipped, and what tables are now in main-memory. To avoid idleness between feedback and new assignment, servers can be extended to buffer *one* query while processing the previously assigned. The feedback together with the fact that servers do not maintain own query queues ensures that the impact of a few, inaccurate cost estimates, which can never be completely avoided, is kept down to a minimum.

Finally, the query *execution* we proposed does not allow for multi-programming, i.e. running several queries concurrently on one server. This choice was motivated by two facts. Firstly, multi-programming is not very beneficial in main-memory databases like Monet as concurrently processed queries often get into each other's way, unlike in I/O dominated database systems. Secondly, and more importantly as this holds for other database back-ends too, the potential gains of multi-programming where I/O of one query and CPU intensive computation of another one can be aligned is very limited as it is our foremost goal to avoid costly I/O operations at all.

8 Conclusion

Web-enabled databases and database back-end technology for large web-base information systems are one of the fastest growing segments of the database market. Those systems challenge the traditional repertoire of optimization techniques used in database technology. Powerful, user interfaces for multi-media object retrieval concurrently submit large numbers of queries to the database back-end which make throughput optimization a primary optimization goal.

In this paper, we propose a parallel query processing architecture and investigated the possibility to exploit data sharing by clever scheduling of the arriving queries. We have developed MAS, a scheduling strategy that tries to maximize the re-use of data resident in main memory across the database cluster. The algorithm is distinguished by its simplicity and robustness on one hand—the information needed to make MAS work is easy to obtain, accurate, and needs only little effort to be kept up-to-date—and its effectiveness on the other hand.

Our experiments show superior results compared to conventional list scheduling in terms of both query throughput and scaling behavior confirming our considerations. Moreover, by re-using the data available rather than assigning data actively, the scheduling algorithm adapts to changing hotspots.

Our future work is geared toward extending the scheduling schema to consider intermediate results and exploit similarities among queries.

Acknowledgements. Thanks are due to Albrecht Schmidt who provided us with a Monet database instance of the ACM Anthology.

References

[BK95]   P. A. Boncz and M. L. Kersten. Monet: An Impressionist Sketch of an Advanced Database System. In *Proc. Basque International Workshop on Information Technology*, San Sebastian, Spain, 1995.

[BK99]   P. A. Boncz and M. L. Kersten. MIL Primitives for Querying a Fragmented World. *The VLDB Journal*, 8(2):101–119, 1999.

[BMK99]   P. A. Boncz, S. Manegold, and M. L. Kersten. Database Architecture Optimized for the new Bottleneck: Memory Access. In *Proc. of the Int'l. Conf. on Very Large Data Bases*, pages 54–65, Edinburgh, UK, 1999.

[CHM95]   C. Chekuri, W. Hasan, and R. Motwani. Scheduling Problems in Parallel Query Optimization. In *Proc. of the ACM SIGACT-SIGMOD-SIGART Symposium on Principles of Database Systems*, pages 255–265, San Jose, CA, USA, May 1995.

[DG92]   D. J. DeWitt and J. Gray. Parallel Database Systems: The Future of High Performance Database Systems. *Communications of the ACM*, 35(6):85–98, June 1992.

[FGND93]   D. F. Ferguson, L. Georgiadis, C. Nikolaou, and K. Davies. Goal Oriented, Adaptive Transaction Routing for High Performance Transaction Processing Systems. In *Proc. of the Int'l. Conf. on Parallel and Distributed Information Systems*, pages 138–147, San Diego, CA, USA, January 1993.

[GI96]   M. N. Garofalakis and Y. E. Ioannidis. Multi-dimensional Resource Scheduling for Parallel Queries. In *Proc. of the ACM SIGMOD Int'l. Conf. on Management of Data*, pages 365–376, Montreal, Canada, June 1996.

[GI97]   M. N. Garofalakis and Y. E. Ioannidis. Parallel Query Scheduling and Optimization with Time- and Space-Shared Resources. In *Proc. of the Int'l. Conf. on Very Large Data Bases*, pages 296–305, Athens, Greece, September 1997.

[Gra69]   R. L. Graham. Bounds on Multiprocessing Timing Anomalies. *SIAM Journal on Applied Mathematics*, 17(2):416–429, March 1969.

[Gra95]   J. Gray. A Survey of Parallel Database Techniques and Systems. In *Tutorial Handouts of the 21st Int'l. Conf. on Very Large Data Bases*, Zurich, Switzerland, September 1995.

[HM94]   W. Hasan and R. Motwani. Optimization Algorithms for Exploiting the Parallelism-Communication Tradeoff in Pipelining Parallelism. In *Proc. of the Int'l. Conf. on Very Large Data Bases*, pages 36–47, Santiago, Chile, September 1994.

[HM95]   W. Hasan and R. Motwani. Coloring Away Communication in Parallel Query Optimization. In *Proc. of the Int'l. Conf. on Very Large Data Bases*, pages 239–250, Zurich, Switzerland, September 1995.

[HS93]   W. Hong and M. Stonebraker. Optimization of Parallel Query Execution Plans in XPRS. *Distributed and Parallel Databases*, 1(1):9–32, 1993.

[MBK00]   S. Manegold, P. A. Boncz, and M. L. Kersten. What happens during a Join? - Dissecting CPU and Memory Optimization Effects. In *Proc. of the Int'l. Conf. on Very Large Data Bases*, Cairo, Egypt, September 2000. Accepted for publication.

[MD93]   M. Mehta and D. J. DeWitt. Dynamic Memory Allocation for Multiple-Query Workloads. In *Proc. of the Int'l. Conf. on Very Large Data Bases*, pages 354–367, Dublin, Ireland, September 1993.

[MSD93]   M. Mehta, V. Soloviev, and D. J. DeWitt. Batch Scheduling in Parallel Database Systems. In *Proc. of the IEEE Int'l. Conf. on Data Engineering*, pages 400–410, Vienna, Austria, April 1993.

[NZT96]   M. G. Norman, T. Zurek, and P. Thanisch. Much Ado About Shared-Nothing. *ACM SIGMOD Record*, 25(3):16–21, September 1996.

[PMC⁺90]   H. Pirahesh, C. Mohan, J. Cheng, T. S. Liu, and P. Selinger. Parallelism in Relational Data Base Systems: Architectural Issues and Design Approaches. In *Proc. of the Int'l. Symp. on Databases in Parallel and Distr. Systems*, pages 4–29, Dublin, Ireland, July 1990.

[Rah92]   E. Rahm. A Framewok for Workload Allocation in Distributed Transaction Processing Systems. *Systems Software Journal*, 18:171–190, 1992.

[RBS00]   U. Röhm, K. Böhm, and H.-J. Schek. OLAP Query Routing and Physical Design in a Database Cluster. In *Proc. of the Int'l. Conf. on Extending Database Technology*, Lecture Notes in Computer Science, pages 254–268, Konstanz, Germany, March 2000.

[SD89]   D. A. Schneider and D. J DeWitt. A Performance Evaluation of Four Parallel Join Algorithms in a Shared-Nothing Multiprocessor Environment. In *Proc. of the ACM SIGMOD Int'l. Conf. on Management of Data*, pages 110–121, May 1989.

[SD90]   D. A. Schneider and D. J. DeWitt. Tradeoffs in Processing Complex Join Queries via Hashing in Multiprocessor Database Machines. In *Proc. of the Int'l. Conf. on Very Large Data Bases*, pages 469–480, Brisbane, Australia, August 1990.

[SKWW00]   A. R. Schmidt, M. L. Kersten, M. A. Windhouwer, and F. Waas. Efficient Relational Storage and Retrieval of XML Documents. In *International Workshop on the Web and Databases*, pages 47–52, Dallas, TX, USA, May 2000.

[SSN94]   K. Shim, T. Sellis, and D. Nau. Improvements on a Heuristic Algorithm for Multiple-Query Optimization. *IEEE Trans. on Knowledge and Data Engineering*, 12(2):197–222, March 1994.

[Sto86]   M. Stonebraker. The Case for Shared-Nothing. *IEEE Data Engineering Bulletin*, 9(1):4–9, March 1986.

[Tho87]   A. Thomasian. A Performance Study of Dynamic Load Balancing in Distributed Systems. In *Proc. of the IEEE Int'l. Conf. on Distributed Computing Systems*, Berlin, Germany, 1987.

[WFA95]   A. N. Wilschut, J. Flokstra, and P. M. G. Apers. Parallel Evaluation of Multi-Join Queries. In *Proc. of the ACM SIGMOD Int'l. Conf. on Management of Data*, pages 115–126, San Jose, CA, USA, May 1995.

Inferring the Principal Type and the Schema Requirements of an OQL Query

A. Trigoni and G.M. Bierman

University of Cambridge Computer Laboratory, UK

Abstract. In this paper, we present an inference algorithm for OQL which both identifies the most general type of a query in the absence of schema type information, and derives the minimum type requirements a schema should satisfy to be compatible with this query. Our algorithm is useful in any database application where heterogeneity is encountered, for example, schema evolution, queries addressed against multiple schemata, inter-operation or reconciliation of heterogeneous schemata. Our inference algorithm is technically interesting as it concerns an object functional language with a rich semantics and complex type system. More precisely, we have devised a set of constraints and an algorithm to resolve them. Our resulting type inference system for OQL should be useful in any open distributed, or even semi-structured, database environment.

1 Introduction

The ODMG Standard [6] (hereafter referred to as simply the Standard) presents, rather informally, some details of a type system for checking OQL queries using type information about the classes, extents, named objects and query definitions from a given database schema. Recently there have been some efforts to formalise this type system [2,3]. This paper builds on our earlier work [3] and considers the problem of inferring the most general type of an OQL query in the absence of any schema information.

For example, consider the following OQL definition and query:

```
define Dept_Managers(dept) as
  select e
  from    Employees as e
  where   e.position="manager" and e.department=dept;

select d
from    Departments as d
where   count(Dept_Managers(d))>5
```

This query yields those departments that have more than five managers. It is interesting to notice that this information could be drawn by running the query against databases with significantly different schemata. For instance, consider schema A, which has two classes, `Employee` and `Department`, defined as follows.

B. Read (Ed.): BNCOD 2001, LNCS 2097, pp. 185–201, 2001.

```
class Employee (extent Employees)          class Department (extent
{ attribute string      name;              Departments)
   attribute string     position;          { attribute string id;}
   attribute int        year_of_birth;
   attribute float      salary;
   attribute Department department;}
```

On the other hand, consider a second schema B, which has a class `Employee` and a named collection object `Departments` of type `List(int)`.

```
class Employee (extent Employees)
{ attribute string name;
   attribute string position;
   attribute int    department;}
```

The query could potentially run against both A and B without causing any type errors. In the case of schema A, the result of the query would be a bag of `Department` objects. In a database with schema B, the result of the query would be a bag of integers. Two vital questions arise at this point. First, how we can draw limits, or put restrictions, on the properties of a schema, so that a certain query is well-typed with respect to it? Second, what information we can derive about the type of the result of the query, supposing that we have no specific schema in mind? In this paper, we study these two questions in detail, but first let us consider the setting where this could be important.

For example, this information could be exploited in distributed database applications. Suppose we have time critical queries addressed against multiple schemata. If frequent updates on parts of these schemata are likely to occur, then many of the queries will inevitably fail to be executed. In order to avoid this situation, we should register interest in specific updates of each schema –at least in those that would affect the critical queries– and resolve the type incompatibility in due course and not at the time the queries get executed.

Our work is equally useful in contexts where we need to achieve inter-operation between heterogeneous sources. There has been a lot of research on reconciling schemata with semantic heterogeneity [4,7]. One approach to this problem identifies the semantic inconsistencies of the ontologies in different domains and creates a global ontology that combines all of them. Another approach identifies the intersection of domains where the inconsistencies occur and tries to resolve them by introducing matching rules between them. In both cases, queries that are initially written to be executed on one domain need to be rephrased to fit the needs of more domains. Knowing the schema requirements of a query and the schema mappings to a (global or just different) ontology, the task of rephrasing queries becomes a trivial automatic process. Suppose that a group of airline companies cooperate to create a single uniform system for booking tickets. In order to do that they define a global ontology that is very close to each of the distinct ontologies. Each query is initially phrased to conform to the global ontology and is then transformed to appropriate queries addressed to the individual schemata. The transformation is much easier to perform if besides the schema mappings (from one ontology to the other), we are aware of the query schema requirements. The latter effectively point out the exact mappings we need to use.

This paper is organised as follows. In section 2 we recall our earlier [3] definition of a core OQL—a fragment of the language defined in the Standard, but which has the same expressive power. We give a brief overview of the type system of OQL, including the notion of subtyping. In section 3, we study the type system of our inference model introducing a new relation between types, called *more specific*. In section 4, we describe the kinds of constraints generated by our type inference algorithm, and in section 5, we present an algorithm for resolving these constraints. The core of our inference system, the inference rules, are given in section 6. Finally, in section 7, we present the inference algorithm which yields the most general type of a query along with its type schema requirements.

2   Core OQL

In this section we fix the syntax and type system for OQL. This is explained in greater detail in an earlier paper [3]; space restrictions mean that here we simply give the syntax for queries and definitions[1] in Figure 1. An OQL **program** consists of a number (maybe zero) of named definitions followed by a query.

The syntax for OQL types is also given in Figure 1. In what follows we will write $Col(\sigma)$, to denote an arbitrary collection type (set, bag, list or array), with elements of type σ.

Implicit in the ODMG model is a notion of subtyping; the underlying idea is that σ is said to be a subtype of τ, if a value of type σ can be used in any context in which a value of type τ is expected. This we shall write $\sigma \leq \tau$ and define as the least relation closed under the rules given in Figure 1.

We use the $\sqsubseteq$ symbol to denote single inheritance between two classes, referred to in the Standard as the "*derives from*" relation. To simplify our presentation we do not consider interfaces.

An interesting feature of our subtype relation is the treatment of structures. A type $\sigma = \texttt{struct}(\texttt{l}_1\!:\!\sigma_1,\ldots,\texttt{l}_m\!:\!\sigma_m)$ is considered to be a subtype of $\tau = \texttt{struct}(\texttt{l}_1\!:\!\tau_1,\ldots,\texttt{l}_n\!:\!\tau_n)$ if τ is obtained from σ by dropping some labels. (In fact, we generalise this a little and also allow subtyping between the label types). This so-called width-subtyping is an extension to the Standard, but we feel it offers considerable flexibility.

The type system and the subtype relation are given in detail in an earlier paper [3]. In that work, we aimed at deriving the type of an OQL query given specific schema information. In order to do that, we defined typing judgements of the form:

$$\mathcal{S}; \mathcal{D}; \mathcal{N}; \mathcal{Q} \vdash \textsf{q}\!:\!\sigma$$

---

[1] Naturally as we are interested in *inferring* types we drop the requirement that definition parameters be explicitly typed.

Queries $q ::= b \mid f \mid i \mid c \mid s$
$\qquad \mid \quad$ x
$\qquad \mid \quad$ bag(q,...,q) $\mid$ set(q,...,q) $\mid$ list(q,...,q) $\mid$ array(q,...,q)
$\qquad \mid \quad$ struct(l:q,...,l:q)
$\qquad \mid \quad$ C(l:q,...,l:q) $\mid$ q.l $\mid$ (C)q
$\qquad \mid \quad$ q[q] $\mid$ q in q $\mid$ q() $\mid$ q(q,...,q)
$\qquad \mid \quad$ forall x in q:q $\mid$ exists x in q:q
$\qquad \mid \quad$ q $binop$ q $\mid$ $unop$(q)
$\qquad \mid \quad$ select [distinct] q
$\qquad \qquad$ from (q as x, $\cdots$, q as x)
$\qquad \qquad$ where q
$\qquad \qquad$ [group by (l:q, $\cdots$, l:q)]
$\qquad \qquad$ [having q]
$\qquad \qquad$ [order by (q asc|desc, $\cdots$, q asc|desc)]

Definitions $d ::=$ define x as q
$\qquad \mid \quad$ define x(x,...,x) as q

Here b, f, i, c, s range over booleans, floats, integers, characters and strings respectively, x is taken from a countable set of identifiers, l is taken from a countable set of labels, and C ranges over a countable set of class names. We assume sets of unary and binary operators, ranged over by $unop$ and $binop$ respectively.

Types $\sigma ::=$ int $\mid$ float $\mid$ bool $\mid$ char $\mid$ string $\mid$ void
$\qquad \mid \quad \sigma \times \cdots \times \sigma \to \sigma$
$\qquad \mid \quad$ bag(σ) $\mid$ set(σ) $\mid$ list(σ) $\mid$ array(σ)
$\qquad \mid \quad$ struct(l:σ, $\cdots$, l:σ)
$\qquad \mid \quad$ C

We assume a distinguished class name Object.

Sub-typing

$$\frac{}{\text{C} \le \text{Object}} \; \text{Top} \quad \frac{\text{C} \sqsubseteq \text{C}'}{\text{C} \le \text{C}'} \; \text{Sub-Class}$$

$$\frac{\sigma_1' \le \sigma_1 \cdots \sigma_k' \le \sigma_k \qquad \tau \le \tau'}{\sigma_1 \times \cdots \times \sigma_k \to \tau \le \sigma_1' \times \cdots \times \sigma_k' \to \tau'} \; \text{Sub-Fun} \quad \frac{\sigma \le \tau}{\text{Col}(\sigma) \le \text{Col}(\tau)} \; \text{Sub-Coll}$$

$$\frac{\sigma_1 \le \tau_1 \qquad \cdots \qquad \sigma_k \le \tau_k}{\text{struct}(l_1:\sigma_1, \ldots, l_k:\sigma_k, \ldots, l_{k+n}:\sigma_{k+n}) \le \text{struct}(l_1:\tau_1, \ldots, l_k:\tau_k)} \; \text{Sub-Struct}$$

$$\frac{}{\sigma \le \sigma} \; \text{Sub-Refl} \quad \frac{\sigma \le \sigma' \qquad \sigma' \le \sigma''}{\sigma \le \sigma''} \; \text{Sub-Trans}$$

Fig. 1. Syntax, Types and Subtyping for Core OQL

where $\mathcal{S}$ are the class definitions, $\mathcal{D}$ are the persistent query definitions and $\mathcal{N}$ are the named objects of a specific schema. $\mathcal{Q}$ represents the query typing environment, i.e. it contains the types of any free identifiers in q. A simple example of the typing rules used to derive the type of a query is the following:

$$\frac{\mathcal{S};\mathcal{D};\mathcal{N};\mathcal{Q} \vdash q\colon \mathtt{list}(\sigma)}{\mathcal{S};\mathcal{D};\mathcal{N};\mathcal{Q} \vdash \mathtt{first}(q)\colon \sigma} \quad \text{First-list}$$

In the current context, we have no information about the classes, the query definitions, and the named objects, as we have no schema information. The problem we address can thus be written $? \vdash q\colon ?$, i.e. given an arbitrary query q, can we infer its type and the type of any supporting schemata?

3 Type and Schema Inference

In this section, we present the extended type system behind our inference algorithm and a new relation between types called *Generalisation-Specialisation* relation. We also discuss the notions of *Least Upper Bound* and *Greatest Lower Bound* of two types that occur frequently in our inference algorithm.

3.1 Extended Type System

It turns out to be convenient to extend the notion of type given in Figure 1; an example should make this clear. Consider the following:

```
define q1 as select x from Students as x;
define q2 as set(first(Students));
q1 union q2
```

Considering the query q1 union q2 first, we can infer immediately that q1 and q2 should be either sets or bags of elements. To represent this we introduce a new type constructor set/bag$(-)$. Moreover, the elements of this collection cannot be of a *function* type, since the Standard does not allow functions to be members of a collection; thus we introduce the types nonfunctional and function. From the definition q1 we infer that Students is some collection (set, bag, list or array) of elements of any (non-functional) type. Considering the definition q2 we can infer further information about Students. As it is the argument of a first operation it must be an *ordered* collection, i.e. a list or an array. Again we introduce a new type constructor list/array$(-)$. In summary, the algorithm should infer that Students is a list or an array of a nonfunctional member type τ, and that the query q1 union q2 is of type bag(τ).[2]

The above example motivates our need to extend the initial *specific* types (given in Figure 1) with the following so-called *general* types.

---

[2] The Standard [§4.10.11] states that merging a set and a bag results in a bag.

$\{\texttt{any}, \texttt{nonfunctional}, \texttt{atomic}, \texttt{orderable}, \texttt{int/float}\}\cup$
$\{\texttt{collection}(\tau), \texttt{set/bag}(\tau), \texttt{list/array}(\tau), \texttt{constructor}(l_i\!:\!\tau_i)\}\cup$
$\{\text{all types from the core type system with at}$
$\text{least one component type being a general type, e.g. } \texttt{set}(\texttt{any})\}$

where τ, τ_i are *specific* or *general* types.

Given these general types the resulting type system is then as follows:

$$
\begin{aligned}
\sigma ::=\ & \texttt{int} \mid \texttt{float} \mid \texttt{bool} \mid \texttt{char} \mid \texttt{string} \mid \texttt{void} \\
& \mid \ \sigma \times \cdots \times \sigma \to \sigma \\
& \mid \ \texttt{bag}(\sigma) \mid \texttt{set}(\sigma) \mid \texttt{list}(\sigma) \mid \texttt{array}(\sigma) \mid \texttt{struct}(\texttt{l}\!:\!\sigma, \cdots, \texttt{l}\!:\!\sigma) \\
& \mid \ \texttt{C} \\
& \mid \ \texttt{any} \mid \texttt{nonfunctional} \\
& \mid \ \texttt{atomic} \mid \texttt{orderable} \mid \texttt{int/float} \\
& \mid \ \texttt{constructor}(\texttt{l}\!:\!\sigma, \cdots, \texttt{l}\!:\!\sigma) \\
& \mid \ \texttt{collection}(\sigma) \mid \texttt{set/bag}(\sigma) \mid \texttt{list/array}(\sigma)
\end{aligned}
\tag{1}
$$

This extended type system (1) is coupled with the type hierarchy illustrated in Figure 2. It is worth noting that the *general* types, which are the internal nodes of the tree, are not types that can be found in a database schema, but rather abstractions or families of types that encapsulate the common features of their children.

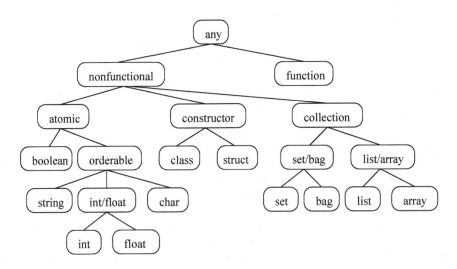

Fig. 2. Type Hierarchy

A type is said to be *specific*, if it can be derived by the type system given in Figure 1. Otherwise, it is said to be *general*. All the leaves of the hierarchy tree (in Figure 2) are specific types, if they are nullary (non parametric) types (int, float, char, string, bool) or if they are parametric types with all the parameter types being specific types (e.g. set(int)).

Given this more general type system, we need to extend our notion of subtyping given earlier. We define a new relation, GSR (Generalisation-Specialisation Relationship). Given types σ, τ, we write $\sigma \sqsubseteq \tau$ to express that σ is *more specific* than τ.

$$\frac{\sigma \leq \tau}{\sigma \sqsubseteq \tau} \; \text{GSR} - \text{Type} \qquad \frac{\sigma_1' \sqsubseteq \sigma_1 \cdots \sigma_k' \sqsubseteq \sigma_k \quad \tau \sqsubseteq \tau'}{\sigma_1 \times \cdots \times \sigma_k \to \tau \sqsubseteq \sigma_1' \times \cdots \times \sigma_k' \to \tau'} \; \text{GSR} - \text{Fun}$$

$$\frac{\texttt{coll}_1 \text{ is child of } \texttt{coll}_2 \quad \sigma \sqsubseteq \tau}{\texttt{coll}_1(\sigma) \sqsubseteq \texttt{coll}_2(\tau)} \; \text{GSR} - \text{Coll}$$

where $\texttt{coll}_1, \texttt{coll}_2$ are nodes in the sub-tree (figure 2) with root $\texttt{collection}$ and is child of signifies that $\texttt{coll}_2$ is a direct or indirect parent of $\texttt{coll}_1$ or that $\texttt{coll}_1$ and $\texttt{coll}_2$ are the same.

$$\frac{\texttt{constr}_1 \text{ is child of } \texttt{constr}_2 \quad \sigma_1 \sqsubseteq \tau_1 \cdots \sigma_k \sqsubseteq \tau_k}{\texttt{constr}_1(\texttt{l}_1\!:\!\sigma_1, \ldots, \texttt{l}_k\!:\!\sigma_k, \ldots, \texttt{l}_{k+n}\!:\!\sigma_{k+n}) \sqsubseteq \texttt{constr}_2(\texttt{l}_1\!:\!\tau_1, \ldots, \texttt{l}_k\!:\!\tau_k)} \; \text{GSR} - \text{Constr}$$

where $\texttt{constr}_1, \texttt{constr}_2$ are nodes in the sub-tree (figure 2) with root $\texttt{constructor}$, and is child of signifies that $\texttt{constr}_2$ is a direct parent of $\texttt{constr}_1$ or $\texttt{constr}_1$ and $\texttt{constr}_2$ are the same.

$$\frac{\texttt{atom}_1 \text{ is child of } \texttt{atom}_2}{\texttt{atom}_1 \sqsubseteq \texttt{atom}_2} \; \text{GSR} - \text{Atomic}$$

where $\texttt{atom}_1$ and $\texttt{atom}_2$ are nodes in the sub-tree (figure 2) with root $\texttt{atomic}$ and is child of signifies that $\texttt{atom}_2$ is direct or indirect parent of $\texttt{atom}_1$ or $\texttt{atom}_1$ and $\texttt{atom}_2$ are the same.

$$\frac{}{\sigma \sqsubseteq \sigma} \; \text{GSR} - \text{Refl} \qquad \frac{\sigma_1 \sqsubseteq \sigma_2 \quad \sigma_2 \sqsubseteq \sigma_3}{\sigma_1 \sqsubseteq \sigma_3} \; \text{GSR} - \text{Trans}$$

$$\frac{\sigma \neq \tau_1 \to \tau_2}{\sigma \sqsubseteq \texttt{nonfunctional}} \; \text{GSR} - \text{NonFun} \qquad \frac{}{\sigma \sqsubseteq \texttt{any}} \; \text{GSR} - \text{All}$$

Given this definition, we can define the *Greatest Lower Bound* (GLB) and the *Least Upper Bound* (LUB) of two types τ_1 and τ_2. Insight into these concepts can be gained through the following simple example. Consider the types $\tau_1 = \texttt{set(atomic)}$ and $\tau_2 = \texttt{set/bag(int)}$. The GLB of the two types is derived by taking the most specific of the collection constructors, $\texttt{set}$, and the most specific of the parameter types, $\texttt{int}$. Thus $\text{GLB}(\tau_1, \tau_2) = \texttt{set(int)}$. Likewise, for the LUB, we take the most general of the two collection constructors, $\texttt{set/bag}$, and the most general of the two parameter types, $\texttt{atomic}$. Thus, $\text{LUB}(\tau_1, \tau_2) = \texttt{set/bag(atomic)}$.

We may now formally present GLB and LUB. In the following definitions, we assume that $\texttt{constr}_1$, $\texttt{constr}_2$ are nodes in the sub-tree (figure 2) with root $\texttt{constructor}$ and that $\texttt{constr}_1$ is a child of $\texttt{constr}_2$ or $\texttt{constr}_1 = \texttt{constr}_2$. Moreover, $\texttt{coll}_1$ and $\texttt{coll}_2$ are nodes in the sub-tree (figure 2) with root $\texttt{collection}$ and $\texttt{coll}_1$ is a child of $\texttt{coll}_2$ or $\texttt{coll}_1 = \texttt{coll}_2$.

$$\text{GLB}(\tau_1, \tau_2) \stackrel{\text{def}}{=} \tau_1 \text{ if } \tau_1 \subseteq \tau_2 \wedge \tau_2 \subseteq \text{atomic}$$

$$\text{LUB}(\tau_1, \tau_2) \stackrel{\text{def}}{=} \tau \text{ if } \tau_1 \subseteq \text{atomic} \wedge \tau_2 \subseteq \text{atomic} \wedge$$
$$(\text{there exists no } \tau' \text{ s.t. } (\tau' \neq \tau \wedge \tau_1 \subseteq \tau' \wedge \tau_2 \subseteq \tau' \wedge \tau \subseteq \tau'))$$

$$\text{GLB}(\text{constr}_1(l_1 : \sigma_1, \ldots, l_k : \sigma_k), \text{constr}_2(l_1 : \sigma'_1, \ldots, l_k : \sigma'_k, \ldots, l_{k+n} : \sigma'_{k+n})) \stackrel{\text{def}}{=}$$
$$\text{constr}_1(l_1 : \text{GLB}(\sigma_1, \sigma'_1), \ldots, l_k : \text{GLB}(\sigma_k, \sigma'_k), \ldots, l_{k+n} : \sigma_{k+n})$$

$$\text{LUB}(\text{constr}_1(l_1 : \sigma_1, \ldots, l_k : \sigma_k), \text{constr}_2(l_1 : \sigma'_1, \ldots, l_k : \sigma'_k, \ldots, l_{k+n} : \sigma'_{k+n})) \stackrel{\text{def}}{=}$$
$$\text{constr}_2(l_1 : \text{LUB}(\sigma_1, \sigma'_1), \ldots, l_k : \text{LUB}(\sigma_k, \sigma'_k))$$

$$\text{GLB}(\text{coll}_1(\sigma_1), \text{coll}_2(\sigma_2)) \stackrel{\text{def}}{=} \text{coll}_1(\text{GLB}(\sigma_1, \sigma_2))$$

$$\text{LUB}(\text{coll}_1(\sigma_1), \text{coll}_2(\sigma_2)) \stackrel{\text{def}}{=} \text{coll}_2(\text{LUB}(\sigma_1, \sigma_2))$$

$$\text{GLB}(\tau_1 \times \cdots \times \tau_k \to \sigma, \tau'_1 \times \cdots \times \tau'_k \to \sigma') \stackrel{\text{def}}{=} \text{LUB}(\tau_1, \tau'_1) \times \cdots \times \text{LUB}(\tau_k, \tau'_k) \to \text{GLB}(\sigma, \sigma')$$

$$\text{LUB}(\tau_1 \times \cdots \times \tau_k \to \sigma, \tau'_1 \times \cdots \times \tau'_k \to \sigma') \stackrel{\text{def}}{=} \text{GLB}(\tau_1, \tau'_1) \times \cdots \times \text{LUB}(\tau_k, \tau'_k) \to \text{LUB}(\sigma, \sigma')$$

$$\text{LUB}(\sigma, \tau) \stackrel{\text{def}}{=} \text{any, if } \sigma \subseteq \text{function} \wedge \tau \subseteq \text{nonfunctional}$$

$$\text{LUB}(\sigma_1, \sigma_2) \stackrel{\text{def}}{=} \text{nonfunctional, if } \forall \tau_1, \tau_2 . \sigma_1 \subseteq \tau_1 \wedge \sigma_2 \subseteq \tau_2 \wedge \tau_1 \neq \tau_2 \wedge$$
$$\tau_1, \tau_2 \in \{\text{atomic}, \text{constructor}(), \text{collection}(\text{any})\}$$

4 Type Compatibility - Constraints

The inference algorithm we present in section 7 analyses an OQL construct and infers the most general type of the query and the schema requirements that should be satisfied so that the query is well-typed. Before being able to present the inference algorithm, we first discuss an important mechanism that the algorithm is based upon—the generation of constraints. When the inference algorithm analyses a certain query construct, it often infers several relations or associations amongst the types of the query and its subqueries. These associations are given in the form of constraints.

For example, the analysis of a query q_1 union q_2 would generate the constraint that the type τ of the query is the merge result of the types τ_1 and τ_2 of the two subqueries, i.e. $\tau = \text{Merge\_Result}(\tau_1, \tau_2)$. In section 5, we show how this constraint is simplified and is *assimilated* in the set of the existing constraints.

Analysing the query exists x in Customers: x.income $> 40,000$ our algorithm generates the following constraints. First, it introduces the constraint $\tau_1 = \text{Member\_Type}(\tau_2)$, where τ_1 is the type of x and τ_2 is the type of Customers. The type of x is expected to be the same as that of the members of the collection Customers. Second, the constraint $\tau_3 = \text{Constructor\_Member\_Type}(\tau_1, \text{income})$ is generated, where τ_3 is the type of x.income. This signifies that x is a constructor type (a structure or a class) with at least one member income of type τ_3. Another interesting constraint is that the types of x.income (τ_3) and of the literal $40,000$ (int) should be compatible in the sense that they than can be compared for inequality. This is expressed by the constraint $\text{Greater\_Less\_Than\_Compatible}(\tau_3, \text{int})$. Later, we will show how this constraint is simplified to the constraint $\tau_3 \subseteq \text{int/float}$.

In section 6, we give a set of inference rules, one for each query construct. Each rule starts with an existing set of constraints and generates a number (possibly zero) of new constraints. The different kinds of constraints generated by the rules in our inference algorithm are given below:

1. Equality_Compatible$(\tau_1, \ldots, \tau_n)$	6. $\tau_0 = $ Merge_Result(τ_1, τ_2)
2. Greater_Less_Than_Compatible$(\tau_1, \ldots, \tau_n)$	7. $\tau_0 = $ Distinct_Result(τ_1)
3. $\tau_1 = \tau_2$	8. $\tau = $ Member_Type(σ)
4. $\tau_1 \subseteq \tau_2$	9. $\tau = $ Constructor_Member_Type$(\sigma, 1)$
5. $\tau_0 = $ Arith_Result(τ_1, τ_2)	

We briefly explain the constraints used in our inference model. The constraint Equality_Compatible$(q_1, \ldots, q_n)$ is analysed in section 4.1. The constraint Greater_Less_Than_Compatible(q_1, q_2) is useful for ensuring typability for queries like $q_1 < q_2$. Type equality, and GSR (Generalisation-Specialisation Relationship) are handled by constraints 3 and 4. $\tau_0 = $ Arith_Result(τ_1, τ_2) is needed for the type inference of queries of the form $q_1 \, op \, q_2$ where $op \in \{+, -, /, *\}$. Likewise, $\tau_0 = $ Merge_Result(τ_1, τ_2) arises as a constraint from inferencing the type of **union**, **intersect** or **except** query expressions. The constraint $\tau_0 = $ Distinct_Result(τ_1) implies that both τ_0 and τ_1 are collection types and the collection constructor of τ_0 is the distinct equivalent of the collection constructor of τ_1. Moreover, $\tau = $ Member_Type(σ) implies that σ is a collection type and that τ is the type of its members. Finally, the constraint $\tau = $ Constructor_Member_Type$(\sigma, 1)$ is used to denote that σ is a **class** or **struct** type with at least one member 1 of type τ. If σ is a **class** type then 1 can be any of its properties, relationships or methods.

4.1   Collections - Membership Type Compatibility

The first two constraints refer to type compatibility w.r.t. equality or non-equality comparison. These constraints arise in OQL constructs that involve a merge of two or more elements, or a membership test. For instance, the first constraint results from considering a query of the form **set**$(q_1, \ldots, q_n)$, which includes the merge of n query results.

First of all, we should stress the fact that in order for two values (objects or literals) to be eligible as members of the same collection, they should be eligible for *equality comparison*. If two types are compatible (membership-wise), two values of these types may be members of a set. In order to insert an element into a set, we need to test if its value is equal to any existing value. Thus, we need to ensure that these values have types which are compatible (equality-wise). Inversely, if two types are compatible equality-wise, then their values may be inserted into any collection, therefore these types are also compatible membership-wise.

The Standard [§4.10] defines recursively when two types are compatible, and thus when elements of these types can be put in the same collection. The Standard then defines the notion of least upper bound (LUB) of two types to derive the type of the collection elements. In a context where we need to check and derive the type of a query based on *specific* type information (from a schema), this approach is sufficient and straightforward. However, in our context, where we aim to infer the type of a query without any schema information, the compatibility issue becomes more complicated. The use of LUB to infer the type of a query like $\mathtt{set}(q_1, \ldots, q_n)$ does not yield the appropriate result, for example consider the following.

```
define q1 as struct(x:12,y:30);
define q2 as element(select z from People as z where z.x=14);
set(q1,q2)
```

If we call the inference algorithm on q1 and q2 the inferred types (IT) would be $\mathtt{struct}(x : \mathtt{int}, y : \mathtt{int})$ and $\mathtt{constructor}(x : \mathtt{int})$ respectively. The least upper bound of these two types is $\mathtt{constructor}(x : \mathtt{int})$. Thus, the inferred type of the query $\mathtt{set}(q1,q2)$ would be $\mathtt{set}(\mathtt{constructor}(x : \mathtt{int}))$.

However, the correct inferred type should be $\mathtt{set}(\mathtt{struct}(x : \mathtt{int}))$, since we may not merge objects and structures in the same collection, and therefore we know that the constructor should be a struct and not a class.

To overcome this problem we define another relation between types, namely CUB (*Compatible Upper Bound*). Intuitively, CUB combines the behaviour of both LUB and GLB (Greatest Lower Bound). In the previous example, the CUB of the two types $\mathtt{IT}(q_1)$ and $\mathtt{IT}(q_2)$ would be derived by taking the most specific of the two constructor types (constructor and struct), but the least general of the element types ($(x : \mathtt{int})$ and $(x : \mathtt{int}, y : \mathtt{int})$). Before we define CUB, we define *compatibility* (Membership- or Equality- wise) for our typing system.

Compatibility is recursively defined as follows:

- τ is compatible with τ
- if σ is compatible with τ
  and $\mathtt{coll}_1, \mathtt{coll}_2 \in \{\mathtt{collection}, \mathtt{set/bag}, \mathtt{list/array}, \mathtt{set}, \mathtt{bag}, \mathtt{list}, \mathtt{array}\}$
  and either the collection constructors are the same or one is child of the other in the hierarchy tree then $\mathtt{coll}_1(\sigma)$ is compatible with $\mathtt{coll}_2(\tau)$.
- Any two class types $\mathtt{class\_name}_1$ and $\mathtt{class\_name}_2$ are compatible.
- If σ_i is compatible with τ_i, $\forall\, i = 1, \ldots, n$
  and $\mathtt{constr}_1, \mathtt{constr}_2 \in \{\mathtt{constructor}, \mathtt{struct}\}$
  and no labels other than $l_1, \ldots, l_n$ are common in both constructor types
  then $\mathtt{constr}_1(l_1 : \sigma_1, \ldots, l_n : \sigma_n, l_{11} : \sigma_{11}, \ldots, l_{1k} : \sigma_{1k})$ and
  $\mathtt{constr}_2(l_1 : \tau_1, \ldots, l_n : \tau_n, l_{21} : \tau_{21}, \ldots, l_{2m} : \tau_{2m})$ are compatible.
- If σ_i is compatible with τ_i, $\forall\, i = 1, \ldots, n$ and $\mathtt{class\_name}$ is a class type such that $\mathtt{Constructor\_Member\_Type}(\mathtt{class\_name}, l_i) = \tau_i$, $\forall\, i = 1, \ldots, n$, then the types $\mathtt{class\_name}$ and $\mathtt{constructor}\,(l_1 : \sigma_1, \ldots, l_n : \sigma_n, l_{11} : \sigma_{11}, \ldots, l_{1k} : \sigma_{1k})$ are compatible, provided that no labels other than $l_1, \ldots, l_n$ are common members in the two types.
- If $\sigma, \tau \in \{\mathtt{atomic}, \mathtt{orderable}, \mathtt{int/float}, \mathtt{int}, \mathtt{float}, \mathtt{char}, \mathtt{string}, \mathtt{bool}\}$
  and either they are the same, or one is a child of the other in the hierarchy tree, or one is int and the other is float
  then σ is compatible with τ.

- If either of the types is **nonfunctional** and the other type is not a function type then these types are compatible.
- If either of two types is **any**, then these types are compatible.

Note that we do not define compatibility for function types, as no two function values may be members of the same collection or may be compared for equality. Only the results of function application may be considered for compatibility.

Given that two types are compatible (based on the recursive definition above), their CUB is defined recursively and in accordance with the compatibility category that they fall into.

- $\text{CUB}(\tau, \tau) = \tau$.
- If $\text{coll}_1(\sigma)$ is compatible with $\text{coll}_2(\tau)$ and coll_1 is a child of (or the same as) coll_2, then $\text{CUB}(\text{coll}_1(\sigma), \text{coll}_2(\tau)) = \text{coll}_1(\text{CUB}(\sigma, \tau))$.
- If the types τ_1 and τ_2 are class types, then $\text{CUB}(\tau_1, \tau_2)$ is the least common superclass of the two classes.
- If the types $\sigma = \text{constr}_1(l_1: \sigma_1, \ldots, l_n: \sigma_n, l_{11}: \sigma_{11}, \ldots, l_{1k}: \sigma_{1k})$ and $\tau = \text{constr}_2(l_1: \tau_1, \ldots, l_n: \tau_n, l_{21}: \tau_{21}, \ldots, l_{2m}: \tau_{2m})$ are compatible, where $\text{constr}_1, \text{constr}_2 \in \{\text{constructor}, \text{struct}\}$ then $\text{CUB}(\sigma, \tau) = \text{constr}_1(l_1: \text{CUB}(\sigma_1, \tau_1), \ldots, l_n: \text{CUB}(\sigma_n, \tau_n))$.
- If $\sigma = \text{class\_name}_1$ and $\text{Constructor\_Member\_Type}(\text{class\_name}_1, l_i) = \sigma_i$, $\forall\, i = 1, \ldots, n$ and $\tau = \text{constructor}(l_1: \tau_1, \ldots, l_n: \tau_n, l_{21}: \tau_{21}, \ldots, l_{2m}: \tau_{2m})$ then $\text{CUB}(\sigma, \tau)$ is the least superclass of class_name_1, say class_name_2, satisfying the following condition: For all l'_j, l'_j is a property or a relationship of class_name_2, if $\text{Constructor\_Member\_Type}(\text{class\_name}_2, l'_j) = \phi_j$ then there exists $k, 1 \leq k \leq n$, s.t. $l'_j = l_k \wedge \text{CUP}(\tau_k, \sigma_k) \subseteq \phi_j$, $\forall\, j = 1, \ldots, m, m \leq n$.
- If σ is compatible with τ, then
    1. if either of them is **int/float** or one is **int** and the other is **float** then $\text{CUB}(\sigma, \tau) = \text{int/float}$
    2. else $\text{CUB}(\sigma, \tau) = \text{GLB}(\sigma, \tau)$.
- If $\sigma = \text{nonfunctional}$ and $\tau \subseteq \text{nonfunctional}$ then $\text{CUB}(\sigma, \tau) = \tau$.
- If $\sigma = \text{any}$ then, for any type τ, $\text{CUB}(\sigma, \tau) = \tau$.

As discussed earlier, the notion of CUB is used for the inference of the types of queries like $\text{set}(q_1, \ldots, q_n)$. However, the OQL construct q_1 in q_2 raises another issue of a slighly different nature. The Standard [§4.10.8.3] states that if the type of q_2 is $\text{coll}(\tau)$ then the type of q_1 should be τ. This is not the case in our context. Suppose that the type of q_2 is inferred to be $\text{bag}(\text{struct}(x: \text{int}, y: \text{string}))$; then according to the Standard q_1 should have the type $\text{struct}(x: \text{int}, y: \text{string})$. Since a value of type $\text{struct}(x: \text{int})$ could potentially be added in the collection q_2 (that is, since $\text{struct}(x: \text{int})$ and $\text{struct}(x: \text{int}, y: \text{float})$ are compatible types), there is no reason why q_1 could not be of type $\text{struct}(x: \text{int})$ or even $\text{struct}()$.

The same situation occurs when dealing with a collection of objects of different classes. Suppose $\texttt{lub\_class}(\texttt{l}_1\colon\sigma_1,\ldots,\texttt{l}_n\colon\sigma_n)$ is the LUB of all classes of the objects in the collection and $\texttt{Object}$ is the most general class that all other classes derive from (the top of the class hierarchy). We should be able to check whether an object of type $\texttt{object\_class}(\texttt{l}'_1\colon\sigma'_1,\ldots,\texttt{l}'_m\colon\sigma'_m)$ is a member of the collection, even if its class is not a subclass of $\texttt{lub\_class}(\texttt{l}_1\colon\sigma_1,\ldots,\texttt{l}_n\colon\sigma_n)$. This allows more queries to (safely) type-check, for example:

```
select x
from    People as x
where   x.father in School_Teachers
```

does not type-check according to the Standard. In order to be type-correct, $\texttt{x.father}$ requires an explicit type cast, i.e. $(\texttt{School\_Teacher})\texttt{x.father}$. The problem is that this query, despite being well-typed, can generate a runtime error (if the cast does not succeed). We choose not to enforce that $\texttt{x.father}$ has a type which is more specific than the member type or the collection $\texttt{School\_Teachers}$. Rather, we simply ensure that $\texttt{x.father}$ could potentially be a member of $\texttt{School\_Teachers}$. To do this we add the constraint $\texttt{Equality\_Compatible}(\sigma,\tau)$, where σ is the type of $\texttt{x.father}$ and τ is the member type of $\texttt{School\_Teachers}$.

5   Resolving Constraints

Now that we have studied the kinds of constraints that are generated by our inference algorithm, we can discuss how these constraints are resolved. When a constraint is generated by an inference rule, it is added to the set of existing constraints. If this was a simple insertion procedure, we would end up having a huge set of constraints, that would include redundant and often incomprehensible type information; there is obviously a need to resolve the inserted constraints. Due to the complexity of the type system and the expressiveness of the language, we have a wide variety of constraints, that cannot be solved using a standard unification mechanism alone [10]. In our system, the insertion of a new constraint in a set of existing constraints may have one of the following effects:

- A constraint is deleted, if it is always satisfied, e.g. the constraint
  $\texttt{Equality\_Compatible}(\texttt{set(int)},\texttt{set(float)})$
  is always true, so it does not need to be maintained.
- A constraint raises a type error or exception, if it is never satisfied, e.g.
  $\texttt{set(Employee(name : string))} \subseteq \texttt{list/array(Employee(name : string))}$.
- A constraint might be maintained as it is. This usually occurs when some of the types involved are *general*; it may be that when refined, these types no longer satisfy the constraint. Therefore, they must be preserved as required schema information. For instance, if $\tau_i \subseteq \texttt{set/bag}(\tau)\forall~i = 0,1,2$ are in the set of already produced constraints, the constraint $\tau_0 = \texttt{Merge\_Result}(\tau_1,\tau_2)$ needs to be preserved.

- A constraint is often simplified, i.e. replaced by one or more simpler constraints. For instance, the constraint $\mathtt{set}(\sigma) = \mathtt{set}(\tau)$ is replaced by the simpler one $\sigma = \tau$.
- A constraint occasionally implies one or more constraints. The latter need to be added to the set of constraints already produced. For example, the constraint $\mathtt{Greater\_Less\_Than\_Compatible}(\tau_1, \tau_2)$ is inserted as a new constraint along with the implied constraints $\tau_1 \subseteq \mathtt{orderable}$ and $\tau_2 \subseteq \mathtt{orderable}$.

The effect varies depending on the constraint kind, the types involved in the constraint and the already existing constraints on these types. The details of the constraint resolution algorithm will appear in [11].

It is worth pointing out that the resolution of constraints could take place either at the time each constraint is generated (*gradual resolution*) or at the time all the constraints have been produced (*accumulative resolution*).

The *gradual resolution* is very simple, since it usually concerns the insertion of a few constraints whose simplification (*unification*) is straightforward. If their simplification produces new constraints then these are simplified as well, until no more constraints are produced.

The *accumulative resolution* starts from the constraints of the form $\tau_1 = \tau_2$. It simplifies them to constraints of the form $\mathtt{type\_var} = \tau$ and replaces $\mathtt{type\_var}$ by τ in all other constraints that involve $\mathtt{type\_var}$. Then it proceeds to simplify all other kinds of constraints. If a simplification leads to more constraints, the latter are added to the set of unprocessed constraints and are simplified in due course.

6 Type Inference Rules

Having explained the type system underlying our inference model and the various constraints generated and resolved by our algorithm, we are now in a position to present the backbone of our work, the *inference rules*. Note that there is a single rule for each OQL construct, and, therefore, the use of the rules by the inference algorithm is syntax driven. In the remainder of this section, we present a substantial part of the inference rules; the complete set will be given in [11].

In the following rules, $\mathcal{H}$ signifies the *type environment*, that is $\mathcal{H} = \{var_i : \tau_i\}$, and $\mathcal{C}$ denotes the *constraints* added so far. The inference rules for the literal and the identifier queries are given first:

$$\frac{}{\mathcal{H}; \mathcal{C} \vdash b \colon \mathtt{bool} \Rightarrow \mathcal{C}} \qquad \frac{}{\mathcal{H}; \mathcal{C} \vdash i \colon \mathtt{int} \Rightarrow \mathcal{C}} \qquad \frac{}{\mathcal{H}; \mathcal{C} \vdash f \colon \mathtt{float} \Rightarrow \mathcal{C}}$$

$$\frac{}{\mathcal{H}; \mathcal{C} \vdash c \colon \mathtt{char} \Rightarrow \mathcal{C}} \qquad \frac{}{\mathcal{H}; \mathcal{C} \vdash s \colon \mathtt{string} \Rightarrow \mathcal{C}} \qquad \frac{}{\mathcal{H} \cup \{x \colon \sigma\}; \mathcal{C} \vdash x \colon \sigma \Rightarrow \mathcal{C}}$$

There are several rules to deal with various collections (sets, bags, lists, arrays). We just give one representative rule, that concerns the query construct $\mathtt{set}(q_1, \ldots, q_n)$. As expected, the rule generates a constraint that ensures that the types of the queries are compatible equality-wise (or membership-wise). We also give the rules for accessing the first, last or i-th member of an ordered collection, as well as checking whether an element belongs in a certain collection. The constraint $\texttt{Member\_Type}(\sigma) = \tau$ denotes that σ is a collection (set, bag, list or array) with members of type τ.

$$\frac{\mathcal{H}; \mathcal{C} \vdash q_1 : \sigma_1 \Rightarrow \mathcal{C}_1 \quad \dots \quad \mathcal{H}; \mathcal{C}_{n-1} \vdash q_n : \sigma_n \Rightarrow \mathcal{C}_n}{\mathcal{H}; \mathcal{C} \vdash \texttt{set}(q_1, \dots, q_n) : \texttt{set}(\texttt{CUB}(\sigma_1, \dots, \sigma_n)) \Rightarrow \mathcal{C}_n \wedge \{\texttt{Equality\_Compatible}(\sigma_1, \dots, \sigma_n)\}}$$

$$\frac{\mathcal{H}; \mathcal{C} \vdash q_1 : \sigma \Rightarrow \mathcal{C}_1}{\mathcal{H}; \mathcal{C} \vdash \texttt{first}(q_1) : \phi \Rightarrow \mathcal{C}_1 \wedge \{\texttt{Member\_Type}(\sigma) = \phi\} \wedge \{\sigma \subseteq \texttt{list}/\texttt{array}(\phi)\}}$$

$$\frac{\mathcal{H}; \mathcal{C} \vdash q_1 : \sigma \Rightarrow \mathcal{C}_1 \quad \mathcal{H}; \mathcal{C}_1 \vdash q_2 : \tau \Rightarrow \mathcal{C}_2}{\mathcal{H}; \mathcal{C} \vdash q_1[q_2] : \phi \Rightarrow \mathcal{C}_2 \wedge \{\tau = \texttt{int}\} \wedge \{\texttt{Member\_Type}(\sigma) = \phi\} \wedge \{\sigma \subseteq \texttt{list}/\texttt{array}(\phi)\}}$$

$$\frac{\mathcal{H}; \mathcal{C} \vdash q_1 : \sigma \Rightarrow \mathcal{C}_1 \quad \mathcal{H}; \mathcal{C}_1 \vdash q_2 : \tau \Rightarrow \mathcal{C}_2}{\mathcal{H}; \mathcal{C} \vdash q_1 \texttt{ in } q_2 : \texttt{bool} \Rightarrow \mathcal{C}_2 \wedge \{\texttt{Equality\_Compatible}(\sigma, \texttt{Member\_Type}(\tau))\}}$$

The rules for constructing a structure or an object, as well as for accessing a member of a structure or an object are given below. The constraint $\texttt{Constructor\_Member\_Type}(\sigma, \ell) = \tau$ denotes that type σ is a class or a structure with a member called ℓ of type τ.

$$\frac{\mathcal{H}; \mathcal{C} \vdash q_1 : \sigma_1 \Rightarrow \mathcal{C}_1 \quad \dots \quad \mathcal{H}; \mathcal{C}_{n-1} \vdash q_n : \sigma_n \Rightarrow \mathcal{C}_n}{\begin{array}{c} \mathcal{H}; \mathcal{C} \vdash \texttt{class\_name}(l_1 : q_1, \dots, l_n : q_n) : \texttt{class\_name} \Rightarrow \mathcal{C}_n \wedge \\ \{\sigma_1 \subseteq \texttt{Constructor\_Member\_Type}(\texttt{class\_name}, l_1)\} \wedge \dots \wedge \\ \{\sigma_n \subseteq \texttt{Constructor\_Member\_Type}(\texttt{class\_name}, l_n)\} \end{array}}$$

$$\frac{\mathcal{H}; \mathcal{C} \vdash q_1 : \sigma_1 \Rightarrow \mathcal{C}_1 \quad \dots \quad \mathcal{H}; \mathcal{C}_{n-1} \vdash q_n : \sigma_n \Rightarrow \mathcal{C}_n}{\mathcal{H}; \mathcal{C} \vdash \texttt{struct}(l_1 : q_1, \dots, l_n : q_n) : \texttt{struct}(l_1 : \sigma_1, \dots, l_n : \sigma_n) \Rightarrow \mathcal{C}_n}$$

$$\frac{\mathcal{H}; \mathcal{C} \vdash q_1 : \tau \Rightarrow \mathcal{C}_1}{\mathcal{H}; \mathcal{C} \vdash q_1.l : \sigma \Rightarrow \mathcal{C}_1 \wedge \{\texttt{Constructor\_Member\_Type}(\tau, 1) : \sigma\}}$$

The inference rules for the existential and the universal quantification follow. It is worth noting that the variable x is bound in query q_2 to the member type of the collection q_1.

$$\frac{\mathcal{H}; \mathcal{C} \vdash q_1 : \sigma_1 \Rightarrow \mathcal{C}_1 \quad \mathcal{H} \cup \{x : \phi\}; \mathcal{C}_1 \vdash q_2 : \sigma_2 \Rightarrow \mathcal{C}_2}{\mathcal{H}; \mathcal{C} \vdash \texttt{exists } x \texttt{ in } q_1 : q_2 : \texttt{bool} \Rightarrow \mathcal{C}_2 \wedge \{\sigma_2 = \texttt{bool}\} \wedge \{\texttt{Member\_Type}(\sigma_1) = \phi\}}$$

$$\frac{\mathcal{H}; \mathcal{C} \vdash q_1 : \sigma_1 \Rightarrow \mathcal{C}_1 \quad \mathcal{H} \cup \{x : \phi\}; \mathcal{C}_1 \vdash q_2 : \sigma_2 \Rightarrow \mathcal{C}_2}{\mathcal{H}; \mathcal{C} \vdash \texttt{forall } x \texttt{ in } q_1 : q_2 : \texttt{bool} \Rightarrow \mathcal{C}_2 \wedge \{\sigma_2 = \texttt{bool}\} \wedge \{\texttt{Member\_Type}(\sigma_1) = \phi\}}$$

An interesting set of rules concerns the application of methods with or without parameters. The inferred types of the queries used as arguments are not constrained to be the same as the types of the parameters of the method involved. They only need to be their subtypes.

$$\frac{\mathcal{H}; \mathcal{C} \vdash q_1 : \sigma \Rightarrow \mathcal{C}_1}{\mathcal{H}; \mathcal{C} \vdash q_1() : \phi \Rightarrow \mathcal{C}_1 \wedge \{\sigma = \texttt{unit} \rightarrow \phi\}}$$

$$\frac{\mathcal{H}; \mathcal{C} \vdash q_0 : \sigma_0 \Rightarrow \mathcal{C}_0 \ \ldots \ \mathcal{H}; \mathcal{C}_{n-1} \vdash q_n : \sigma_n \Rightarrow \mathcal{C}_n}{\mathcal{H}; \mathcal{C} \vdash q_0(q_1, \ldots, q_n) : \phi \Rightarrow \mathcal{C}_n \wedge \{\sigma_0 = \tau_1 \times \ldots \times \tau_n \rightarrow \phi\} \wedge \{\sigma_1 \subseteq \tau_1\} \wedge \ldots \wedge \{\sigma_n \subseteq \tau_n\}}$$

The rules concerning the query constructs q binop q or unop q are omitted for space reasons. We finish by giving the rule for a simple select query; the judgements dealing with a group by or an order by clause can be found in [11].

$$\mathcal{H}; \mathcal{C} \vdash q_1 : \sigma_1 \Rightarrow \mathcal{C}_1$$
$$\mathcal{H} \cup \{x_1 : \tau_1\}; \mathcal{C}_1 \vdash q_2 : \sigma_2 \Rightarrow \mathcal{C}_2$$

$$\ldots$$

$$\mathcal{H} \cup \{x_1 : \tau_1, \ldots, x_{n-1} : \tau_{n-1}\}; \mathcal{C}_{n-1} \vdash q_n : \sigma_n \Rightarrow \mathcal{C}_n$$
$$\mathcal{H} \cup \{x_1 : \tau_1, \ldots, x_n : \tau_n\}; \mathcal{C}_n \vdash q_{01} : \sigma_{01} \Rightarrow \mathcal{C}_{01}$$
$$\mathcal{H} \cup \{x_1 : \tau_1, \ldots, x_n : \tau_n\}; \mathcal{C}_{01} \vdash q_{00} : \sigma_{00} \Rightarrow \mathcal{C}_{00}$$

$$\overline{\mathcal{H}; \mathcal{C} \vdash \texttt{select } q_{00} \texttt{ from } q_1 \texttt{ as } x_1, \ldots, q_n \texttt{ as } x_n \texttt{ where } q_{01} : \texttt{bag}(\sigma_{00}) \Rightarrow \mathcal{C}_{00} \wedge}$$
$$\{\texttt{Member\_Type}(\sigma_1) = \tau_1\} \wedge \ldots \wedge \{\texttt{Member\_Type}(\sigma_n) = \tau_n\} \wedge \{\sigma_{01} = \texttt{bool}\}$$

7   Inference Algorithm

Having given an overview of the type system, the constraints and the rules involved in our inference model, we may now present the core of our work, which is the inference algorithm. The algorithm takes as input a query q and returns its inferred type, as well as a pair $(\mathcal{H}, \mathcal{C})$ of a type environment and its constraints. This pair is a synopsis of the requirements a schema should satisfy so that the query q can be executed against it without any type-errors.

1. For each free variable var in the query q, $\mathcal{H} = \mathcal{H} \cup \{\texttt{var} : \texttt{new\_type\_var}\}$. Initially $\mathcal{C} = \{\}$.
2. Based on the construct of the query q recursively apply the appropriate inference rule.
3. Depending on the unification strategy, either simplify the constraints as soon as they are produced (gradual unification) or simplify them all in the end after having applied all the inference rules. If the unification process produces a type-error then the query is not typable and the algorithm is interrupted.
4. The final $\mathcal{H}, \mathcal{C}$ include the requirements a schema should have to be compatible with the query q. The type of q, which is the type inferred by the outer inference rule, also satisfies the constraints $\mathcal{C}$.

8   Related Work and Conclusions

Fundamental to the work described in this report is the type system for ODMG OQL described in an earlier paper [3]. Alagić [2] independently gave a number of typing rules for OQL; see our earlier paper for a comparison. The canonical reference for work on type systems for database programming languages is the work of Buneman and Ohori [5]. The goals of their type inference algorithm are identical to ours; both approaches infer the most general type of an expression (if one exists) without accessing any schema information, and in this sense determine the constraints placed on the schema by the query. However, the underlying languages, the type systems, and some parts of the inference algorithms differ considerably. Buneman and Ohori introduce kinded types to infer the type of a record based on selections of fields on this record. Instead, we use the notion of *general* types; in this way we are able to express general type information not only for records, but also for parametric collection types, structures and classes. Moreover, due to the syntax of OQL, we define a wider variety of constraints than those introduced in their framework and therefore a different algorithm to resolve them.

The work most related to ours arises from studying type systems for object oriented programming languages, see for example [8,9,1]. However none of these studies consider the various issues arising from studying *database* type systems; for example, the complications arising from combining parametric collection types with subtyping.

Much research on schema evolution, schema inter-operation, distributed or semi-structured database applications has pointed out that there is a need to run queries in the presence of changing or heterogeneous schemata, or even in the absence of specific schema information. Our work addresses this problem, by proposing an inference algorithm for the ODMG query language OQL. This algorithm infers the most general type of an OQL query and derives the schema information required so that the query can be executed against it without any type errors. In contrast to other work, we deal with a rather complex type system, which includes atomic types, structures, classes, various (parameterised) collection types (set, bag, list, array) and function types. This, in connection with the rich semantics of OQL, results in the generation of a wide variety of constraints by the inference rules. We discuss the semantics of these constraints and provide a mechanism for their solution. Finally, we present a set of inference rules for OQL, which is the core of our type inference algorithm. Based on our experience, this algorithm, as well as all the formalisms prior to it, are easy to implement, and hence, we believe that they could prove to be useful in many applications.

Acknowledgements. Trigoni is funded by the State Scholarships Foundation of Greece and the National Bank of Greece.

References

1. O. Agesen and U. Holzle. Type feedback vs. concrete type inference: a comparison of optimization techniques for object-oriented languages. In *OOPSLA*, pages 91–107, 1995.

2. S. Alagić. Type checking OQL queries in the ODMG type systems. *ACM Transactions on Database Systems*, 24(3):319–360, September 1999.

3. G.M. Bierman and A. Trigoni. Towards a formal type system for ODMG OQL. Technical Report 497, University of Cambridge, Computer Laboratory, October 2000.

4. M.W. Bright, A.R. Hurson, and S. Pakzad. Automated resolution of semantic heterogeneity in multidatabases. *ACM Transactions on Database Systems*, 19(2), 1994.

5. P. Buneman and A. Ohori. Polymorphism and type inference in database programming. *ACM Transactions on Database Systems*, 21(1):30–76, March 1996.

6. R.G.G. Cattell et al. *The Object Data Standard: ODMG 3.0*. Morgan Kaufmann, 2000.

7. R. Hull. Managing semantic heterogeneity in databases: A theoretical perspective. In *PODS*, 1997.

8. J. Palsberg and M. I. Schwartzbach. Object-oriented type inference. In *OOPSLA*, pages 146–161, 1991.

9. J. Plevyak and A.A. Chien. Precise concrete type inference for object-oriented languages. In *OOPSLA*, pages 324–340, 1994.

10. J. A. Robinson. A machine-oriented logic based on the resolution principle. *Journal of the ACM*, 12(1):23–41, January 1965.

11. A. Trigoni. Phd thesis, to appear. 2001.

Immersed Visual Data Mining: Walking the Walk

Ayman Ammoura, Osmar R. Zaïane, and Yuan Ji

Department of Computing Science, University of Alberta, Edmonton, AB, Canada
{ayman, zaiane, jiyuan}@cs.ualberta.ca

Abstract. This paper presents a flexible system, DIVE-ON, for the purpose of visual data mining. A new approach to interactively visualize and explore N-dimensional data warehouses in an immersed virtual environment is put forth. DIVE-ON is capable of constructing a multidimensional data model on a remote system, transporting pertinent views to a CAVE, creating an immersed virtual environment and providing an interactive data mining toolset. DIVE-ON architecture emphasizes the development of two independent subsystems, a visualization environment and a virtual data warehouse. The first objective of our research is to examine the possibility of effective mining, and manipulating views with little or no instructional help by providing an environment that is built around the human's visual, sensorimotor, and spatial knowledge acquisition abilities. The second goal is to create a highly transparent and centralized data warehouse that integrates various distributed data sources. Within the warehouse, DIVE-ON incorporates an XML-based multidimensional query language (XMDQL) to circulate the queries among the distributed data sources.

1 Introduction

Data mining and data visualization have become two essential tools in data analysis. While data mining relies on algorithms, structures and operations for data extraction, visualization techniques rely on advances in computer graphics and the human visual system to convey this extracted knowledge. Datamining in an Immersed Virtual Environment Over a Network, **DIVE-ON**, is the name of a system that utilizes advances in virtual reality, databases, and distributed computing to develop a new approach to visual data mining through the use of Virtual Reality (**VR**). The system's high modularity ensures that deploying various visualization technologies and various data warehouse architectures can be achieved independently of one another.

At an amazing rate, corporations worldwide are mining their data to learn more in many areas including fraud, client purchasing patterns, fleet utilization, credit applications and health care outcome analysis. Significant research efforts have been devoted towards facilitating the ability to access pertinent information, which may be hidden beneath massive data volumes that have been collecting in distributed repositories for many years. Data warehouses have been

B. Read (Ed.): BNCOD 2001, LNCS 2097, pp. 202–218, 2001.

developed to aid in our request for a framework that is well suited for the purpose of Knowledge Discovery in Databases (**KDD**). Data warehouses incorporate a multidimensional data model that is designed for the use of knowledge workers [11] (upper management and analysts) for online analytic processing (**OLAP**) so that historical data can be quickly presented in various views and degrees of abstraction.

Although a notable amount of research and development has been devoted to the research and development of data mining algorithms, distributed DBMS, VR, and data visualization, the amalgamation of all these advances into one body is rather new. Due to very restrictive limitations in hardware technology, multidimensional data visualization applications have been employed towards commercial use only in the early 1990s. DIVE-ON is our attempt to advance this process a step further by combining advances in VR, computer graphics, and data mining into a flexible system that can be used effectively with little or no training. This paper is organized into three main sections. The complete system end-to-end is presented first, then the concept of immersion in a virtual environment is presented along with the state of the art IVE system, CAVE theatre (Section 3). The fourth section presents the architecture of the Virtual Data Warehouse (**VDW**) and illustrates how the XML-based (XMDQL) queries are formed, parsed, and distributed among the various data sources.

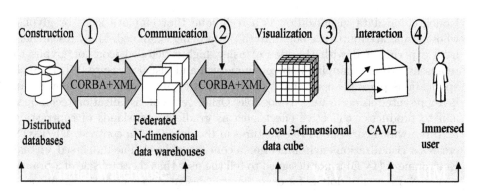

Fig. 1. The three components of the DIVE-ON system.

2   Complete System Overview

DIVE-ON can be abstracted in terms of three task-specific subsystems, which are tightly coupled to provide the services required. Figure 1 shows various layers composing the complete system from the server-side (DBMS) to the client-side (CAVE). The first subsystem is the Virtual Data Warehouse (VDW) (details in Figure 8) which is responsible for creating and managing the data warehouse over the distributed DBMS. A main component of the virtual warehouse is a shell, Data Cube Constructor Shell (DCC-Shell) that fulfills incoming data transportation/query messages (Figure 1 (1) and (2)). The second subsystem is the Visualization Control Unit (**VCU**), which is responsible for the creation and handling of the virtual world in a manner that maximizes the frame rate to ensure that the "reality" in virtual reality is not compromised (Figure 1 (3), details in Figure 6). The ability to provide interactive virtual data mining tools is the task of the third subsystem, the User Interface Manager (**UIM**) (Figure 1 (4), details in Figure 5). Inter and intra subsystem data exchange is handled via a set of specialized interfaces that implement specific protocols to guarantee reliability, extendibility and subsystem independence. This communication is granted though the implementation of client and server applications by using both Common Object Request Broker Architecture (CORBA) [4] over TCP/IP and Simple Object Access Protocol (SOAP) [19] over HTTP. In later stages of our research, we will evaluate and compare the two implementations. Messages between subsystems are transmitted as XML documents, which contain the requests and the corresponding responses (Section 4). In terms of location, the VCU and the UIM exist locally in the graphics research facilities at the University of Alberta, while the VDW can be distributed and remote.

3   Immersed Iconographic Visualization

Iconographic data visualization is a technique that employs icons or glyphs, whose visual attributes are bound to the data being examined. Many researchers have experimented with the idea of using highly detailed icons or glyphs to represent a direct mapping between numerical and visual measure [17] [7]. Such applications place great emphasis on the quantity of a measure and how it can be represented as accurately as possible. Other types of visualization techniques aim to produce a collective effect such as gradients or islands of contrasting textures, which correspond to structures in the data [14]. In contrast, DIVE-ON creates a visualization environment on a conceptual level. The Immersed Virtual Environment (**IVE**) is not designed to tell the user that the total sale of a branch was an X amount of dollars for example; it is designed to convey the significance of this amount.

3.1   The CAVE Environment

While the gathering and building of information can be done from any location, the actual visualization experience takes advantage of the state-of-the-art virtual reality environment in Canada at the University of Alberta. This facility is called VizRoom that is formally known as CAVE Theatre (CAVE and VizRoom are used interchangeably). CAVE is a recursive acronym (Cave Automatic Virtual Environment) [5] and refers to a visualization environment that places the user within three (9.5 X 9.5) feet walls (Figure 2). Each of these walls is back-projected with a high-resolution projector that delivers the rendered graphics at 120 frames per second (Figure 3). The graphics projected are in stereo (60

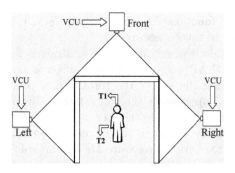

Fig. 2. A CAVE user within the three back-projected walls. T1, T2: The head and hand-held tracker data stream respectively (Real-time).

frames per second for each eye), which enables DIVE-ON to create *stereoscopic* views that can be seen by the user by wearing lightweight shutter glasses. This type of IVE was chosen for the DIVE-ON over other system for several reasons including.

- The user is free to move naturally without the constraints of the head mounted display (HMD).
- As mentioned above, the DIVE-ON is essentially a decision support tool and most likely will be used by a group or a team of analysts.
- Within the CAVE any view at anytime is instantly available to all for examination and discussion (Figure 3.a). Within the walls of the CAVE one is able to naturally communicate with others, like hand use to point out an interesting data item to others.
- It is easier to increase realism in a CAVE environment since both the left view and the right view are already rendered (on the left and right walls). This enables the user access to readily available views in a natural way, by simply turning their head. With the HMD, the head orientation is tracked (T1 in Figure 2) and used to trigger image rotation in correspondence with the user's head rotation.
- From previous experiments, hygienic factors were a big issue for some users. After all, wearing a helmet with an inside display while walking around will definitely make most of us sweat.

3.2   Creating the Virtual Objects

The data presented to the user in the IVE is encoded using graphical objects; these are the objects that actually make up the rendered virtual world. The VCU views the three-dimensional cube it receives from the VDW (Section 4) as a three variable function. Each of the three data dimensions becomes associated with one of the three physical dimensions, namely X, Y, and Z. Since each entry in the data cube is a structure containing two measures M_1 and M_2, the VCU simply plots the two functions $M_1(x, y, z)$ and $M_2(x, y, z)$ in $\Re^3$. Next we will present the meaning of these measures.

Assume that the data warehouse under analysis is built around the theme "dollars sold". An OLAP decision support person is not primarily interested in the fact that during the year t the total sale of product p at store s was $100,000.00; what is important is the context that this measure occurs within. The VCU expresses this context to the user in VR by associating these measures with visual cues that are bound to the virtual objects. The first cue we use is *size*, which is associated with the measure M_1 (dollars sold). After normalization, $M_1(x_t, y_p, z_s)$ is used to render a cube (or a sphere) of that length (or radius) centered at position (x_t, y_p, z_s), for some t, p, and s within the data range. Figure 3 illustrates this criteria. A user walking among these virtual objects in VR becomes almost instantly aware of the relative significance of each value without the need for numeric data.

(a)   (b)

Fig. 3. A team of immersed users discussing the "dollars sold" data cube. (a) Using cubes. (b) A user pointing the direction of flight within 3D-lit spheres.

The second cue used is the object's *colour*. An 8-colour palette is chosen and the range of normalized values of the measure M_2 are discretized and mapped to the palette. The palette extremes are "red", representing a "high" measure value, and "blue" representing a "low" value. As the magnitude of a measure increases in value so does the red content of its associated object. Using colour to encode data attributes has many significant applications. For example, at the lowest level of aggregation (high granularity) colour can be used to represent the deviation from the mean along one of the dimensions, profit margins and availability. This is particularly useful for market fluctuation, utilization and profitability analysis.

Furthermore, if the user is viewing the data in a highly summarized view, the colour can become a very effective tool that helps the user locate anomalies at a lower level. For example, the M_2 value for a month object can represent the maximum M_2 found in all the days it aggregates. In Figure 3, a virtual object representing the total revenue for a given year with the colour "red", could indicate that one of the months has a great deviation from the rest of the year. This will entice the analyst to *reach* in virtual reality and "select" that object [22] to understand the reason and inquire about the exact figures for that year. Alternatively, the user may be interested in knowing that a great stability dominates a product category (a "blue" object).

Figure 3 presents the IVE created by rendering cubes that embody the above-described use of visual cues. The three dimensions X, Y, and Z are mapped to the data cube dimensions Product, Supplier and Location respectively. Colour is associated, in this example, with the profit margin while size with gross revenue [22]. The user may request the data attributes to be encoded using cubes (Figure 3.a) or spheres (Figure 3.b); while rendering cubes is much faster, using spheres reveals more information using the same virtual space.

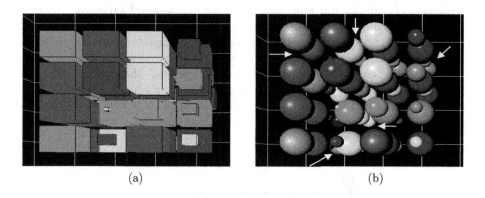

(a)   (b)

Fig. 4. Same data attributes from the same viewpoint using cubes and spheres: (a) Aggregates as cubes (b) The arrows point some of the data objects that are occluded in (a).

Using spheres makes it easier to distinguish between objects that are within close proximity to one another. To illustrate, Figure 4 shows two snapshot of a small-scale version of DIVE-ON running on a PC. Both images represent the same data, from the same viewpoint, and using the same distance between object centres. The arrows in (Figure 4.b) point at few of the objects that were previously invisible in (Figure 4.a). It is apparent that using spheres "exposes" more data items within the same display area. Spheres are indeed a better presentation for the data for two main reasons. First, to be able to distinguish between a "filled circle" and a sphere the graphics engine must perform shading and light calculations of the surface rendered. The variation of the shadow intensity on the surface of the sphere is a significant visual cue that aids the user in locating where one ends and another begins. Second, a sphere occludes fewer objects simply because they require less volume. Suppose that we are representing an aggregate of a size-attribute r using a cube of length r and a sphere of diameter r.

Since the volume of a sphere is approximately $(0.476r^3)$ less than that of a cube, using a sphere instead of a cube clears exactly that amount of volume for the line of sight to penetrate through.

3.3   The User Interface Manager (UIM)

To support various VR devices, tools, and environments it was necessary to separate the creation and the application of the virtual world. The User Interface Manager (UIM) is the subsystem that is responsible for the reception, filtration, formulation, and channeling of all available input streams. All tracker signals feed into the UIM for preprocessing (Figure 5, (TI) Tracker Interface). Constant update of the user's location is necessary to determine the initial location of the floating menu (Figure 3.a), the active menu number, and the current menu choices. This information is used by the VCU to immerse the user with the graphical objects by providing him/her with the sense of presence. To create such an environment, the body motion data collected by the UIM (T1 in Figure 2) is used to translate the stereo graphics in a manner that simulates the real world. For example, if the user walks forward, the appropriate image translation would be backwards to create the illusion of "walking" through the data. The data stream (T2 in Figure 2), emitted from the user's hand, is used to track the position of the 3D menu in the virtual world. This is why they are called "floating menus," because their location is mapped, with six degrees of freedom (6-DOF), to the user's hand [9].

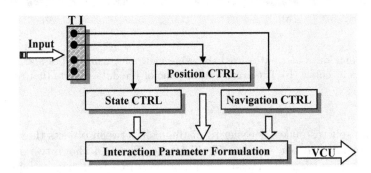

Fig. 5.   User Interface Manager. The Tracker Interface (TI) receives the real-time tracker input stream and channels it according to type. The set of interaction parameters is then fed to the VCU.

In almost every IVE application the essence of computer-human interaction can be categorized as object manipulation, viewpoint manipulation, or application control [12]. The reason for this taxonomy is the fact that simulating reality is all about simulating the changing views around us along with the ability to interact with the objects that make up these views. As a result, an interface that is highly transparent must use the human sensorimotor system to its advantage by providing the proper visual feedback to the user's motion. Understanding these issues helped us provide an interface that requires little or no instructions; however, it should be clear that the user is required to have an understanding of the data source and OLAP operations. All the interactive capabilities of DIVE-ON have been grouped in adherence with the above categorization. The users chosen in our experiments were people that are familiar with the architecture of the data warehouse being viewed and with the terminology and methodologies of data mining.

3.4   The Visualization Control Unit (VCU)

The VCU is the module responsible for generating and managing the Immersed Virtual Environment (IVE) for data visualization and exploration and should be viewed only as such. This means that the specifics of the VDW should be of no concern to the VCU developer and vice versa. To implement this abstract view, each of the VCU and VDW are constructed within a wrapper that provides the only mean of relaying messages between the two subsystems. A simple communication protocol that defines a set of requests (VCU to DCC) and their corresponding replays (DCC to VCU) is implemented in DIVE-ON. This design effectively hides the implementation details and allows the VCU and the DCC to be independent of one another. After the DCC completes the creation of the N-dimensional data cube it signals the VCU (via the DCC-Shell). Since we are generating a 3D virtual world, only a subset of the available dimensions can be viewed at any given time (up to 7 dimensions: 3 physical dimensions in addition to the colour, size, animation and possibly sound [22]). The given dimensions that are chosen by the user are extracted from the N-dimensional data cube and a sub-data cube is passed to the VCU for rendering. In light of the above discussion, what level of abstraction does the sub-cube represent? In other words, is the sub-cube highly summarized or highly abstracted? Since the user will be placed within an IVE, it is imperative that the delay to the user's actions is kept at a minimal. For this reason, DIVE-ON relies on the VCU to perform the data aggregation required (generating less detailed data). This effectively reduces network dependence to a minimum.

As illustrated in Figure 6, the VCU contains a module called "VR Partition." This module is used to provide DIVE-ON with the scalability needed when handling massive amounts of data. As the amount of rendered objects increase, the frame rate of the image transformations decrease. This effectively reduces the sense of presence since the latency between the user's motion and the image update has increased. To prevent such situations, only portions of the virtual world that are visible to the user are actually rendered. Using a special type of Octrees to partition the virtual world based on the user's virtual location is implemented by the VCU. The details of the approach are not within the focus of this paper and will be published separately.

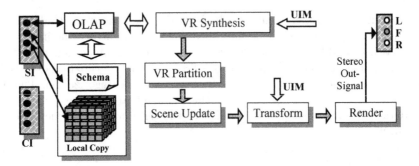

Fig. 6. The VCU Architecture. SI and CI are the SOAP and CORBA client Interfaces respectively. Output is channeled to Left, Front, and Right projection stereo signals.

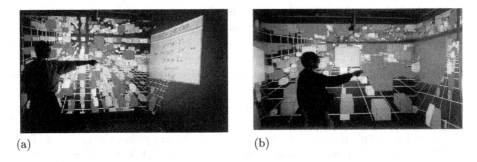

(a)   (b)

Fig. 7. : (a) An exocentric presence within the IVE. (b) Using the hand-held tracker to fly through the data. Once the user locates an "interesting" locality, they may stop the flight mode and start walking for detailed exploration.

4   The Virtual Data Warehouse (VDW)

The Virtual Data Warehouse (VDW) is a conceptualization of a centralized data warehouse that includes a set of distributed data sources and a shell (DCC-Shell) that is responsible for managing and querying these sources (Figure 8). The DCC-shell does not store any actual transaction (raw data). Instead, these transactions are left on their original sites while the DCC builds and updates a global multidimensional model of the available dimensions and measures, hence the name "virtual warehouse". This approach provides the VDW clients a constantly updated and global view of an N-dimensional data cube in a manner that makes the source distribution transparent. Although the DCC-Shell does not store raw data, it maintains a pool of meta-data (cube global schema) that is synchronized with all data sources. These meta-data are prepared when constructing the VDW, and when a part is modified, all sites must be updated to avoid inconsistencies. Besides meta-data, DCC-Shell also maintains a resource allocation table that includes information pertaining to the location, data organization, and the communication method of each data source. All the meta-data and resource allocation data are in XML format, so it is easy to understand and maintain, therefore making the whole system extensible and flexible.

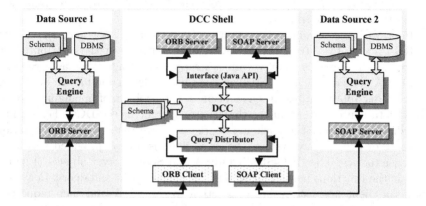

Fig. 8. The Virtual Data Warehouse (VDW) architecture.

Similar to a traditional warehouse, the virtual warehouse provides querying capabilities to a requesting client. There are three classes of query functions that are available to a client. First is the *Warehouse query*, which is designed to provide the client with basic VDW structure including the number of data cubes, and the measures and main theme of each cube. Many phisically or conceptually different data cubes can be services by the virtual data warehouse. The *Cube schema query* provides the meta-data of one specific data cube in the VDW. This meta-data includes a depiction of all available dimensions, measures, and the concept hierarchies that further describe each dimension. Finally, *Cube data query* is used to obtain an entire N-dimensional cube or any subset of it. This is particularly useful in applications such as the VCU that handles low dimensional cubes for visualization sessions (usually 3 dimensions but up to 7 [22]). All query requests and responds are in XML format, analogous to the way meta-data is stored within the DCC-shell. In the next section, the relay of XML messages within the system is presented which is then followed by schema formulation and the XMDQL language.

4.1   Inter/Intra Subsystem Communications

All DIVE-ON internal messages communicated between the VCU and the VDW, and between the VDW and the data sources are formed as XML documents. The VDW is designed as a stand-alone server capable of fulfilling incoming inquires from *any* client. As seen in Figure 8 the server software (CORBA and SOAP servers) is built using a Java API layer, which is regarded as a middleware that interprets incoming requests and encodes outgoing replies between the server modules and the DCC. These server modules are capable of providing their services by constructing a set of objects that a client can remotely call upon (invoke), and awaits the receipt of the XML document containing the response. Adhering to this mechanism, the VCU handles the IVE, OLAP and user interaction by using a client module to invoke the DCC-Shell object responsible for the particular service sought.

Inter-VDW communication is also implemented as client-server using CORBA and SOAP. To allow the DCC-Shell control over the distributed data sources, each source is built within a wrapper working either as a SOAP or a CORBA server. The DCC-Shell in turn uses a client module to access each source. This approach provides a solution to the problem of managing heterogeneous data sources in a manner that is transparent to the DCC. For example, regardless of whether the back-end source is a real data warehouse, relational database or even legacy system, the DCC-Shell is always provided with a uniformed interface. The DCC-Shell CORBA and SOAP server objects (Figure 8) provide the functions needed for warehouse management and query. In a typical session a client first establishes connection to the VDW and then requests information pertaining to its contents. Having learned about the existing entities within the VDW, a client may then initiate a cycle requesting any given available cuboid.

4.2   Schema Formulation

Since the VDW maintains a global and an up-to-date schema that combines all the distribute resources, it is important to choose a representation that facilitates reads, updates, and modifications. For this reason, the schema is represented using XML. Constructing an XML schema for the warehouse general structure is rather simple, consequently we illustrate our method by discussing the data cube schema that is used to fulfill the *cube schema query*.

The *CubeSchema* is defined mainly by a set of measures and dimensions. Within an XML document of the VDW, the root element CubeSchema has sub-elements of Measures and Dimensions, which consist of Measure elements and Dimension elements. Each measure element has a *name* attribute to identify itself, and an *aggregationFunction* attribute with value "SUM" or "COUNT" to express how to aggregate the measure data. Measure also has several sub-elements such as *Title, DataType* and *Description*. Here is an example of Measure elements:

```
<Measures>
  <Measure name="Unit_Sales" aggregationFunction="SUM">
   <Title>Unit Sales</Title>
   <DataType>double</DataType>
  </Measure>
  <Measure name="Store_Cost" aggregationFunction="SUM">
   <Title>Store Cost</Title>
   <DataType>double</DataType>
  </Measure>
```

```
<Measure name="Store_Sales" aggregationFunction="SUM">
 <Title>Store Sales</Title>
 <DataType>double</DataType>
</Measure>
<Measure name="Sales_Count" aggregationFunction="Count">
 <Title>Store Cost</Title>
 <DataType>double</DataType>
</Measure>
</Measures>
```

The concept hierarchy defined on a dimension is expressed using levels of the ontology used. It is straightforward to write down dimension information in XML format given that the attributes forming the concept hierarchy are related by a total order relation (Figure 9). In some instances however, the attributes of a dimension may be organized in a partial order forming a lattice [11]. For example, attributes of the dimension "time" could be organized as a partial relation such as: "$day < \{month < quarter; week\} < year$". In such a relation, a roll-up operation from the level "day" is considered ambiguous since there are two ways to ascend the concept hierarchy, namely "week" or "month". It is hence not possible to represent the concept hierarchy as a tree since partial order produces a cycle. Removing the attribute "week" produces the totally ordered concept hierarchy (Figure 9).

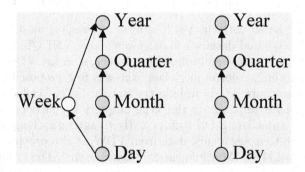

Fig. 9. A lattice (partial order) and a tree (total order) concept hierarchy for the dimension *time*.

To solve the problem of partially ordered concept hierarchies, the attributes that cause partial ordering are considered as *properties* of the dimensions in the XML representation. For example, as in Figure 9 putting "week" into "day" as a property transforms the relation from partial to total order. So the Time dimension has five levels: {Year, Quarter, Month, Day}. Day level has a property "Day-of-Week". The XML fragment could be then written as follows:

```
<Dimension name="Time">
  <Description>Time dimension for Cube</Description>
  <Levels number="4">
   <Level name="Year" Title="Year"/>
   <Level name="Quarter" Title="Quarter"/>
   <Level name="Month" Title="Month"/>
   <Level name="Day" Title="Day" type="base">
    <Property name="Day_of_Week" datatype="String" />
   </level>
  </Levels>
  <Unit name="1997">
   <Unit name="Q1">
    <Unit name="January">
     <Unit name="1" baseID="1"> <Property>Wednesday</Property></Unit>
     <Unit name="2" baseID="2"> <Property>Thursday</Property></Unit>
     <Unit name="3" baseID="3"> <Property>Friday</Property></Unit>


      . . .


    </Unit>
   </Unit>
  </Dimension>
```

4.3   XML Multidimensional Query Language (XMDQL)

To be able to interact with the VDW, a form of querying must be in place. We propose an XML-based declarative query language, XMDQL, a language that allows the user to express multidimensional queries on the VDW. The concept of a special multidimensional query language was first proposed (still not finalized) by Pilot software [18] as an industry standard. They called their language MDSQL. In OLAP terminology this type of query is equivalent to slicing and dicing the data cube. DIVE-ON defines XMDQL as a query language that is formatted in XML to query a cube data from VDW; it also provides functionality similar to that of MDX (Multidimensional Expressions). The result of executing an XMDQL query could be a cell, a two-dimensional slice, or a multidimensional sub-cube. To specify a cube, XMDQL must contain information about the four basic subjects: (1) The cube being queried, (2) dimensions projected in the result cube, (3) slices in each dimension and (4) the members from a non projected dimension on which data will be filtered for members from projected dimensions. The basic form of the XMDQL is as follows:

```
<XMDQL>
  <SELECT>
    Project dimensions and slices
  </SELECT>
  <FROM>
      Which cube to query
```

```
  </FROM>
  <WHERE>
    Filtering constraints
  </WHERE>
</XMDQL>
```

For example, given a data cube with four dimensions: Location, Time, Product and Customer, the following XMDQL query would retrieve the sales of office products in the USA for each quarter in 1997. The Product and Time dimensions are projected dimensions, each in one slice, while the Location dimension is expressed in the WHERE clause as a filter.

```
<XMDQL>
  <SELECT>
    <Measure name="Store_Sales">
    <Axis dimension="Product">
      <Slice type="mono" title="${name}">
        <Path>Office.*</Path>
      </Slice>
    </Axis>
    <Axis dimension="Time">
      <Slice type="mono" title="Quarter ${name}">
        <Path>1997.*</Path>
      </Slice>
    </Axis>
  </SELECT>
  <FROM>
    <Cube name="AllElectronics"/>
  </FROM>
  <WHERE>
    <Condition dimension="Location">
      <Path>N_America.USA</Path>
    </Condition>
  </WHERE>
</XMDQL>
```

The *Axis* element represents projected dimension, and the *Slice* element represents each piece of a slice cut from this dimension. The *Path* element indicates the conceptual level from the concept hierarchy to retrieve the data from, as well as the constituents of the data to retrieve. For instance, the path="Office.*" means showing all children of *Office* such as *computer, fax, copier, etc.*

4.4   Query Distribution and Execution

A VCU query is first received by the DCC-Shell interface (through ORB/SOAP Server) and forwarded to the Query Distributor through the DCC. The Query Distributor analyzes the query and, without translating the XMDQL query, broadcasts it to all the relevant data sources based on the resource allocation table that contains information pertaining to the sources content and their communication protocols. Each data source then translates the incoming query into an appropriate form. A specific wrapper transforms the XMDQL query from the global schema to a set of queries in the local schema after pruning attributes that are not applicable to the local data source. Each data source executes the query (or set of queries) and forms an XML document that contains the needed cube data. This information is relayed back to the VDW via the server software installed on the distributed sites. All the returned information is then merged by the VDW to form an N-dimensional data cube. For our visualization purposes, the DCC then extracts the VCU-requested data cube and sends it back to be rendered in the CAVE. The distribution information could be represented in XML as follows:

```
<Distribution dimension="Store">
 <Component path="N_America.USA"
           mart="DataMart1">USA sales data</Component>
 <Component path="N_America.Canada"
           mart="DataMart1">Canada sales data</Component>
</Distribution>
```

5   Conclusions and Future Directions

In this paper we have presented a system prototype for visual data mining in an immersed virtual environment. Since the very early days of computing science with extremely limited needed technologies, scientists have been fascinated with virtual reality (VR). VR systems are capable of abstracting complex problems or scenarios in an easy to understand way by exploiting the human's natural skills including the visual system. The CAVE theatre is a new technology that maximizes the utilization of the human sensory system. What is novel about our research is the fact that with DIVE-ON we have focused this technology into a new direction, namely remote visual data mining. As was presented in [22], DIVE-ON is indeed capable of creating an IVE that interactively allows the user to explore and learn from a distributed set of data with little or no instructional help. To properly evaluate the effectiveness of this technology, we are currently formally assessing our system by comparing interaction capabilities, discovery opportunities and user satisfaction with implementation on a common screen with OpenGL, the DIVE-ON as described in this paper, and an immersed virtual environment in a smaller version of the CAVE called *Cavelet*. The Cavelet is a set of three flat back-projected screens, approximately 3 x 4 feet each, surrounding the three sides of a desk. The user also uses head and hand-held trackers as in Figure 2 but is sitting down.

A major problem with visualizing data in three dimensions is the problem of occlusion. We have addressed some of these concerns by using spheres in data representation (Section 3.4); however, it is computationally prohibitive to render a large number of 3D spheres while maintaining an interactive frame rate. One research issue we plan to investigate is the use of distortion views, also called fisheye or detail-in-context, in 3D graphics.

So far we have exploited the human visual system to convey information pertaining to data. In the near future we also plan to experiment with *data sonification* techniques to add audible cues to the IVE. After applying a data mining algorithm, if a potentially useful piece of information that has otherwise been unknown is revealed, an audible cue would be generated. The sound attribute would not only indicate the significance of the finding but also aid the user in locating its origin within the data space.

DIVE-ON creates a virtual world that is inhabited by one type of geometric objects (spheres or cubes) each one of which uses its colour and size to tell something about what it represents. We would like to examine the possibility of increasing the number of data mining measures presented by introducing more than one type of geometric objects. For example, a pyramid that points upwards could be used to indicate the existence of monotonic increase somewhere at a lower level, which is particularly useful in market analysis studies. The use of such objects could instantly identify several attributes relating to the ever changing consumer trends and utilization forecasting. Shapes can also be used as a cue, like colour and size, to visualize yet another discretized dimension. We are also investigating extensions to XMDQL based on DMQL [10] in order to include data mining constraints for association rules and classification. These XMDQL extensions would be used for interactive classification as well as interactive evaluation of association rules from within the immersed virtual environment in the CAVE.

References

1. Agarwal S., Agrawal R., Deshpande P., Gupta A., Naughton J. F., Ramakrishnan R. and Sarawagi S., "On the Computation of Multidimensional Aggregates," Proc. of VLDB Conference, 1996, pp 506-521.
2. Baker, M. P., "Human Factors in Virtual Environments for the Visual Analysis of Scientific Data," NCSA Publications: National Centre for Supercomputer Applications.
3. Chaudhuri, S., and Umeshwar, D., "An Overview of Data Warehousing and OLAP Technology," Proc. ACM SIGMOD Record, March, 1997.
4. Common Request Object Broker Architecture (CORBA): http://www.corba.org/
5. DeFanti, T. A., Cruz-Neira, C., and Sandin, D. J., "Surround-Screen Projection-Based Virtual Reality: The Design and Implementation of the CAVE," Proceedings of ACM SIGGRAPH, 1993, http://www.evl.uic.edu/EVL/VR/systems.shtml.
6. Extensible Markup Language (XML): http://www.w3.org/XML/
7. Foley J. and Ribarsky, B., "Next-Generation Data Visualization Tools." In Scientific Visualization Advances and Challenges, chapter 7, pp 103-127. Academic Press/IEEE Computer Society Press, San Diego, CA, 1994.
8. Gary, J., Chaudhuri, S., Bosworth, A., Layman, A., Reichart, D., and Venkatrao, M., "Data Cube: A Relational Aggregation Operator Generalizing Group-by, Cross-Tab, and Sub-Totals," Proc. of the Twelfth IEEE International Conference on Data Engineering, February, 1996, pp 152-159.

9. Green, M. and Shaw, C. develop MR-Toolkit at the University of Alberta: http://www.cs.ualberta.ca/~graphics/MRToolkit.html

10. Han J., Fu Y., Wang W., Koperski K. and Zaïane O. R., "DMQL: A Data Mining Query Language for Relational Databases," Proc. 1996 SIGMOD'96 Workshop Research Issues on Data Mining and Knowledge Discovery (DMKD'96), pp 27-34, Montreal, Canada, June, 1996.

11. Han J., and Kamber M., "Data Mining: Concepts and Techniques," Morgan Kaufmann Publishers, 2001.

12. Hand, C., "A Survey of 3D Interaction Techniques," Computer Graphics Forum, December, 1997, 16(5), pp 269-281.

13. Inmon, W. H., "Date Warehouse - A Perspective of Data Over Time," 370/390 Data Base Management, February, 1992.

14. Jaswal, V., "CAVEvis: Distributed Real-Time Visualization of Time-Varying Scalar and Vector Fields Using the CAVE Virtual Reality Theater," IEEE Visualization, 1997, pp 301-308.

15. Keim D. A., Kriegel H.-P.: VisDB: A System for Visualizing Large Databases , System Demonstration, Proc. ACM SIGMOD Int. Conf. on Management of Data, San Jose, CA, 1995.

16. Keim D. A., Kriegel H.-P., Ankerst M.: Recursive Pattern: A Technique for Visualizing Very Large Amounts of Data, Visualization '95, Atlanta, GA, 1995.

17. Pickett R. M.: "Visual Analysis of Texture in the Detection and Recognition of Objects," in: Picture Processing and Psycho-Pictorics, Lipkin B. S., Rosenfeld A., Academic Press New York, 1970.

18. Pilot Software: http://www.pilotsw.com/news/olap_white.htm

19. Simple Object Access Protocol (SOAP): http://www.w3.org/TR/SOAP/

20. Ward, M. O., Keim D. A.: Screen Layout Methods for Multidimensional Visualization, Euro-American Workshop on Visualization of Information and Data, 1997.

21. Wehrend, S., and Lewis, C., "A Problem Oriented Classification of Visual Techniques," proc. of IEEE Visualization '90:139-143.

22. Zaiane, O. R. and Ammoura, A., "On-Line Analytic Precessing while Immersed in a CAVE," Proc. Second Int. IEEE Conference on User Interfaces for Data Intensive Systems (UIDIS2001), Zurich, Switzerland, May 2001.

Author Index